...quand il est froid, vous y mettez les pêch...

...our les y laisser 24 heures. ensuite vous fait...

...ouiller votre sucre un sec... er y ajou...

...ant une pointe d'eau de ... ne laisser...

... sucre sur le feu. vous vous brouillerez...

...sucre, si vous ne prenez pas cette precau...

...s laisser refroidir le sucre. ensuite vous...

...etter les pêches. le lendemain vous fait...

...ouiller votre sucre, jusqu'à ce que vous voy...

...il soit gras à vos doigts. vous le retirer...

...ser encore la quantité d'eau de vie qu'...

...vous y mettrez vos pêches pour les fai...

...iller un bouillon ou deux. vous les retirer...

...feu pour les laisser refroidir. quand elle...

...t froides, vous les mettez dans des bouteill...

...anc goulot, tout doucement. vous passer...

...au travers d'une serviette, et le verser s...

Dining at Monticello

In Good Taste and Abundance

Edited by
Damon Lee Fowler

THOMAS JEFFERSON FOUNDATION, INC.

Library of Congress Cataloging-in-Publication Data

Dining at Monticello : in good taste and abundance / edited by Damon Lee Fowler.
    p. cm.
  Includes bibliographical references and index.
  ISBN 1-882886-25-9 (alk. paper)
    1. Cookery, American. 2. Jefferson, Thomas, 1743-1826. 3. Cookery--United States--
History. I. Fowler, Damon Lee.
  TX715.D58422 2005
  641.5973--dc22

                                         2004030696

This book was made possible by support from the
Martin S. and Luella Davis Publications Endowment.

Jacket photography by Robert C. Lautman (Dining Room); Renée Comet, styled by Lisa
Cherkasky (foods purchased by Jefferson); Edward Owen (*Thomas Jefferson* by Thomas Sully,
1821). In background: Thomas Jefferson to Stephen Cathalan, Jr., June 6, 1817. Jefferson Papers,
Library of Congress

Coordinated by Beth L. Cheuk
Recipes edited by Jennifer Lindner McGlinn
Designed by Gibson Design Associates
Printed in the United Kingdom by Butler & Tanner
Distributed by
    The University of North Carolina Press
    Chapel Hill, North Carolina 27515-2288
    1-800-848-6224

HGFEDCBA

Contents

THE ESSAYS

THE RECIPES

Thomas Jefferson's Place in American Food History

LOST BETWEEN EXAGGERATION AND INATTENTION, Thomas Jefferson's true place in American food history is difficult to pin down. Popular legend, unbridled by fact and colored by romantic notion, places Jefferson at the very center of our national culinary identity, crediting him with the introduction of ice cream, macaroni, tomatoes, vanilla, French fries, and even French cuisine to the young republic. At the other extreme, scholarly biographers focus their attention almost exclusively on Jefferson's public life, with only the briefest mentions of his elaborate presidential entertaining, neglecting the records of an intense interest in food and the critical role it played in how he conducted his public life.[1] Neither extreme—carelessly enthusiastic or cautiously silent—provides real understanding of Jefferson's role in our country's culinary past. And yet the surviving documentation of Monticello's food culture is marvelously rich, from Jefferson's own notebook describing the kitchen garden, to the family's personal letters and recipe manuscripts, to detailed accounts of food purchases. These documents provide a vivid picture and authentic understanding of Jefferson's curiosity about the growing, preserving, and cooking of fine food, not to mention his real passion for eating well. Although the picture the evidence paints is less of the pioneer of colorful legend than his enthusiasts would perhaps like, to a far greater degree than historians have described, Jefferson made an important impact on our national culinary consciousness as an ever-searching epicure, gathering and incorporating the best elements of the food traditions he encountered in both Old World and New.

DAMON LEE FOWLER is a culinary historian and author of five cookbooks.

One of the most persistent food myths surrounding Jefferson dates to his own day, at least from the time an outraged Patrick Henry purportedly claimed that "he has abjured his native victuals in favor of French cuisine."[2] Modern writers sometimes suggest that Jefferson's years as minister plenipotentiary to France completely revolutionized his culinary thinking. It is easy to see why: Jefferson went abroad with eyes and notebooks wide open, eager to observe and record his impressions of life on the Continent. His experiences with Roman architecture, English gardens, and European wines did in

fact transform life at Monticello, where the house, gardens, and wine cellar were redesigned and augmented after his return from France.

It is therefore tempting to argue that the same is true of food—that Jefferson's experiences in France opened a new gastronomical world for him. However, it is also important to remember that the French were in America long before this particular American was in France, and Jefferson was no stranger to French cooking. Decades before he lived in Paris, he enjoyed meals prepared by Frenchmen both at the Governor's Palace in Williamsburg, where he dined regularly during his student days, and at the residence he and James Monroe shared in Annapolis. Like other Virginians of his class, he inherited from Europe an understanding of French food as an "international culinary language" that communicated status and style.[3] Just as the language of France had become the language of diplomacy, its cuisine was the culinary equivalent. Eager to make this stylish French fare a lifelong element of his own table, Jefferson brought his slave James Hemings to Paris "for the particular purpose of learning French cookery."[4] In other words, Jefferson's early experiences with French cuisine at home had already inspired him to take advantage of the culinary opportunities that awaited him in France.

In fairness, dining every Tuesday on the refined cuisine of the court of Louis XVI can only have deepened Jefferson's love for French cooking. Just as he brought home eighty-six crates of European art, books, silver, furniture, and porcelain, he also brought such foodstuffs as mustard, vinegar, raisins, nectarines, macaroni, almonds, cheese, anchovies, olive oil, and 680 bottles of wine.[5] This passion for the best elements of Continental cuisine stayed with Jefferson for life: he continued to enjoy French-influenced cuisine in Philadelphia, Washington, and even Charlottesville; Monticello's pantries

and cellars were stocked annually with European delicacies; and many of the recipes he recorded are written in French or are French-influenced. Even as president, he found time to send some of his French butler's recipes to his daughters at Monticello, noting that the "orthography will be puzzling and amusing: but the receipts are valuable."[6] Clearly, then, Jefferson's years in Paris made a permanent imprint on his food habits.

What we often neglect to remember is that Jefferson's time in Paris was a *two-way* cultural exchange. At the same time that he eagerly sought European ideas, plants, and technologies—food-related and otherwise—to enrich his own life at home and to share with his fellow Americans, he was also a vocal defender of the New World and its natural products. Assessing the fruit available in Paris, he concluded that "[t]hey have no apple here to compare with our Newtown pippin," and requested that James Madison arrange shipment of both a barrel of the apples and fifty to one hundred of

Jefferson's silver service pieces included this sugar bowl, coffee urn, and cream pot, made, respectively, in England, France, and America, demonstrating his access to table wares made around the world.

its grafts, presumably less for his own use than to establish the American product in France.[7] In his Parisian garden, Jefferson grew "Indian corn for the use of my own table," and requested that seeds for additional corn, cantaloupe, watermelon, and sweet potatoes be sent to him, along with Virginia hams, which were "better than any to be had on this side [of] the Atlantic."[8] Even surrounded by haute cuisine, Jefferson still wanted to eat "in our manner," requesting shipment of such quintessentially American foods as pecans and cranberries. Contrary to Patrick Henry's accusation, it's evident that Jefferson's culinary adventures in France did not supplant his own American food traditions, but only broadened them; clearly, he relished the best from both sides of the Atlantic.

During his years at Monticello, nowhere is Jefferson's search for "the best" more plainly revealed than in his Garden Book, where he recorded the planting of hundreds of varieties of fruits, vegetables, and herbs in search of improved varieties of existing plants or new and useful additions to his collection. His plantings were a catholic and highly experimental amalgamation of wheat from Ireland, grapes from Italy, and tarragon from France, alongside peppers from Texas and cucumbers from Ohio, so that Charles Willson Peale wrote that "Your gardens must be a Museum to you."[9] Bound to the seasons in a way most Americans have long forgotten, Jefferson celebrated the addition of sprout kale to his garden because it "furnishes a vast crop of sprouts from the beginning of December through the whole winter, which are remarkably sweet and delicious."[10] Similarly, he shared his discovery of asparagus bean with his son-in-law John Wayles Eppes: "It is a very valuable [vegetable], much more tender and delicate than the snap, and may be dressed in any form in which Asparagus may, particularly fried in batter, or chopped to the size of the garden pea, and dressed as such in the French way."[11] Unhappily, some of his experiments like the asparagus bean were not to take root in American gardens, but others did.

Jefferson's letter and notes describing the source, cultivation, and kitchen possibilities of the asparagus bean suggest that he was deeply aware of his family's food culture on all levels. Despite the recollection of his

Newtown (or Albemarle) Pippins grow at Monticello today in the restored South Orchard. When Jefferson was in France, he noted that "[t]hey have no apple here to compare with our Newtown pippin" and arranged for the apples and grafts to be shipped overseas.

WAS THOMAS JEFFERSON A VEGETARIAN?

JEFFERSON CANNOT BE CALLED a vegetarian, as we understand the term today. In his own time, however, he was unusually moderate in his consumption of meat and was notable for the variety as well as the quantity of vegetables he ate. The documentary record includes several descriptions, including Jefferson's own, of his eating habits:

Harvested vegetables in front of the Garden Pavilion, restored to Monticello's vegetable garden in 1984.

Thomas Jefferson:
"I have lived temperately, eating little animal food, and that not as an aliment, so much as a condiment for the vegetables which constitute my principal diet."

Ellen W. Coolidge, granddaughter:
"He ate a great many vegetables and little meat, contrary to the custom of his countrymen."

Thomas J. Randolph, grandson:
"He ate heartily, and much vegetable food, preferring French cookery, because it made the meats more tender."

Daniel Webster:
"He enjoys his dinner well, taking with meat a large proportion of vegetables."

Edmund Bacon, Monticello overseer from 1806-1822:
"He never eat [sic] much hog meat. He often told me, as I was giving out meat for the servants, that what I gave one of them for a week would be more than he would use in six months…. He was especially fond of Guinea fowls; and for meat he preferred good beef, mutton, and lambs…. He was very fond of vegetables and fruit and raised every variety of them."[21]

Note: Records show that most adult slaves received a half or one pound of salt pork a week.

— L.S.

slave Isaac Jefferson that he never entered the kitchen at Monticello except to wind the clock, Jefferson's records show that, at the least, he was keenly interested in how the food served at Monticello was both grown and prepared. Jefferson's Garden Book provides careful charts noting, for instance, that in 1811, artichokes (a vegetable that popular legend would claim was unknown in Virginia until much later) came "to table" on May 28 and the "last dish" was eaten on July 28. Further, we have correspondence and invoices detailing his personal role in acquiring ordinary food staples and more exotic European imports. Beyond that, he made drawings of a pasta machine, an apple press, tureens, coffee urns, and cruets; his designs for goblets were executed in silver and used

at Monticello. He also recorded recipes, ten of which survive. One entitled "Observations on Soup" reveals a key element of Jefferson's personality, whether culinary or otherwise: observation. He had a natural and active curiosity about everything, and foodstuffs were no exception, as can be so clearly seen in his records of the produce from his gardens, in the recipes he gleaned from French chefs (and often took the trouble to copy out himself), and in his reading of essays with titles such as "On the Construction of Kitchen Fireplaces and Kitchen Utensils" and "Of the Construction of Saucepans and Stewpans for Fixed Fireplaces."[12]

To portray Jefferson as purely an academic, intellectual observer of food culture, however, belies the words of his guests,

Jefferson designed the thousand-foot-long vegetable garden as a ferme ornée, *to serve as a functional kitchen garden while incorporating ornamental features, whether built, such as the pavilion, or natural, such as adjacent rows of purple, white, and green sprouting broccoli.*

Restored in 2004, the Monticello kitchen combined traditional elements such as the brick oven (at left) with an inventory of French copper cookware.

OPPOSITE: Thomas Jefferson *by Thomas Sully (1821). Jefferson retired to Monticello in 1809, following forty years of public service.*

together would promote "harmony and mutual confidence" among the statesmen.[14] Both publicly at the President's House and more privately at Monticello, dinners featured unusual elements to enhance conversation, such as the use of dumbwaiters to eliminate interruptions and of round or oval tables so that diners could see one another better. That these conversations continued long past the meal and "carried us far into the night" (in a day when dinner was served around three o'clock) is a true hallmark of good hospitality.[15]

The natural consequence of Jefferson's avid interest in and commitment to fine food was a table with "every thing in superb stile."[16] This is easier to document at the President's House, where visitors chronicled the "elegant and rich" food in detail.[17] There an extensive staff—including Edith Hern Fossett and her sister-in-law Fanny Gillette Hern, two enslaved cooks from Monticello—worked to create impressive fare. As one guest wrote of the then-president, "He is accused of being very slovenly in his dress, … but however he may neglect his person he takes good care of his table. No man in America keeps a better."[18] After Jefferson's retirement, Fossett and Hern brought their culinary knowledge back to Monticello, with its newly developed French-style kitchen and its well-stocked storage rooms. From

whether at the President's House or Monticello, who noted that he "performed the honors of the table with great facility," that "[h]e always renders his company easy and agreeable," and was "very fond" of the "easy flow of after dinner conversation."[13] Jefferson well understood the social value of good food. While president, he hosted frequent dinners for both fellow Republicans and Federalists in a conviction that sharing meals the first days of Jefferson's retirement until the last years of his life, visitors continued to celebrate the offerings, describing the table as "genteely and plentifully spread" and "in good taste and abundance."[19] Certainly it's hard to imagine other homes of the period in remote frontier locations where highly trained cooks produced dinners that were "always choice, and served in the French style."[20] The large numbers of visitors who flocked to the mountaintop home are, in part, a testament to the quality and distinctiveness of the hospitality.

Thomas Jefferson resonates with food lovers across the ages not because he *mastered* haute cuisine, but because he understood its principles. He embraced the relationship between garden and table; he sought out quality ingredients both from home and abroad; he understood both the simplicity of classic dishes as well as the adventure of new foods; he preserved his own food roots and reached out to the cuisines of other cultures; he encouraged the connection between food and sociability and cherished lingering conversation over fine wine. Within these ideas is nothing revolutionary or unique; to presume so is to miss Thomas Jefferson's true role in American culinary history, which is simply this: in this brilliant and complex man is a timeless articulation of the role and value of food in our lives.

Th. Jefferson
presents his compliments to

and requests the favour of his company
to dinner on   next
at half after three o'clock

The favour of an answer is requested

Nourishing the Congress: Hospitality at the President's House

ON MARCH 4, 1801, AFTER WALKING to the Capitol to take the oath of office, the new president returned to his New Jersey Avenue lodgings for dinner. Thomas Jefferson took his usual place, "the lowest and coldest seat," at a long table where he and thirty others dined on boarding-house fare. Two weeks later he set up his own household on Pennsylvania Avenue and soon began to offer much grander meals to residents of the federal city. "Never before had such dinners been given in the President's House," remembered one of his guests, "nor such a variety of the finest and most costly wines."[1] President Jefferson's entertainments—for legislators and diplomats, citizens of Washington and Georgetown, European philosophers, and Cherokee chiefs—were unprecedented in their frequency and bountiful elegance.

Jefferson's best-known printed invitation card and objects he used at Monticello—including a silver chocolate pot in the form of a Roman askos—recall the many dinners he hosted at the President's House in Washington, shown (above) in an 1811 watercolor by Benjamin H. Latrobe.

Before he took up residence in the unfinished stone palace lately vacated by John and Abigail Adams, Jefferson started to assemble the largest domestic staff he had employed since his years as minister to France. His five years in Paris had profoundly influenced his taste in everything from architecture to wine, and it was to France that he turned in his quest for the two most important members of his household. When Jefferson asked for assistance from Philippe Létombe, French envoy in Philadelphia, he acknowledged that a suitable maitre d'hôtel did not exist "among the natives of our country."[2] The ideal household administrator was eventually found in Etienne Lemaire, a "portly well-mannered frenchman" who had served both European aristocrats and wealthy Americans.[3] For the position of *chef de cuisine* Létombe hired forty-two-year-

---

LUCIA STANTON is Shannon Senior Historian at the Thomas Jefferson Foundation, Inc.

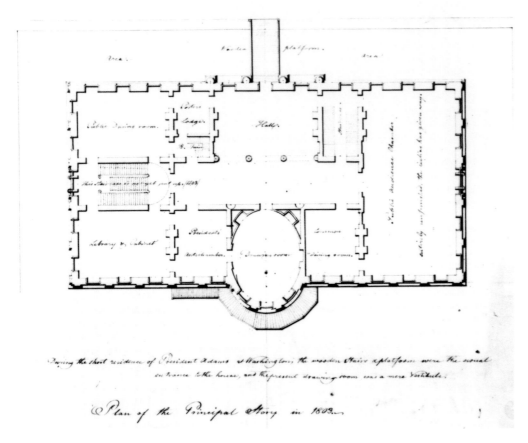

Benjamin H. Latrobe's 1803 plan of the main floor of the President's House shows the location of Jefferson's dinners: the "Public Dining Room" (now the private dining room) and "Common Dining Room" (now the Green Room).

old Honoré Julien, who—with four months of experience in George Washington's Philadelphia kitchen—was already familiar with presidential entertaining.[4]

Soon after the inauguration, Jefferson retreated to Monticello for a month. On April 17 he wrote back to Washington expressing the hope that his new chef had arrived and that everything was ready "for the entertainment of company."[5] By December, when members of the Seventh Congress arrived in the capital for the first session, the Jeffersonian approach to hospitality was well established. Among the many innova-

tions the senators and congressmen found at the Republican court were frequent informal dinners replacing the weekly levees of Washington and Adams. Since each member was invited at least once, and many more often, the bulky Congress of almost 150 men dictated a crowded social calendar at the President's House—three dinners a week during the three-to-five-month session.

Jefferson's motives for systematically wining and dining the legislators were a constant subject of debate. Hospitable by nature, he also felt an obligation to brighten the lives of the wifeless public servants billeted in the boardinghouses that had sprouted on the raw expanses of the new capital. A British observer remarked that the president's house and those of cabinet members were almost essential to the senators and congressmen, "unless they chose to live like bears, brutalized and stupefied."[6] Jefferson also believed that rational conversation at a table where political discussion was discouraged would promote his declared object of restoring harmony to a society agitated by party strife.[7]

Three times a week, therefore, the president's secretary sent up to Capitol Hill a dozen printed invitations, which specified a dinner hour of "half after three, or at whatever later hour the house may rise."[8] Most of the congressional diners gathered in parties of no more than twelve—Federalists one day, Republicans another—in what is now the Green Room, with its chintz curtains and green floorcloth. Margaret Bayard Smith, wife of the editor of the Washington *National Intelligencer*, applauded the use here of a round or oval table, "a great influence on the conversational powers of Mr. Jefferson's guests," and of course—with no clear head or foot—a democratic solution to the issue of precedence.[9] The room was also equipped with a number of dumbwaiters, small tables with tiered shelves, that minimized the need for servants. Many witnesses reported that Jefferson himself did the serving. "He performed the honors of the table with great facility," observed Massachusetts senator William Plumer, while architect Benjamin Latrobe noted that "Mr. Jefferson said little at dinner besides attending to the filling of plates, which he did with great ease and grace for a philosopher."[10]

In the northwest corner of the President's House was the large "public" dining room, furnished with a rectangular table, massive sideboards, and a second type of dumbwaiter—a revolving serving door similar to one installed at Monticello. In 1803 Hetty Ann Barton found it second only in interest to the "mammoth cheese," the 1,235-pound gift of the republican citizens of Cheshire, Massachusetts. This dumbwaiter

was "so contrived that but a few minutes and all appeared or disappeared at once. This machine, fixed in the wall, held all *one course*, and was turned into the room in a minute."[11]

These two rooms became the arenas for displaying the arts of both Julien and Lemaire, as a maitre d'hôtel was also expected to have culinary skills. Jefferson's grandson Thomas Jefferson Randolph recalled the ritual of presentation in 1805: "The maitre d'Hotel announced dinner, remained in the room, seeing that the servants attended to every gentleman but not waiting himself, placing on the first dish of the second course," that is, the dessert.[12] Lemaire, in the attire of a gentleman, was assisted by waiters in the presidential livery—blue cloth coats with scarlet facings and gilt buttons, scarlet waistcoats, and corduroy pantaloons.[13]

Honoré Julien labored invisibly in Jefferson's basement at a large built-in coal-burning stew-range, assisted by a succession of scullions and three apprentices. Thinking ahead to his retirement, Jefferson had young

A revolving serving door like this one at Monticello simplified dinner service in the "public" dining room at the President's House. All the dishes of one course could be transferred into the room without a number of servants passing to and fro.

WHAT IS SERVICE À LA FRANÇAISE?

THROUGHOUT THE eighteenth and early nineteenth centuries, *service à la française*, or French-style service, remained de rigueur in elite American homes, and visitors' accounts suggest that dining at Jefferson's table was no exception. This mode of entertainment gained favor in France among medieval nobility and soon spread throughout much of Europe. Although dining etiquette developed over the centuries, the tenets of *service à la française* remained largely unaltered and were heralded in early America. Fashionable hosts strictly followed the

divided into classes and hierarchically arranged, with those belonging to lesser classes surrounding those of greater stature. The number of diners determined the quantity of dishes served. A three-course dinner for eight, for example, could require as many as twenty-four separate dishes. As the number of guests increased, so did the variety of foods presented.

Service à la française was more than simply a style of eating; it was a mode of entertainment—one that began the moment guests entered the dining room. There to greet them stood a table fully set with silver, glass, and great platters and tureens filled and at the ready, encouraging the appetite and impressing the senses. Above all, *service à la française* emphasized an orderly and grand presentation of dishes that showcased a host's resources and culinary savoir-faire.

Evidence suggests that Jefferson regarded French-style service as at once the epitome

Service à la française *shown in a design of sweetmeats and fruits. Note the hierarchy of larger and smaller dishes symmetrically arranged around a grand centerpiece. Courtesy Winterthur Library.*

style's edicts, which reflected the hierarchy, balance, and symmetry so admired in the period.

French-style service commonly dictated two to four courses, each consisting of an even number of dishes placed symmetrically around a centerpiece, such as a large roast or a decorative serving vessel. Dishes were

of fashionable entertaining *and* a mere template. It guided his decisions and influenced his taste, but, in the end, he used the principles of this revered service to create a dining style that was uniquely his own. Jefferson combined French-style elegance and cuisine with his own democratic sense of style, inspiring one guest to note, "In his entertainments, republican simplicity was united to Epicurean delicacy."[28]

—J.L.M.

enslaved women—Ursula Hughes (briefly), Edith Fossett, and Fanny Hern—brought at different times from Monticello to learn French cookery in the presidential kitchen.

The meals produced by Lemaire, Julien, and their assistants inspired many of Jefferson's guests to take up their pens when they returned to their lodgings. An early and unusually comprehensive account is that of Massachusetts congressman Manasseh Cutler, after a dinner in February 1802: "Rice soup, round of beef, turkey, mutton, ham, loin of veal, cutlets of mutton or veal, fried eggs, fried beef, a pie called macaroni which appeared to be a rich crust filled with the strillions of onions, or shallots, which I took it to be, tasted very strong, and not agreeable. Mr. [Meriwether] Lewis told me there were none in it; it was an Italian dish, and what appeared like onions was made of flour and butter, with a particularly strong liquor mixed with them. Ice cream very good, crust wholly dried, crumbled into thin flakes: a dish somewhat like a pudding—inside white as milk or curd, very porous and light, covered with cream sauce—very fine. Many other jimcracks, a great variety of fruit, plenty of wines, and good."[14]

At subsequent dinners Cutler enjoyed the beef *bouilli*, Latrobe singled out larded venison for notice, and William Plumer regretted the appearance of portions of

the "mammoth cheese" three years after its arrival (it was "very far from being good," he wrote).[15] Other commentators merely described the main courses as "handsome," "neat and plentiful," "very good," "excellent," "very elegant," and "elegant and rich."[16] Mrs. Smith summarized the impression made by the meals when she declared that "the excellence and superior skill of [Jefferson's] French cook was acknowledged by all who frequented his table."[17]

Once a month Jefferson entered his analysis of the accounts of his maitre d'hôtel, Etienne Lemaire, into his Memorandum Books. Here, in the spring of 1806, he recorded the amount spent each week on "prov[isio]ns" for the kitchen and, on the right, calculated the average cost of each guest's dinner.

Jefferson's secretary, twenty-seven-year-old Isaac Coles, was a daily diner at the President's House. Six months after his arrival, he suddenly began to record the dinner menu. For just four days in the spring of 1807 the jottings in his diary reveal the principal dishes: *bouilli*, mutton (once "with a very rich stuffing"), loin of veal, beef steaks, and even a quarter of bear. Secondary dishes included ducks, partridges, fowls "with oyster sauce," a bacon ham, sausages "with a rich onion sauce," and fish, and the vegetables were cabbage, spinach, potatoes, turnips, carrots, beans, salad, and pickles. The desserts that Lemaire ceremoniously placed on the table included omelets, jellies, stewed apples, apples *à la française*, apples "inclosed in a thin toast," "a kind of custard with a floating cream on it," and various cakes.[18]

When seeking to fill Lemaire's position, Jefferson had specified that "honesty and skill in making the dessert are indispensable qualifications."[19] And it was the dessert course that drew from his guests their most enthusiastic comments and most detailed descriptions. Latrobe described it as "extremely elegant," Plumer as "rich & various," and New York congressman Samuel Latham Mitchill was moved to record the unusual apparition of frozen ice cream inside warm pastry "as if the *ice* had just been taken from the *oven*."[20] At the two annual presidential open houses on New Year's Day and the Fourth of July, the sideboards of the public dining room were covered with sweet offerings that found their way into the chronicles of those in attendance: a rich variety of cakes, apple pies and other confectionery, and, always, ice cream—even in July, since Jefferson had an ice house excavated shortly after taking of-

fice. On Independence Day in 1806 Lemaire had to hire an extra servant to turn the ice cream maker. For these occasions—when the company numbered in the hundreds—he purchased many dozens of eggs for making petits fours and Savoy biscuits.[21]

Very early on most mornings, in order to provide the ingredients for Julien's and his own creations, Lemaire set out in a horse-drawn wagon to the Washington and Georgetown markets. His record of purchases from January 1806 itemizes payments for immense quantities of meat and poultry; seafood such as shad, sturgeon, rockfish, and oysters; a variety of wild game including wild ducks, pigeons, and squirrels; every imaginable vegetable, from asparagus and peas in spring to tomatoes and squash in August; exotic fruits like oranges and pineapples as well as local strawberries and watermelons; and miscellaneous items from hickory nuts to Havana chocolate.[22] What Jefferson called "groceries"—storage items including cheese, crackers, preserves, tea, and spices—were purchased from his friend and private banker, John Barnes of Georgetown. And what Barnes could not provide had to be ordered from France. A large shipment received from Bordeaux in 1806 included olives and olive oil, anchovies, three kinds of almonds, artichoke hearts, tarragon vinegar, Maille mustard, seedless raisins, figs and

TABLE OF VEGETABLE MARKET &c

ABOVE: *Jefferson recorded the first and last appearances of vegetables in the Washington markets, compiling his information into this chart. He also distributed seeds to district market-gardeners to encourage the cultivation of a wider variety of vegetables.*

OPPOSITE: *Jefferson's guests remarked on the fine wines at presidential dinners. In his first two years in the President's House, he spent more than four thousand dollars on wine.*

prunes, Bologna sausage, and a Parmesan cheese.[23]

Many of the imported delicacies figured in the final course, when the tablecloth was removed, the wines brought in, and the table laid with an array of small dishes containing filberts, pecans, and walnuts, and candied and preserved fruits, along with cheese and crackers.[24] Decanters of Hermitage, Tokay, and Nebbiolo promoted "the easy flow of after dinner conversation" so prized by Jefferson and contributed to the harmonizing effect of his presidential dinners, tempering differences and kindling common interests.[25]

For eight years French food, French wine, and French servants lightened Jefferson's political labors. After he retired to Monticello in 1809 he continued to send off annual orders for French wine and foodstuffs to his agent at Marseilles, and the skills of Julien and Lemaire were perpetuated by their enslaved "pupils." Julien even made a special journey to Monticello to help set up the new kitchen and provide further instruction.[26] Thereafter Edith Fossett and Fanny Hern produced meals noted for their elegance and abundance. Yet the dining experience was evidently never quite the same. In 1821 Jefferson wrote: "I envy M. Chaumont nothing but his French cook and cuisine. These are luxuries which can neither be forgotten nor possessed in our country."[27]

Like Clockwork: French Influence in Monticello's Kitchen

A FORMER MONTICELLO SLAVE, ISAAC JEFFERSON, recalled that "Mr. Jefferson had a clock in his kitchen at Monticello; never went into the kitchen except to wind up the clock. He never would have less than eight covers [dishes] at dinner—if nobody at table but himself: had from eight to thirty-two covers for dinner ...."[1] Recounted here from an enslaved worker's point of view, these details of food production and dining at Monticello are significant for what they omit: the great amount of day-to-day planning and labor that took place between Jefferson's visits to the kitchen every eight days to wind the tall case clock. The Monticello cooks and their sophisticated workspace acted as a clockwork-like domestic mechanism, fulfilling Jefferson's long-standing intent to replicate at Monticello the sophisticated style of dining that he saw in France and knew from the President's House. The fully developed kitchen at Monticello straddled two worlds, combining some of the conventional elements of kitchens in colonial Virginia with aspects of French design and organization, resulting in dinners served "in half Virginian, half French style, in good taste and abundance."[2]

The kitchens on Virginia plantations in the late eighteenth and early nineteenth centuries typically emphasized architectural separation, both physical and visual, from public or formal interior spaces. Placing food-related activities in outbuildings met practical needs (e.g., fire and heat containment) while simultaneously removing the enslaved domestic labor force from the view and proximity of the main house. Following this convention, Monticello was separated from its dependencies (or service areas, including the kitchen, dairy, smokehouse, and storage

The restoration of Monticello's kitchen was guided by evidence such as the 1790 Grevin packing list (above), which includes a detailed inventory of more than sixty pieces of copper cookware and iron utensils.

JUSTIN A. SARAFIN is Project Coordinator for the restoration of Monticello's dependencies.

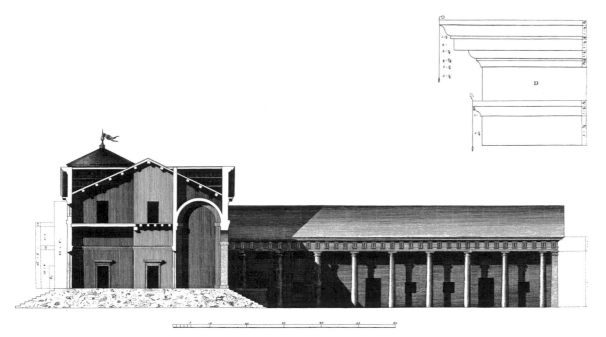

cooking, and transporting dishes to the dining room. Such inter-related tasks made the kitchen a bustling locus of activity, as well as the point where the "above stairs" population of Jefferson, his family, and occasionally guests interacted with hired laborers and with the enslaved African-American community living and working on the cellar level of the house or along Mulberry Row (between the kitchen yard and the garden, parallel to the south wing of dependencies).

Restored by the Thomas Jefferson Foundation in 2004, the present kitchen (marked on opposite page as space G) is actually Monticello's second kitchen. The original was located in the cellar of the South Pavilion (A), the first structure erected on the mountaintop, begun in 1769. After her

cellars for beer, wine, and foodstuffs). Jefferson achieved this spatial division with an architectural arrangement atypical in Virginia, in contrast to the usual assortment of free-standing outbuildings. Taking cues from the sixteenth-century Italian architect Andrea Palladio, he located Monticello's dependencies in two office wings built into the hillside, with terraces that serve the main house above and conceal the work spaces below.[3] An all-weather passageway runs laterally beneath the main level of the house, connecting the wings of the dependencies to form a U shape of work and storage spaces.

This network of pragmatically arranged rooms was located near the food production activities on the mountaintop, including gardening, tending livestock, purchasing provisions from both free and enslaved suppliers, monitoring beverage and food stores,

marriage to Thomas Jefferson in 1772, Martha Wayles Skelton Jefferson managed, with help from certain slaves, the demands of their relatively small household in this original kitchen. One of the few references to Martha Jefferson describes her "with cookery book in hand" reading directions to Ursula, a slave trained as a pastry cook and a "favorite house woman."[4] This small, somewhat rudimentary kitchen remained in service for decades, even after the enslaved cook James Hemings returned from Paris trained "in the art of cookery."[5]

As part of a redesign of Monticello, construction of the south wing of the dependencies commenced in 1801, and when the South Pavilion was remodeled in 1808, the kitchen moved to its second, final location at the L-shaped intersection of the all-weather passage (H) and the south wing of dependencies. By the spring of 1809, specially ordered ironwork arrived to complete the kitchen's new stew stove, at which point the space was fully equipped.[6] Jefferson's relocation of the kitchen reflected a desire to create a skilled and specialized culinary operation, capable of meeting the increased demand for hospitality prompted by his return to Monticello in 1809 after his retirement from the presidency. His years at the President's House were marked by French-influenced cuisine and a style of dining and entertaining that Jefferson intended to maintain upon returning to Albemarle County.

Organized in the spirit of haute cuisine of eighteenth-century France, Monticello's second kitchen and the staff who worked in it were characterized by a high degree of order and specificity with regard to cooking equipment, staff skills and administration, and spatial arrangement. The organization of Monticello's kitchen appeared analogous to the French *cuisine*, or kitchen, equipped

Plan of Monticello's dependencies. The north and south wings of the service areas were connected to the cellars located beneath the house itself via a covered, all-weather passageway (the axis labeled H). The network of service-oriented spaces contains dwellings for enslaved workers (spaces C, D, and F), storage rooms (I, K, and M), a beer cellar (J), a wine room (L), a smokehouse (E), dairy (B), icehouse (Q), the kitchen (G), and the office (N, O, P), or area for staging dishes en route to the Dining Room, reached by a flight of stairs (in space N).

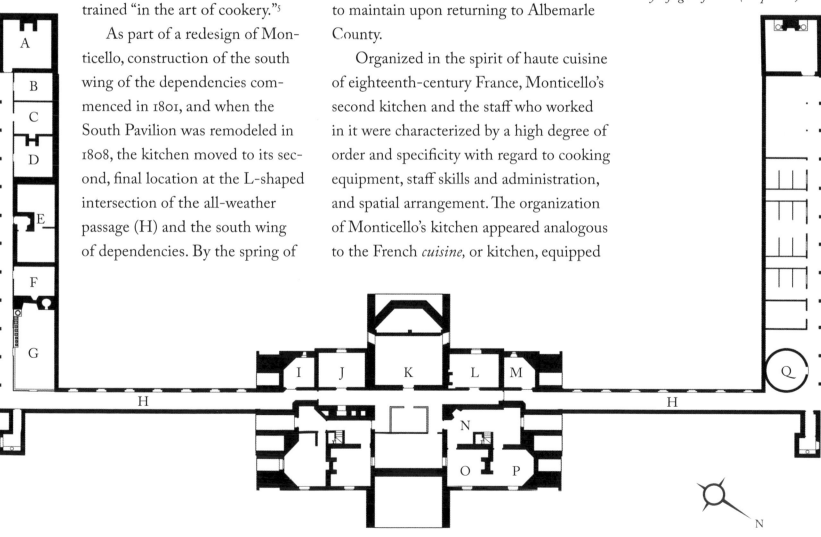

with built-in architectural features such as an eight-opening stew stove, counter-like work surfaces, and an extensive inventory of specialized cookware. William Verral's *Complete System of Cookery*, written in 1759 by an Englishman skilled in French culinary techniques, describes varied types of activities that likely took place in the bustling Monticello kitchen:

Food preparation at Monticello was a time-consuming affair: cooks and assistants used various utensils for the dressing and roasting of meats (above) and for the processing of large quantities of vegetables (below right).

First then, my brethren, take care to begin your work betimes. Your broth and gravy for your soups and sauces should be the first thing in hand: your little matters in the pastry way may be done whilst that is going on; next prepare your fowls, collops [slices of meat], cutlets, or whatever it may be; put them upon plates, and range them in neat order upon the dresser before ye; next see that your meat and roast in the English way be all cleverly trimmed, trussed and singed, and ready for the spit. In like manner get all your garden things cut, pared, pick'd, and washed out into a cullender; and … be sure you provide a plate of green onions, shallots, parsley, minced very fine, pepper and salt always ready mixed, and your spice-box always at hand; so that every thing you want may be ready at a moment's call, and not to be hunting after such trifles when your dinner should be ready to send to table. When your stewpans, &c., make their appearance, place them all in proper arrangement, and you cannot easily err.[7]

Working with the enslaved cooks who organized and executed these activities, Jefferson's daughter or one of his granddaughters would have coordinated the day's menu, essentially serving as maitre d'hôtel, or the person in charge of a French-style kitchen operation.

In addition to the *cuisine*-style kitchen space, Monticello featured an *office* (N, O, and P) or a smaller-scale staging area for plating and preparing dishes for presentation, as well as storing table linens and ceramic tablewares. The cellar-level *office*

How do we know what Monticello's kitchen looked like?

THE ARCHITECTURAL DETAILS and fittings of Monticello's kitchen were restored in 2003 and 2004, re-creating a workspace that represents the pinnacle of culinary technology in Virginia during the early nineteenth century. Renovation work on the kitchen had not been undertaken since 1941, when some original elements were mistakenly removed and incorrectly reconstructed. Almost two hundred years after the kitchen's completion, how did scholars know what to recreate?

Physical investigation provided one means of recapturing the past. Study of the building revealed *when* and *how* the workspaces developed, and the dismantling of incorrect restoration efforts from 1941 allowed the close examination of original construction techniques and materials. Further, comparisons with kitchens at sites where Jefferson's builders are known to have worked also provided design precedents for the re-construction of kitchen details.

Surviving documents, including a series of architectural drawings in Jefferson's own hand, provided additional guidance. A 1796 drawing of the kitchen clearly shows the range of stew stove openings, drawn between the door of the southeast partition wall and the fireplace wall, exactly where the stove is located today. In addition, correspondence between Jefferson and a Georgetown founder describes the cast-iron fittings for the stew stove and thus aided in their reproduction.[14] Even modern documents are helpful: a photograph taken around 1941 shows the outline of the original stew stove in the kitchen's brick floor, which guided the installation of the range.

In order to furnish this workspace accurately, re-

Photograph of Monticello's kitchen, circa 1941, showing the footprint of the stew stove, visible in the brick floor along the left wall, which helped confirm other physical and documentary evidence.

searchers turned to three inventories detailing the contents of Monticello's kitchen. The Grevin packing list of 1790 records the exact types and quantities of copper saucepans and other specialized cooking vessels that were shipped from Paris and eventually sent to Monticello.[15] In 1796, the enslaved chef James Hemings created an updated inventory, reiterating most of the 1790 list and adding more traditional and basic kitchen and fireplace tools.[16] Martha Jefferson Randolph's "Inventory of the furniture in the house at Monticello," compiled around 1826, repeats the contents of previous inventories, confirming that the core collection of kitchen objects was still in use at the time of her father's death.[17]

—J.A.S.

Monticello's re-constructed stew stove featured a copper set kettle much like a basin incorporated into the brick structure. The set kettle provided a constant supply of hot water for cooking and cleaning. The window over the stew stove provided ventilation for the charcoal that burned in eight openings.

was likely located adjacent to the north stairs that lead directly to the revolving serving door of the dining room on the main floor. French architectural plans, published while Jefferson lived in Paris, similarly locate the *cuisine* and *office* apart from one another, with the latter conveniently located en route to the dining room. Such French-style spaces for food preparation facilitated the serving and clearing of meals.

In 1784, as Jefferson prepared to assume the responsibilities of minister plenipotentiary to France, he brought the slave James Hemings with him for the "particular purpose" of learning French cooking methods.[8] Later Hemings gained emancipation on the condition that he convey his knowledge of French cuisine to his brother, Peter

Hemings, who served as cook at Monticello from 1796 to at least 1809. His successor as head cook, Edith Hern Fossett, and another cook apprentice, Fanny Gillette, were brought to Washington, D.C., to learn French cooking techniques from Jefferson's chef at the President's House, Honoré Julien, and Jefferson's maitre d'hôtel, Etienne Lemaire.[9]

Such a highly skilled staff required more extensive equipment than was typically available in the Virginia kitchen of the day, which was usually limited to that necessary for open-hearth cooking. The most significant built-in feature of Monticello's revised *cuisine*, or main kitchen, was the eight-opening stew stove with an integrated set kettle that provided a constant supply of hot water. Essentially the precursor to later nineteenth-century cast-iron ranges and modern multi-burner stovetops, the stew stove was constructed of brick and featured a set of cast-iron cheeks, or square inserts that taper inward toward the bottom, that hold grates for each opening. In operation, cooks placed charcoal onto the grate from above and cleaned ashes from the ash-pit opening below. In contrast to the roaring heat normally associated with traditional open-hearth cooking, the stew stove allowed cooks to regulate the heat beneath stew pans, making possible the delicate elements of French dishes like *bouilli* with *sauce hachée*.

Although relatively rare in America at this time, the stew stove, in one form or another, had been used since antiquity.[10] In addition to his experiences in Europe, where stew stoves were more common, Jefferson also owned a book describing recommendations for kitchen arrangements aimed at increasing efficiency and conserving fuel.[11] In light of this literature, the Monticello stew stove as it has been reconstructed is rather straightforward and traditional in design: each stew opening has its own ash pit, fuel must be loaded from above, and there are no exhaust flues integrated into the brick-masonry structure. Without flues, the openings exhausted through the top or the ash-pit below; the exhaust gases escaped via the

window directly above the counter level and through the two kitchen doors, if opened. The lack of flues presented a known hazard, even if the ill effects of carbon monoxide inhalation were not yet recognized scientifically.[12] However, the stew stove, with its comfortable work height, was more convenient and presumably safer than open-hearth cooking, with its ever-present risk of accidental fire.

Unlike the stew stove, the accompanying set kettle—placed between the fireplace wall and the two largest stew holes—does contain its own flue. Located approximately ten inches above the floor level at the rear of the firebox, it would effectively draw heated air and smoke (from a wood-fueled fire) around the curved bottom of the copper set kettle and ultimately out through the main fireplace chimney. The heat conductivity of the copper boiler coupled with the firebox and flue design minimized the fuel required to keep a constant supply of hot water for cooking and cleaning.

Copper cookware, relatively rare in American kitchens due to its high initial cost and its rigorous maintenance needs, appeared prominently in Monticello's kitchen

The collection of French copper cookware used to furnish Monticello's restored kitchen replicates the inventory of kitchen items appearing in the 1790 Grevin packing list, including a tourtière, *or tart pan (above). The heat conductivity of copper pans made them ideal for use on the stew stove, which allowed cooks far better temperature control than traditional open-hearth cooking.*

ABOVE: *A kitchen scene from Bailey's* Dictionarium Domesticum *illustrates the manner in which the dresser was used for preparing or dressing meats for roasting, and in this case, fish for poaching. Large storage vessels or cooking pots could be stored on shelves beneath the dresser, while smaller and more frequently used items could be stored on the shelves above.*

OPPOSITE: *The restored fireplace wall houses a clock-work spit-jack that mechanized the turning of meats roasting on spits in front of the fireplace. The bake oven to the right of the fireplace was reconfigured during the kitchen restoration.*

inventories. Compared to cast iron, copper is lighter and, more importantly, has superior heat conductivity, maximizing the heat regulation afforded by the stew stove. This collection of copper was essential for French-style cooking, and consisted of a range of saucepans along with individual pieces that served specific functions, such as the *tourtière* (tart pan), *poissonnière* (fish cooker), and *réchaud en cuivre* (copper chafing dish), all of which appear in a list of items that Jefferson had shipped from France to America.[13]

Cooks at Monticello also employed older and less fashionable but otherwise effective technologies and methods, including a clock-work spit-jack mounted on the fireplace wall. Powered by gravity via a series of weights—analogous to the movement of a tall case clock—the spit-jack mechanism slowly turned meat roasting on spits suspended across the hearth on andirons equipped with hooks. Other long-held practices included hanging pots and kettles from the moveable crane in the fireplace and supporting skillets and pans on trivets in the hot ashes of the hearth floor. Incorporated into the fireplace wall, a brick oven enabled baking with radiant heat: a wood fire was built inside the domed interior, and exhausted through the flue located at the opening to the oven. After the oven reached the correct operating temperature, the fire was

cleared out, the food item placed inside, and a wooden door placed in the antechamber to block off the flue and prevent heat from escaping.

Like most well-equipped kitchens of the period, Monticello's probably featured a built-in dresser with integrated shelves. Much like a modern countertop, the dresser's work surface accommodated multiple food preparation tasks, and its shelves held most of the copper inventory. Dressers appear in numerous French and English illustrations of the period, but since such pieces of permanent furniture were usually considered part of the kitchen architecture, they do not appear regularly in kitchen inventories.

Equipped with such an array of culinary tools and work spaces, Monticello's kitchen can be seen as an interpretation or translation of the cooking practices of refined, ordered, and fashionable upper-class English and French kitchens into the decidedly rural setting of Albemarle County, Virginia. With a kitchen specifically designed and outfitted for the purpose of replicating the hospitality that Jefferson and his guests enjoyed at the President's House, the domestic work force on the mountaintop attempted to recreate sophisticated meals in the finest French tradition. These meals were as remarked upon in Jefferson's day as they are worthy of study in our own.

Carrying the Keys: Women and Housekeeping at Monticello

PASTED IN THE COMMONPLACE BOOK of one of Thomas Jefferson's granddaughters is a poem by her father, Thomas Mann Randolph, Jr., in which he describes the housekeeping practices of his daughters Mary and Cornelia Randolph at Monticello:

The Randolph women managed Monticello's domestic operations, including supervising locked storage spaces, selecting menus, and making daily purchases. Granddaughters' letters make clear that they preferred to pursue other activities, such as reading or drawing, as evidenced by this sketch by Cornelia Randolph.

While frugal Miss Mary kept the stores of the House
Not a rat could be seen, never heard was a mouse
Not a crumb was let fall
In kitchen or Hall
For no one could spare one crumb from his slice
The rations were issued by measures so nice
When April arrived to soften the air
Cornelia succeeded to better the fare
Oh! the boys were so glad,
And the Cooks were so sad,
Now puddings and pies everyday will be made,
Not once a month just to keep up the trade.[1]

Even with its teasing fatherly tone, Randolph's poem highlights the emphasis placed on food and the care taken with household provisions. Due to the traditions and expectations of Virginia plantation hospitality, the size of the extended family in residence, and Jefferson's approach to dining, household management was important business at Monticello.

When Jefferson retired from the presidency in 1809 and went to live again at

ELIZABETH V. CHEW is Associate Curator of Collections at Monticello.

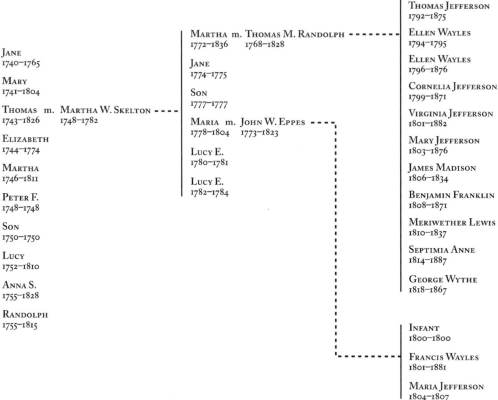

PETER JEFFERSON
1708–1757
m.
JANE RANDOLPH
1720–1776

JANE
1740–1765

MARY
1741–1804

THOMAS m. MARTHA W. SKELTON
1743–1826   1748–1782

ELIZABETH
1744–1774

MARTHA
1746–1811

PETER F.
1748–1748

SON
1750–1750

LUCY
1752–1810

ANNA S.
1755–1828

RANDOLPH
1755–1815

MARTHA m. THOMAS M. RANDOLPH
1772–1836   1768–1828

JANE
1774–1775

SON
1777–1777

MARIA m. JOHN W. EPPES
1778–1804   1773–1823

LUCY E.
1780–1781

LUCY E.
1782–1784

ANNE CARY
1791–1826

THOMAS JEFFERSON
1792–1875

ELLEN WAYLES
1794–1795

ELLEN WAYLES
1796–1876

CORNELIA JEFFERSON
1799–1871

VIRGINIA JEFFERSON
1801–1882

MARY JEFFERSON
1803–1876

JAMES MADISON
1806–1834

BENJAMIN FRANKLIN
1808–1871

MERIWETHER LEWIS
1810–1837

SEPTIMIA ANNE
1814–1887

GEORGE WYTHE
1818–1867

INFANT
1800–1800

FRANCIS WAYLES
1801–1881

MARIA JEFFERSON
1804–1807

James Westhall Ford painted Martha Jefferson Randolph at Monticello in September, 1823. Aged 51, Randolph was the mother of 11 children and the grandmother of 8.

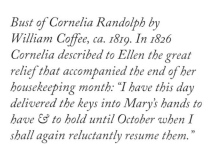

Bust of Cornelia Randolph by William Coffee, ca. 1819. In 1826 Cornelia described to Ellen the great relief that accompanied the end of her housekeeping month: "I have this day delivered the keys into Mary's hands to have & to hold until October when I shall again reluctantly resume them."

Monticello, women and children dominated his large household. His wife, Martha Wayles Skelton Jefferson, had been dead for almost twenty-seven years, but their oldest and only surviving child, Martha Jefferson Randolph, moved her large family to live with her father at her childhood home.[2] Randolph, then aged thirty-six, was the mother of eight children between the ages of one and eighteen; she gave birth to three more at Monticello between 1810 and 1818.[3] Upon Jefferson's death in 1826, thirteen other people resided in the Monticello house, including three great-grandchildren.

Martha Jefferson Randolph managed the household while her father supervised the plantation operations. Only ten years old when her own mother died in 1782, Randolph had not received, before her marriage in 1790, the domestic training necessary for a future plantation mistress. She attended an elite convent school in Paris while her father was serving as American minister there from 1784 to 1789. In a diary entry written in

1839, Randolph's daughter Ellen Randolph Coolidge contrasted her own domestic education with her mother's. Coolidge notes that her mother received instruction in "the useful branches of education, arithmetic, geography, history and modern languages" from "the best masters in Paris," but learned no practical skills for running a household. Her mother, she writes, felt this omission severely, "having to acquire with painful conscientiousness, a knowledge of many matters certainly not taught in the Abbaye Royal de Panthemont, Faubourg Saint-Germain, Paris."[4]

Martha Randolph sought to compensate for the gaps in her own education by providing her daughters with hands-on experience in housekeeping at Monticello, along with their academic lessons. By the mid 1810s, when they were in their later teens, Randolph required her as-yet unmarried daughters Ellen, Cornelia, Virginia, and Mary to perform the duties of housekeeper at Monticello for a month at a time on a rotating basis.

The Randolph women's responsibilities included overseeing the kitchen, supervising the numerous secure storage spaces in the dependencies, and accounting for all the foodstuffs kept under locks to guard against theft, a constant threat. Housekeeping also entailed coordinating with the enslaved butler, Burwell Colbert, the myriad other details of domestic management for a large household with many visitors. While the tasks varied, the month-long turn seemed monotonous to the young women, as Mary Randolph described in an 1821 letter: "[T]he functions I perform … are exactly such as a machine might be made to perform with equal success, locking and unlocking doors, pouring out tea and coffee and in the interim plying my needle."[5]

The Randolphs called the task of housekeeping "keeping" or "carrying the keys." Their shorthand highlights the importance placed on keys in a plantation household and the centrality of locked storage to the duties of the plantation mistress.[6] References to the responsibilities accompanying "the keys" are frequent topics in their surviving letters. In 1823 Virginia Randolph wrote, "I took the keys and entered upon the hardships of keeping house." Two years later Mary Randolph had "an unfinished frock upon the stocks which I have not thought

Martha Jefferson Randolph's red leather "housewife" held pins, needles, a pencil, and pages for notes. On these pages Randolph recorded a silver inventory and made a to-do list.

WHO WAS BURWELL COLBERT?

IN 1809, WHEN JEFFERSON retired from public life, the Monticello butler was a twenty-nine-year-old enslaved man named Burwell Colbert. In this role Colbert, who was described by overseer Edmund Bacon as "the main, principal servant," coordinated Monticello's domestic arrangements with Martha Randolph and her daughters. He supervised the enslaved house maids and teenaged boys who laid fires and helped with table service. Colbert's work was so efficient that Jefferson's granddaughter Ellen Randolph once complained, "We never have the comfort of a clean house whilst Burwell is away."[17] In addition to his general house responsibilities, Colbert acted as Jefferson's personal servant and was one of only two slaves allowed regular access to his private rooms.[18]

The complexities of master-slave relations and their impact on domestic arrangements are borne out in Burwell Colbert's connections with the Jefferson family. Colbert, the enslaved person with the most responsibility in the Monticello house, had control over keys that safeguarded tablewares and foodstuffs. Colbert's commitment to his responsibilities shows itself in an 1819 letter written from Poplar Forest by Ellen Randolph, the day after Colbert learned of his wife Critta's death back at Monticello: "Burwell as you may suppose is overwhelmed with grief…. But although h[e] did not shew [sic] himself, he came out early in the morning and did all his business as usual. He did not lay by and send us the keys as I expected he would."[19] Part of the granddaughters' roles as housekeepers would have been to negotiate with Colbert control over keys and locked rooms, subtleties which are very difficult for historians to ascertain from the distance of time.

Colbert was the son of Betty Brown, a housemaid who also did needle work. His maternal grandmother was Elizabeth (Betty) Hemings, matriarch of the enslaved family that lived and worked at Monticello for five generations. Colbert was one of two enslaved workers to whom Jefferson gave an annual premium for his services, and he was the only slave to receive immediate freedom on Jefferson's death. In the codicil to his will Jefferson wrote, "I give to my good, affectionate, and faithful servant Burwell his freedom…."[20] Before becoming butler, Colbert had trained as a painter and glazier, trades which supported him in freedom.

— E.V.C.

This detail from The Dinner Party, *Henry Sargent, ca. 1821, depicts a waiter at a formal gathering in Boston. As butler at Monticello, Burwell Colbert served as head waiter and supervised other servants assisting with the meal. Photograph © 2005 Museum of Fine Arts, Boston.*

of touching since I carried the keys."[7]

Monticello's daily operations necessitated continual interaction between the members of Jefferson's white family and their enslaved domestic servants. To enable and facilitate the lives of the occupants of the Monticello house in the mid 1820s, approximately sixteen enslaved people, including butler Burwell Colbert, seamstress and ladies' maid Sally Hemings, nurse Priscilla Hemings, and cook Edith Fossett, performed the work required above and below stairs to keep the house functioning.[8]

The kitchen in particular was always a main crossroads of the household. Isaac Jefferson, who lived in slavery at Monticello from 1781 until 1826, recalled his mother Ursula telling him that "Mrs. Jefferson would come out there [to the kitchen] with a cookery book in her hand and read out of it… how to make cakes, tarts, and so on."[9] This rare reference to Jefferson's wife, Martha Wayles Skelton Jefferson, places her in the kitchen instructing the cook. By 1823 Jefferson's twenty-year-old granddaughter Virginia Randolph had taken her grandmother's place in the kitchen. She wrote her fiancé Nicholas Trist that she had received a letter from him "seated upon my *throne* in the kitchen, with a cookery book in my hand."[10] The person working under Virginia's regal supervision would likely have been Edith

Hern Fossett, who by this time had been cooking for Jefferson and his family since shortly after Virginia was born. Trained at the President's House in Washington by Jefferson's French chef, Fossett took over the Monticello kitchen in Jefferson's retirement.

As housekeepers, Martha Randolph and her daughters managed supplies of flour, sugar, tea, bacon, ham, and the more exotic foodstuffs Jefferson imported from Europe, including anchovies, pasta, olive oil, Parmesan cheese, and wines. They also routinely purchased provisions from slaves to use in the house. Accounts kept intermittently in the 1820s by Martha Randolph and her daughter Mary detail this dynamic cash economy that further connected the enslaved people and those who held them on the Monticello plantation.[11]

The Randolphs' purchasing activities at Monticello mirror typical practices across the Chesapeake and Low Country, where slaveholders habitually paid cash to slaves for the fowl, eggs, and garden produce raised on their own time. The Monticello accounts record year-round payments to slaves for

The Randolph women selected menus and read recipes to the Monticello cooks, who then executed the dishes using sophisticated equipment such as the set kettle (above), part of a built-in stew stove, unusual in early American kitchens.

The all-weather passageway underneath Monticello connected the kitchen and other cellar-level work and storage rooms. Staircases led up to the Dining Room and family living spaces. The kitchen and passageway served as major locations of interaction between the enslaved community and Jefferson's family in the main house.

great quantities of eggs and chickens and for smaller quantities of fish, ducks, and soap. Martha Randolph noted seasonal payments for produce including cabbages, cucumbers, watermelons, potatoes, sweet potatoes, apples, and chestnuts. Her purchases in the 1820s correspond closely with those recorded in an earlier account book by her oldest daughter, Anne Cary Randolph, during periods Jefferson spent at Monticello in his second term as president.[12]

Household accounts also suggest that in the years before her father's death Martha Randolph regularly borrowed money from John and Priscilla Hemings. John Hemings was a highly skilled enslaved joiner and his wife a nurse and child-minder; both were favorites of the Randolph grandchildren.

This financial relationship between slave and slave holder bespeaks the meagerness of the housekeeping budget with which the Randolph women provided for the large Monticello household and its many visitors.

Compounding the difficulties of household management was Jefferson's debt, which grew over the years, strained in part by the burden of expected hospitality. The stream of visitors turned the responsibilities of maintaining inventories and selecting menus into challenging tasks. Overseer Edmund Bacon recalled: "After Mr. Jefferson returned from Washington, he was for years crowded with visitors, and they almost ate him out of house and home.... I have killed a fine beef, and it would be all eaten in a day or two."[13]

Their letters indicate that the younger Randolph women considered housekeeping an onerous and time-consuming responsibility that dulled their minds and took them away from reading, writing letters, playing musical instruments, and other activities they preferred. In 1822 Mary wrote: "I could tear my hair and disparage myself to think of the precious time I am wasting from my precious studies...."[14] Virginia wrote to Nicholas Trist in 1822: "I have not much command of my time at present, for it is divided between the duties of hospitality..., keeping house ... and the sewing work I am always obliged to do. Books have been quite out of the question lately, and the harpsichord even has been silent for several months."[15] In 1824, Ellen apologized for a letter she wrote to Trist, saying she "undertook to write during the latter days of my house-keeping month, when I am so overwhelmed with business that … to think of any thing but beef and pudding at present is out of the question."[16]

The Randolph women's written legacy suggests that Monticello's hospitality and signature French-influenced cuisine was created through collaboration between the skilled enslaved workers and the white female housekeepers of the Jefferson family. Though the young white women bemoaned their responsibilities as housekeepers, they had vastly more control over their own time than the enslaved people they directed. At Monticello today, the lively voices of Jefferson's Randolph granddaughters can still speak to us across two centuries through their surviving writings. The voices of their enslaved contemporaries are not so easy to hear. Our challenge is to listen carefully and to tell the most complete story possible.

The beer room in the Monticello cellar was one of many secured storage areas. The importance of locked spaces in the management of Monticello is made clear in the granddaughters' shorthand for their domestic responsibilities: "carrying the keys."

African Americans and Monticello's Food Culture

ALTHOUGH CHIEFLY RESPONSIBLE for the celebrated cuisine enjoyed at Monticello, African Americans were—by design—somewhat invisible to those seated around the table. Farm laborers who raised the crops and livestock that helped supply the table typically lived in quarters at a distant remove from the main house. Cooks and house servants often lived and worked in rooms adjoining Monticello—but even so, these spaces were buried in the hillside, covered and hidden by terraces. Even during meals, the use of service dumbwaiters limited the face-to-face contact between servers and diners, so that those seated at the table could perhaps become blind to the individuals who raised, harvested, prepared, and served the elegant meals they enjoyed. These African Americans—some of whom remain invisible to us today because of our lack of knowledge about their lives—created a lasting, dual culinary legacy, whether the fine cuisine served at Monticello, or the enslaved community's own rich food traditions, cultivated amid adversity.

Some of the house servants listed in Jefferson's Farm Book in 1810 (above, left column) were charged with food-related responsibilities, including food preparation in the technologically sophisticated kitchen at Monticello (opposite).

Today we might associate only a small number of enslaved house servants with the meals served at Monticello—cooks and waiters, for instance. However, virtually all of Jefferson's slaves participated in the food culture. The first and broadest point of involvement was the cultivation of crops, what Jefferson called working "in the ground." After the 1790s, enslaved men and women raised wheat as the main cash crop, and although most of the wheat was sold, some of the flour certainly ended up on the table at Monticello. The wheat harvest in particular shows

DIANNE SWANN-WRIGHT is Curator at the Frederick Douglass–Isaac Myers Maritime Park in Baltimore, Maryland.

Gardeners, such as Goliah or John, were responsible for tending Jefferson's fruit and vegetable gardens. They also supervised the efforts of older workers, dubbed the "veteran aids."

that virtually every member of the enslaved community would have contributed to Monticello's food culture, since all able-bodied men, women, and children over the age of nine laid aside their ordinary responsibilities to participate in the harvest. The only exceptions were female domestic servants, who presumably stayed at the main house to put food on the table in a more direct fashion.

Closer to the Monticello kitchen, enslaved workers created and tended the thousand-foot-long vegetable garden and nearby fruitery to provide for the Jefferson table. Squire and Great George were the first in a series of workers who cultivated Jefferson's mountaintop gardens. They worked newly

cleared, sloping land, not the terraced garden later hewed from the mountaintop by African Americans leased from other farms. Within these fruit and vegetable plots, enslaved gardeners raised not only kitchen plants typical to the region, but they also coaxed life out of seeds from around the world. The men assigned as head gardeners received training for this challenging task from European horticulturalists hired by Jefferson. Scottish gardener Robert Bailey instructed Wormley Hughes and John, for example, and Great George, Monticello's only enslaved overseer, learned about fruit trees from the Italian Antonio Giannini. African-American gardeners then became teachers in their own right, passing on their knowledge and techniques to others. Jefferson assigned elderly women and men—dubbed the "senile core" or "veteran aids"—to weed and work under the supervision of experienced gardeners such as Goliah.

Aside from cultivating fields and gardens, African Americans also tended Jefferson's livestock for the production of milk and eggs, as well as raising and slaughtering animals such as rabbits, poultry, sheep, pigs, and cows. Overseer Edmund Bacon recalled that the foremen on Monticello's several quarter farms would compete to see "which would make the largest crops" or the "best lot of pork." The winner received a premium of "an extra barrel of flour…, a fine Sunday suit…, [or] an extra hundred and fifty pounds of bacon." Bacon remembered that a black foreman, James Hern, "always had the best pork, so that the other overseers said it was no use for them to try anymore."[1]

These activities—raising crops, cultivating gardens, tending animals—were tasks required of the enslaved community, part of the routine Jefferson established when he assigned responsibilities such as plowing, spinning, or making nails. But with their daily tasks completed, the enslaved people of Monticello worked on their own time in their own gardens. More than seventy enslaved men, women, and children harvested enough vegetables and raised enough chickens to sell what may have been their surplus to Jefferson and those who lived in the Monticello house. Peter Hatch notes that "Squire, for example, … represented the most sophisticated garden. He sold thirteen different commodities, including cymlins (a patty-pan-shaped squash), potatoes, lettuce,

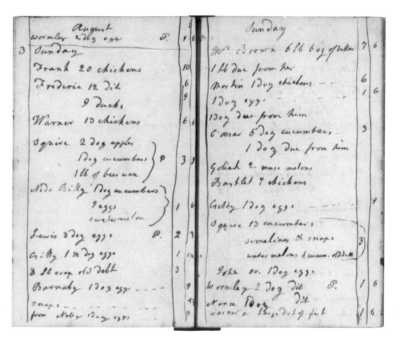

In their own time, enslaved men and women hunted, fished, raised vegetables, and tended poultry yards, selling a variety of goods to Jefferson's family. The account book of Jefferson's granddaughter Anne Cary Randolph (above) shows that in August 1807, slaves sold chicken, ducks, apples, cucumbers, beeswax, eggs, and watermelon, among other items.

How were the Monticello cooks trained?

IN THE SPRING OF 1784, Jefferson considered engaging a French chef in Annapolis to train one of the Monticello slaves. However, soon afterward he found himself preparing for a diplomatic appointment in France, and he decided "for a particular purpose to carry my servant Jame with me."[19]

On his arrival in Paris, nineteen-year-old James Hemings began his culinary apprenticeship. He studied first with Monsieur Combeaux, the caterer who provided Jefferson's meals. His training continued under a female cook Jefferson hired in 1786, amplified by periodic "workshops" with a pastry chef and a cook in the household of the Prince de Condé. After three years of study, James Hemings took charge of the kitchen in Jefferson's residence on the Champs-Elysées. His creations were served to authors and scientists, and a succession of European aristocrats from the Duc de la Rochefoucauld to the Princess Lubomirska.

Back in America, James Hemings was Jefferson's chef in Philadelphia and at Monticello. When he asked to be freed, his manumission was made contingent on training another Monticello slave in the "art of cookery."[20] His brother Peter was thus the next head cook at Monticello. Peter Hemings not only received his brother's training in cookery, but later learned brewing and malting from an English brewer detained in Albemarle County during the War of 1812.

A Frenchman, however, became the chef in the President's House when James Hemings declined the post in 1801. Soon African-American apprentices from Monticello were at work in Washington under chef Honoré Julien and maitre d'hôtel Etienne Lemaire. Edith Fossett and Fanny Hern spent several years at the President's House, and took over the Monticello kitchen on Jefferson's retirement in 1809. There, using the copper *batterie de cuisine* imported from France twenty years before, the two women transformed what

Hanging rack in the Monticello kitchen, with sieves, lids, utensils, and towel.

Jefferson called "plantation fare" into "choice" meals. In 1809 Lemaire wrote, "I am quite happy, Edy and Fanny are good workers, they are two good girls and I am convinced that they will give you much satisfaction."[21]

— L.S.

beets, watermelons, apples, and muskmelons. He sold a cucumber to Jefferson on January 12, 1773, suggesting either that the fruit was pickled and preserved, or that artificial heat in a cold frame or hot bed was used to bring this tender vegetable to fruition in the middle of winter, a rather remarkable feat in eighteenth-century Virginia."[2] While women may have tended these home gardens, account books suggest that men more often sold the goods. Ursula and Wormley Hughes, regular workers in the Monticello house and gardens, appear to have handled the transactions of unnamed others. Children as young as eight years old became sellers of fruits and nuts gathered from the land. Even though chickens, eggs, cucumbers, and cabbage were the most frequently sold items, the Jefferson family also purchased corn, ducks, onions, potatoes, watermelon, sprouts, and strawberries, among other fruits, vegetables, and household items such as beeswax. While in most instances currency changed hands, slaves also exchanged chicken and greens for highly valued pork and coffee. In addition, enslaved people netted bounties from nearby woods and waters, selling fish and game birds. Although at least one enslaved person, Great George, was known to own livestock, no slaves were listed as the sellers of cattle, sheep, or hogs.

African Americans' involvement in food culture began with food production and continued with its preparation. Highly skilled cooks and their assistants worked together to create the French-influenced cuisine that was served in the Dining and Tea Rooms. Men and women, the young and the old, worked from dawn until late into the night. Even the infirm performed light duties such as shelling corn. While men most often salted, hung, smoked, and carved meat, women milked cows and made butter. Young boys like Israel Gillette (whose sister Fanny was a cook) retrieved ice, water, coal, and firewood, or helped in the kitchen peeling, slicing, or turning the ice cream freezer. Tasks also varied from the daily to the periodic, such as the arduous wintertime task of filling the icehouse with sixty-two wagonloads of ice cut from the Rivanna River and transported to the top of the mountain. At given intervals, enslaved workers prepared beer and cider, the beverages served with meals at Monticello. Jefferson preferred Ursula for bottling cider, since "there is nobody there but Ursula who unites trust and skill to do it."[3]

Later Monticello cooks—many of whom

As shown in this circa 1833 lithograph from Life in Philadelphia, *enslaved workers continued working long after dinner concluded, washing dishes, cleaning the kitchen, and making preparations for the next day's meals.*

Shortly after his manumission in 1796, James Hemings recorded an important inventory of "Kitchen Utincils," showing the wide array of culinary equipment that he and other highly trained cooks used at Monticello.

were French-trained—also united trust and skill in their responsibilities. Brothers James and Peter Hemings and sisters-in-law Edith Hern Fossett and Fanny Gillette Hern would have both relied on their training and also added their own touches, preparing dishes with which they are associated even today. Among the Jefferson family recipes, snow eggs and three types of creams are credited to James Hemings, who perhaps learned them in Paris. From Washington, Jefferson wrote home, "Pray enable yourself to direct us here how to make muffins in Peter's method. My cook here cannot succeed at all in them, and they are a great luxury to me."[4] Apparently even the French chef at the President's House could not satisfy Jefferson's desire for Peter Hemings' muffins at breakfast. Similarly, when Jefferson's granddaughter Ellen married and moved to Boston, she requested that her mother send her favorite Monticello recipes, including "gingerbread such as Edy makes."[5] No family recipes credit Edith Fossett as their source, but one for "Fanny's crisp ginger bread"—a possible reference to Fanny Hern—does survive.[6]

Enslaved people not only prepared these favorite dishes, but they also served them. Servants would carry freshly prepared food (on warming plates filled with hot water or sand) from the kitchen through an all-weather passageway and into a French-style staging area, or *office*. There, workers plated and garnished food on porcelain or silver dishes before carrying meals upstairs and loading them onto the Dining Room's revolving service door. Upstairs, service was the domain of the Monticello butler, a position held for decades by members of the enslaved Hemings family, first Martin Hemings and later his nephew Burwell Colbert. Trusted with the keys to locked storage rooms containing foodstuffs, alcohol, and tablewares, these men supervised the young men and boys who set and waited on tables. Perhaps the clearest portrait of the role of butler arises from a time when server Israel Gillette filled in for the sick Burwell Colbert. Jefferson's granddaughter recalled, "Israel has shone, during B's illness. Has kept himself as clean and genteel as possible, and in the pride of being chief waiter has followed Miss Edgeworth's rules of doing every thing in its proper time, putting every thing to its proper use, and everything in its proper place, with as much exactness, as if he had studied them with every desire of edification."[7]

Aside from the long hours of preparing and serving food for Jefferson's table, enslaved workers—primarily women—also tended to their own families' meals. Social custom, personal preference, and economic realities shaped the dietary lives of enslaved people at Monticello. Archaeological investigations suggest that the diets of enslaved people on Jefferson's farms had much in common with others living in Maryland, Virginia, and North Carolina. Pork and beef served as the main sources of protein, vegetables were eaten in abundance, and cornmeal and wheat flour formed a predominance of the grain. Jefferson rationed foods according to the age, gender, and the work assigned to the person. Each week, most adult workers received a half-pound of pork or pickled beef, a peck of cornmeal, and four fish, with whiskey and molasses distributed on special occasions. Other records allude to the periodic allocation of salt, peas, potatoes, and milk.[8]

By far, pork bones dominate the archaeological remains found at slave sites, followed by beef, and then mutton, all raised for use at Jefferson's table as well as for the meat rations distributed to workers. Enslaved cooks would have used all of the meat provided, including the feet, heads, and organs. In addition to carefully managing their rations, excavations show that slave families

Snow eggs (above), along with chocolate, coffee, and tea creams, are attributed to James Hemings in the recipe manuscripts of Jefferson's granddaughters, as shown (at left) in the cookbook of Virginia Randolph Trist.

supplemented their meals by raising poultry, by catching fish, and by hunting game such as venison, opossum, rabbits, and squirrel.

These supplied and hunted meats were augmented by a wide variety of vegetables grown in individual garden plots. If people sold what they themselves favored on their tables, then cabbage, white and sweet potatoes, beans, greens, and cucumbers would have filled pots in slave cabins. Jefferson instructed one overseer to give "to each grown negro a pint [of salt] a month for their snaps, cymlins and other uses."[9] Women would have simmered these vegetables for hours until the meat that seasoned it became tender, and Jefferson's granddaughter recalled that when the enslaved Critta Colbert was ill, she requested "some meat out of the soups" prepared by her mother, a weaver who cooked for her own family in her time away from the loom.[10]

Jefferson's instructions to his overseers document grain rations of cornmeal along with rye and wheat flour. In his Farm Book he observed that "the labourers prefer receiving 1. peck of flour to 1½ peck of Indian [or corn] meal."[11] Despite their preference for

wheat flour, African Americans typically received the latter. Hoecake made from the meal was a staple at regional plantations; one traveler through Virginia described a "group of slaves sitting on some logs at the end of a harvest field baking a very large cake of Indian meal."[12] Jefferson directed overseer Jeremiah Goodman to "give to [the workers'] breadmaker a pint [of salt] a month for each grown negro to put into their bread."[13] The breadmakers were perhaps the middle-aged women assigned to prepare noon meals for gangs working in fields, and given the availability of cornmeal, hoecake was likely the standard bread.[14]

Documentary and archaeological evidence also provides a glimpse into the material culture of the enslaved community. Jefferson periodically distributed Dutch ovens and grain sifters to enslaved workers, such as on the occasion of the marriage of "Bedford John and his wife Virginia."[15] Archaeologists have also unearthed fashionable ceramics such as Chinese porcelain at slave cabins. Research suggests that enslaved people purchased many of these dishes themselves, though they perhaps also received some chipped or discarded items from the main house.

The quality of the fare prepared by the African Americans at Monticello is perhaps best captured by a recollection of Jefferson's

ABOVE: *In freedom, Peter Fossett was one of Cincinnati's most prominent caterers, likely using skills and recipes gleaned from his mother, Edith Fossett, who cooked both at the President's House and Monticello.*

OPPOSITE: *Peter Hemings was the first resident of the cook's room adjacent to the kitchen. Following Jefferson's retirement in 1809, either Edith Fossett or Fanny Hern—both trained at the President's House— moved into the space with her family.*

grandson. He described joining enslaved men as they gathered honey from a bee tree and then returned to a cabin to find that "Old Betty had a pot of hot coffee, fried meat and eggs, and a dish of honey … at a little table covered with the best."[16] This notion of a "table covered with the best" recalls guests' descriptions of the tables over which Jefferson presided. It also foretells the legacy that Monticello slaves would foster after gaining their freedom. Edith Fossett not only mastered culinary skills as a slave in kitchens at the President's House and at Monticello, she also passed them on to her children. After gaining their freedom and settling in Cincinnati, Ohio, her sons Peter and William Fossett became prominent caterers in the city, known for the delicious food they served and the excellent service they rendered. Peter Fossett was an "indispensable major domo at wedding feasts and entertainments," and he used his financial resources to build a Cincinnati church and orphanage.[17] His brother William—described as "active in anything to benefit his people"—later left Ohio and supervised food service at a hotel in Niagara Falls.[18] These names, their lives, and their stories—and in the case of Peter Fossett, even his picture—help to pierce the blanket of invisibility that shrouds the skills and contributions of the enslaved community at Monticello.

"A Declaration of Wants": Provisioning the Monticello Table

WHEN THOMAS JEFFERSON WOULD arrive home from Washington for his twice-yearly visits at Monticello, after inquiring about everyone and talking briefly, his thoughts would turn to food, and he would ask, "What have you got that is good?" Such was the recollection of his overseer of sixteen years, Edmund Bacon, who also remembered that "He was never a great eater, but what he did eat he wanted to be very choice."[1]

Bringing a "choice" meal to table depended, certainly, upon a skilled staff working in a well-appointed kitchen, but equally important was the adequate provisioning of quality foodstuffs. With orchards, an extensive vegetable garden, and livestock production that included cattle, sheep, hogs, rabbits, and fowl, Jefferson's farms served as the primary source for the foods that came to the table at Monticello. However, existing records and correspondence indicate there was always an active exchange between the Monticello kitchen and the surrounding neighborhood, with purchases such as butter and beef from Mr. and Mrs. Craven next door and hams from Meriwether Lewis's mother, among many others. In addition, according to family account books, Monticello's enslaved community either sold or bartered fresh fish, eggs, poultry, and a variety of vegetables. Aside from this local produce, Jefferson supplemented what he termed "plantation fare" with foods from national and international markets and remained active in the acquisition of foodstuffs for the Monticello table throughout his life.

During his political career, Jefferson had prepared for his extended visits to Mon-

Jefferson procured foods from both domestic and international markets, including sugar cones, vinegar, olive oil, cinnamon, anchovies, mustard, Parmesan cheese, raisins, nutmeg, pasta, and almonds. Jefferson's 1821 shipping bill from Dodge & Oxnard (above) shows delivery of wine and food from Marseilles to Boston.

GAYE WILSON is research historian at the Robert H. Smith International Center for Jefferson Studies at Monticello.

A 1772 broadside for a Philadelphia merchant is suggestive of the holdings kept in Jefferson's storage rooms in the cellar at Monticello. The kitchen scales are one of the few original kitchen artifacts that survive from Monticello's well-equipped kitchen.

ticello by sending grocery items ahead that could be more easily obtained in either the Washington area or more likely Philadelphia, Baltimore, or New York. These shipments of what he termed "necessaries" often included coffee, tea, chocolate, sugar, cheese, mustard, raisins, and spices.[2] Then a note to his overseer would request that various kinds of meats, fowl, and other foods produced on the plantation be on hand in anticipation of family members and visitors who would join him during his stay. But after his retirement from the presidency and his permanent move back to Monticello, there was the problem of where to obtain the "necessaries." In other words, where was he to buy groceries?

His cousin, George Jefferson, had been acting as his agent in Richmond for several years, taking care of his sales of wheat, tobacco, and other business matters, but rather than trouble his cousin with grocery orders, Jefferson wrote, "It becomes necessary for

me to establish a correspondence somewhere for the supply of my groceries … and I believe Richmond will be more convenient than Baltimore, Philadelphia, & New York, if to be had there on nearly equal terms." He requested the name of a reputable supplier and estimated that over the year he would want about nine hundred to a thousand pounds of sugar, from one hundred to two hundred pounds of coffee, about twenty-five pounds of tea, and fifteen to twenty barrels of fish in addition to other smaller items.[3]

George Jefferson suggested the name of a Richmond firm, Gordon, Trokes and Company. Jefferson promptly wrote to set up his account and placed an order for a quarterly supply of groceries. His initial order contained many of the same "necessaries" he had shipped home for his bi-annual visits and provides a profile of staple grocery items that stocked the Monticello kitchen. He began his list with eight pounds of tea, preferably Hyson, and fifty pounds of coffee. In this and in other orders Jefferson was very explicit as to his preference in coffee: "Bourbon or E. India would always be preferred, but good West India will give satisfaction, always excepting against what is called Green coffee which we cannot use."[4] In other correspondence he would explain that even though "Green" coffee had become very popular in the United States, "The genuine well ripened coffee of the W. Indies, that of Java, of Bourbon, of Moka rise in different degrees of superiority over it."[5] Jefferson continued his order to Gordon, Trokes and Company with twelve loaves of white sugar, two hundred pounds of best brown sugar, ten pounds of raisins, and two pounds of black pepper, along with lesser amounts of cinnamon, mace, and nutmeg. To this he added ten pounds of pearl barley, twenty pounds of rice, and a keg of crackers. He wanted one "best cheese for the table" and a "poorer" cheese for cookery and noted that "the rich cheeses do not answer for this." He completed his order with a keg of French brandy, three dozen bottles of "Syrop of

Punch," and several barrels of different kinds of fish, "best quality."[6]

Jefferson was especially fond of fish and often included barrels of salted and pickled fish in grocery orders. Salted cod and shad were particular favorites, along with oysters and what he termed a "great delicacy," the tongues and sounds (air bladder) of the cod fish. To insure fresh fish on the Monticello table, he had two fish ponds built in the spring of 1812 and petitioned local acquaintances to help him stock the new ponds: "I have just made me a fish pond and am desirous to get some carp fish to stock it." Most of the fish contributed did not survive, yet Jefferson did not give up, "The obtaining

Jefferson ordered salted and pickled fish regularly and designed several fish ponds at Monticello in the hopes of stocking a fresh supply. Family account books show frequent purchases of fish from enslaved men and boys.

How can one 'provision the table' today?

PROVISIONING THE TABLE in our modern world is in many regards far easier today than it was for Jefferson. We can be particularly thankful that Americans have lately rediscovered the delights of high-quality olive oil, mustards, vinegars, and pastas, along with whole spices such as vanilla beans or nutmeg. While Jefferson did not introduce those items to America, he does appear strikingly "modern" in the degree to which he embraced these largely imported and therefore rare foods.

Yet while it has become far easier to obtain the more "exotic" provisions that made their way to Jefferson's table, we do well to recall that most of the food served at Monticello was produced directly on its farms or within its neighborhood. It was not the easy, idyllic life that romantics imagine, instead requiring the hard labor of both free and enslaved people. However, wholesome foods—stone-ground flour, freshly harvested vegetables, naturally raised meats and dairy products—were more generally incorporated into daily life than today.

Modern grocery stores are glutted with food choices, but shoppers must be very discriminating if they wish to find the sorts of whole foods that were a daily part of eighteenth- and nineteenth-century life. Notes on selecting such ingredients—both imported and regional—appear throughout the recipe section of this book.

The best way to recreate Monticello's table, then, is to embrace a seasonal approach to dining, seeking out naturally raised meats, supporting local farm and dairy networks—in short, becoming as passionate about quality as Jefferson himself was.

—D.L.F

While Jefferson did not introduce foods such as European pasta, olive oil, and mustard to America, he does appear strikingly "modern" in the degree to which he embraced them.

[of] breeders for my pond being too interesting to be abandoned."[7] The second pond was stocked with chub, but heavy spring rains of 1814 carried away many of the fish from both ponds.[8] Nevertheless, neighbors continued to supply him from time to time with local varieties, and an entry in his *Garden Book* for May 1819 mentions three fish ponds: one for carp, one for chub and one for eels.[9] In addition, Monticello household records reflect frequent purchases of fresh fish from enslaved men and boys living on the plantation.[10]

The variety of foods produced on the plantation or purchased within the neighborhood or from a local supplier were enhanced with specialty items and condiments that Jefferson ordered directly from Europe. While living in France, Jefferson became acquainted with American consuls serving at various European ports, and after his return to the United States, he used these political connections for direct purchases of wine and special grocery items. The War of 1812 interrupted overseas commerce, but at its conclusion, Jefferson soon resumed communication with Stephen Cathalan, American consul at Marseilles. He began his first letter with an analysis of Bonaparte's downfall, continued it with a lofty proclamation about the independence of nations, and concluded it with an order for wine and pasta, stating:

"I resume our old correspondence with a declaration of wants."[11] A typical "declaration of wants" could include such items as Smyrna raisins, Parmesan cheese, almonds, anchovies, Maille mustard, olive oil, and "macaroni," the term Jefferson used for all pasta. Improved quality and lower cost seemed to be the primary motivation for these overseas purchases, as some of the items such as mustard, raisins, and even anchovies he would occasionally purchase from merchants in Charlottesville, Richmond, or Williamsburg. He tried obtaining pasta from local sources as well but without apparent success and attempted to cultivate the sesame plant for a domestic alternative to olive oil.

One motivation for raising and producing his own oil was freshness. He remarked upon the disadvantage of having it "brought across the Atlantic and exposed in hot warehouses."[12] Getting goods to Monticello was always a challenge. The nearest Virginia seaport, Norfolk, was almost two hundred miles away. From there, goods were shipped up the

Jefferson used American consuls in France to procure groceries for him. On June 6, 1817, Jefferson wrote this list of food and wine (requesting goods for both him and his grandson) to Stephen Cathalan in Marseilles.

James River to Richmond, where they might be stored until transportation to Monticello could be arranged, either by water or wagon.

If shipped by water, the goods would travel up the James River and then onto one of its branches, the Rivanna. At the Rivanna's upper terminus, the goods would be unloaded in the village of Milton, about three to four miles from Monticello. But in summers, drought could detain the food-stuffs in Richmond until the rivers were navigable again, and in the winter, ice could slow river traffic.

Shipment by wagon was an alternative, with goods carted along the Three Notched Road from Richmond to Charlottesville and then to Monticello. Jefferson employed several of the enslaved men on his plantation as wagoners to carry goods between Monti-cello and Richmond and to move goods and livestock between Monticello and his plan-tation in southern Virginia, Poplar Forest.

He reported from Monticello in January 1815 that "Dick arrived here on the 4th with but-ter, salt, beef and hogs."[13]

Post was another method of shipment, but available only to very small items. Short-ly after his retirement from the presidency, Jefferson wrote his former maitre d'hôtel, Etienne Lemaire, then living in Philadel-phia, for salad oil and vanilla. He advised that the oil would have to go by boat via Richmond, but the vanilla could be sent by post. Lemaire's return letter contained a half pound of vanilla and a reminder to Mon-ticello's cook, Edith Fossett, whom he had helped train, to use the beans sparingly.[14]

Proper packing was a vital part of ship-ping, and often Jefferson gave detailed in-structions, requesting, for instance, that salad oil be "packed in *much straw* to protect it from the heat of the sun."[15] He also directed that items be packed in "an outer case or barrel for greater safety."[16] This "outer case" would curtail breakage or water damage, and Jefferson also hoped it would protect his goods against "the system of plunder which our watermen carry on."[17] After experiencing problems with barrels of wine being tapped and diluted with water, Jefferson advised that molasses be put "in a double case in sound & good condition or it will be no better than a hogshead of water when it arrives."[18] Despite the risk of theft, Jefferson often expressed a preference for shipment by boat, especially if breakage was a consideration, but he specified boatmen that are "deemed trusty," and if available, he preferred the boats of his son-in-law, Thomas Mann Randolph, or those of his cousin, Thomas Eston Randolph. At least with the Randolph watermen, he reasoned, "Their credit with the family, the certainty and responsibility on detection, will give a security which we can have with no others."[19]

In his final years, with his health worsening, still Jefferson remained involved in the provisioning of the Monticello kitchen. After 1819, his eldest grandson and namesake, Thomas Jefferson Randolph, took over much of the running of his farms, and the daily supplies for the kitchen, under the supervision of his daughter and granddaughters, relied heavily upon purchases of chickens, eggs, butter, and a variety of vegetables from neighbors and the enslaved community of Monticello. However, overseas orders for wine and specialty foodstuffs continued to be in Jefferson's own hand, and as his debts mounted in his last months, he juggled payments to local Charlottesville merchants for staple grocery items. In January 1826, just six months before his death, Jefferson authorized payment of freight and duties on what would be his last shipment from Marseilles. His final cellar inventory listed: "Virgin oil of Aix, Anchovies, and 112¾ lb Maccaroni."[20]

Thomas Jefferson's Favorite Vegetables

IN 1819 THOMAS JEFFERSON WROTE, "I have lived temperately, eating little animal food, and that … as a condiment for the vegetables, which constitute my principal diet."[1] His one-thousand-foot-long kitchen garden terrace was an experimental laboratory where he cultivated 70 different species and 330 varieties of vegetables. Although he loved fine fancy fruit and the ornamental "pet trees" that graced his mountaintop home, the vegetable garden, because of its dramatic scale and scope, was Thomas Jefferson's chief horticultural achievement at Monticello. Here, Jefferson himself sowed peas, cabbages, and okra and recorded in his garden "Kalendar" when the lettuce "came to table" or how the broad beans were "killed by bug."

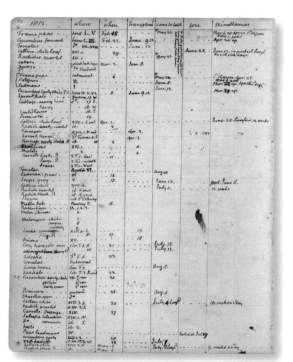

The 1812 Garden Kalendar reflects an unusually active planting season: multiple plantings of "tomatas" and lettuce, and the cultivation of such Jefferson favorites as eggplant ("Melongena"), sesame ("Benni"), tarragon, and Pani (i.e., Pawnee) corn collected by Meriwether Lewis.

What were Thomas Jefferson's favorite vegetables? Although his unabashed enthusiasm for many garden plants was readily expressed by sweeping pronouncements about how the Marseilles fig was "incomparably the finest fig I've ever seen," or that the flowering acacia was "the most delicious flowering shrub in the world," only a few vegetables received such accolades.[2] Instead, the frequency with which Jefferson planted a certain variety or species is perhaps a more objective criterion for tabulating his favorite garden plants. Also, Jefferson's notes on gardening extended from 1767 until 1824, fifty-seven years, and the enduring merits of many vegetables can be measured by their appearance in the more mature gardens planted in his retirement. Two more keys to Jefferson's vegetable world can be identified by examining family recipes and by tabulating the purchases of vegetables made for Jefferson's table. At Monticello, three generations of Jefferson women purchased vegetables from slaves, who cultivated gardens out in the five-thousand-acre plantation and maintained an

---

PETER J. HATCH is the Director of Gardens and Grounds at Monticello.

alternative economy based on the production and sale of foodstuffs. When Jefferson was president, his butler, Etienne Lemaire, purchased produce in the markets of Washington.[3]

The English or Garden pea is usually described as Jefferson's favorite vegetable because of the frequency of plantings in the Monticello kitchen garden, the amount of garden space devoted to it (three entire "squares"), and the character-revealing playfulness of his pea contests: according to family accounts, every spring Jefferson competed with local gentleman gardeners to bring the first pea to the table, with the winner then hosting a community dinner that included a feast on the winning dish of peas. Among the twenty-three pea varieties Jefferson documented sowing were Early Frame, planted annually from 1809 until 1824; Hotspur, named for its quick, frantic growth; Marrowfat, a starchier and later variety; and Blue Prussian, which Jefferson obtained from the premier American nurseryman of his day, Bernard McMahon. Monticello's seed catalog, *Twinleaf*, offers Prince Albert, indistinguishable from Early

ABOVE: *Ripening garden peas,* Pisum sativum. *Jefferson planted peas with such passionate consistency, year after year, that the species has the unchallenged distinction of being his favorite vegetable.*

OPPOSITE: *Newly planted rows of Paris White Cos lettuce, a Romaine type grown in the nineteenth century.*

Frame and introduced into American gardens in the 1840s.

Lettuce was the most common vegetable purchased in the Washington markets for presidential dinners: Jefferson's butler Lemaire purchased it over ninety times in 1806. Between 1809 and 1824, lettuce was planted an average of eight times annually at Monticello. Brown Dutch appeared most frequently, often in fall for winter harvests. This is a handsome, loose-headed variety, with leaves ruffled and tinged reddish-brown, worthy of a place in any gourmet market today. "Ice" lettuce, presumably a solid-heading Iceberg type, and Tennis-ball, a parent of modern Boston lettuce, were also prominent.

Monticello salads consisted of a mixed bouquet of greens, including spinach and endive for winter use, orach, corn salad or mache, pepper grass, French sorrel, cress, and "sprouts." According to Jefferson's relative Mary Randolph in her 1824 *The Virginia House-wife*, greens were gathered early in the morning, laid in cold water, sometimes including ice, then only removed hours later at dinner. Her salad dressing included oil, common and tarragon vinegar, hard-boiled egg yolks, mustard, sugar, and salt. Salads were garnished with sliced egg whites and scallions, "they being the most delicate of the onion tribe."[4]

Salad oil was a perennial obsession for

Thomas Jefferson. He referred to the olive as "the richest gift of heaven" and "the most interesting plant in existence."[5] When he found domestic olive oil imperfect and imported olive oil too expensive, Jefferson turned to the possibilities of a salad oil extracted from the seed of the sesame plant, or benne (*Sesamum orientale*). Jefferson acclaimed the species "among the most valuable acquisitions our country has ever made," and attributed its American introduction to African-American slaves.[6] Jefferson sowed the seed annually from 1809 until 1824, and purchased or concocted three different sesame oil presses. He was disappointed by the low yield of seed to oil and by the problems of extracting chaff and leaves during the pressing.

Jefferson was a pioneer grower of "tomatas." Tomatoes were purchased in 1806 for presidential dinners, and beginning in 1809 he recorded the planting of this grudgingly accepted vegetable yearly, usually in square X near the midpoint of the garden. Jefferson's daughter, Martha, and her daughters, Virginia and Septimia, recorded numerous recipes that involved tomatoes, including different kinds of gumbo soup, cayenne-spiced tomato soup, green tomato pickles, tomato preserves, and tomato omelettes. In an 1824 speech before the Albemarle Agricultural Society, Jefferson's son-in-law, Thomas

Mann Randolph, discussed the progress and transformation of Virginia farming due to the introduction and popularization of new crops. He mentioned how tomatoes were virtually unknown ten years earlier, but by 1824 everyone was eating them because they believed they "kept blood pure in the heat of summer."[7] Jefferson grew a variety described as "Spanish tomato (very much larger than the common kinds.)"[8] This was probably typical of the heavily lobed, ribbed, and flattened tomatoes generally grown in the early nineteenth century. Today, our collection includes Costoluto Genovese, an Italian variety with a shape that resembles a patty-pan squash, and Purple Calabash, which has a deep, dark, almost black skin.

Jefferson documented planting twenty-seven varieties of kidney bean (*Phaseolus vulgaris*). Unfortunately, bean varieties at Monticello were usually identified by their geographical source ("dwarf beans of Holland"), or a basic physical description ("long haricots"), making their retrieval today difficult. *The Virginia House-wife* discussed "French" or snap beans, which should be picked young and prepared with the strings plucked, not "Frenched" by slicing them longitudinally. "Those who are nice," Mary Randolph wrote, "do not use them at such a growth as to require splitting."[9]

The Scarlet Runner bean (*Phaseolus*

coccineus) and its flowering variants was the species Jefferson had in mind when in 1812 he recorded planting "Arbor beans white, crimson, scarlet, purple ... on [the] long walk of [the] garden."[10] Still common in northern European kitchen gardens, most Americans today grow Scarlet Runners as ornamentals. Another ornamental bean species, the Caracalla, or snail flower (*Vigna caracalla*), was described by Jefferson as "the most beautiful bean in the world."[11]

Cabbage was the second most commonly purchased vegetable bought by the Jefferson family from Monticello slaves, and it was the second most purchased vegetable in the Washington markets (fifty-one purchases in 1806). Jefferson recorded planting eighteen varieties at Monticello in thirty different locations. Mary Randolph recommended boiling cabbage: "With careful management, they will look as beautiful when dressed as they did when growing."[12] Early York was the most frequently planted cabbage variety; its early-season heading and small, conical head suggest qualities found in the still-popular Early Jersey Wakefield. Ox Heart, a larger, later, pyramid-shaped cabbage documented in the Garden Book, was introduced into the Monticello gardens in 1999.

Like many savvy gardeners, Jefferson seemed to prefer perennial flowers and vegetables to annuals. An 1815 entry in the Garden Book includes a chart detailing the dates of harvests for perennials such as artichokes, asparagus, and sea kale. Surprisingly, cold-tender artichokes were harvested thirteen of twenty-two years, a higher percentage than our success rate at Monticello today. Artichokes were prepared similarly to their presentation today: the flower heads boiled, and the leaves trimmed and served with melted butter. Asparagus is a harbinger of spring, and Jefferson noted its arrival at the table twenty-two times, the average date being April 8. Rather than purchasing established plants, Jefferson sowed asparagus seed, patiently awaiting a harvestable crop in four years. Mary Randolph's directions for the preparation of asparagus were more elaborate than for any other vegetable: stalks were meticulously scraped, bundled carefully in lots of 25, and immersed in boiling water. The cooking was delicately timed so "their true flavour and colour" is preserved: "a minute or two more boiling destroys both."[13] Asparagus was served on buttered toast.

Sea kale (*Crambe maritima*), a perennial cabbage native to the seashore of Great Britain, was another yearly favorite at Monticello. Spring shoots were blanched with sea kale pots to moderate their inherent *Brassica* bitterness, and harvested when six to ten inches long in April. The stalks were then bundled and prepared like asparagus.

ABOVE: *With their ridges, deep lobes, and flattened shape,* Costoluto Genovese *duplicate the characteristics of an early nineteenth-century tomato. Jefferson was a pioneer in the cultivation of "tomatas."*

OPPOSITE: *Red cabbage growing between recently installed bean poles and young, twining Caracalla beans.*

The Monticello kitchen garden in autumn with ripening Texas Bird peppers, sent to Jefferson by Captain Samuel Brown, who was stationed with American forces in San Antonio. This handsome, dwarf, and extremely hot pepper was planted by Jefferson in pots and in Square XII of the garden in 1814.

Jefferson was probably inspired to grow sea kale after reading Bernard McMahon's *The American Gardener's Calendar*, 1806, sometimes called his "Bible" of horticulture. Jefferson ordered sea kale pots from a Richmond potter in 1821.[14]

Although I've singled out numerous vegetable species as Thomas Jefferson's favorites, it would be folly to dismiss others of the vegetable tribe. Cucumbers were sowed yearly in the Monticello kitchen garden, sometimes in hogsheads, and they were the most commonly purchased vegetable from the Monticello slave community. Chartreuse, according to a surviving family recipe, consisted of "all roots… cut in slices and arranged in a fanciful way, alternating carrots and white vegetables, in a straight sided vessel.

It was turned out in a beautiful form and made a very pretty dish for a ceremonious dinner."[15] Jefferson obtained the Texas bird pepper in 1812 and was instrumental in its distribution throughout southeastern Pennsylvania, where regional recipes emerged for hot spicy sauces, vinegars, pickles, and cake-like pepper pots. Nasturtiums—with the leaves harvested for greens, the flowers picked for salads, and the seeds used as substitute capers—were planted annually from 1812 to 1824, when Jefferson requested a quantity of seed necessary to plant a 1,800-square-foot bed. Among herbs, French tarragon is generally recognized as his favorite. Was there a vegetable in the civilized western world that Thomas Jefferson did not embrace?

WHY DID THE JEFFERSON FAMILY BUY VEGETABLES?

MONTICELLO'S THOUSAND-FOOT-LONG kitchen garden is legendary for the variety and scope of its vegetable production, so the question immediately arises, "Why did the Jefferson family require outside sources to provide for the table?"

One explanation might lie in the experimental focus of the Jefferson garden. Although over three hundred vegetable varieties were documented, the emphasis was on using the garden as a laboratory rather than on production for the dinner table. In addition, no matter how large the garden, chefs inevitably find shortfalls when a large number of guests are imminent: a few cucumbers will hardly suffice when quantities of pickles are on the menu. As well, much of the produce purchased from Monticello slaves was out of season: potatoes were sold in December and February, hominy beans and apples purchased in April, and cucumbers bought in January. Archaeological excavations of slave cabins at Monticello indicate the widespread presence of root cellars, which not only served as secret hiding places, but surely as repositories for root crops and other vegetables amenable to cool, dark storage. Conversely, inventories of the Monticello cellars curiously omit garden produce, and are dominated by fancy, imported delicacies like capers, olive oil, and Parmesan cheese. Produce harvested from slave gardens at Monticello seemed to be more purposefully directed toward the out-of-season table, and the vegetables included everyday garden staples like cabbages and potatoes, rather than the new and unusual gourmet vegetables like artichokes and sea kale found in the Jefferson garden.

Monticello was a five-thousand-acre plantation organized into a series of four or five satellite farms, and the African-American gardens were likely associated with quarter farm communities or isolated cabins out on the farm. Except for watermelons, and perhaps sweet potatoes, few of the sold fruits and vegetables were either African in origin, or closely associated with African-American food culture. Neither documentary nor archaeological evidence has illuminated the character of these gardens. One exception was an intriguing reference, three years after Jefferson's death, to the distribution of peach pits to slaves at Edgehill, a Jefferson family estate adjacent to Monticello, "and thus in a few years there will be two or three trees about every cabin."[16]

— P.J.H.

Cymlins, "one of our finest and most innocent vegetables," according to Jefferson, were occasionally purchased from Monticello slaves.

Thomas Jefferson's Table: Evidence and Influences

THOMAS JEFFERSON'S GARDEN BOOK is filled with references to food coming "to table," including his April 24, 1767, notation: "forwardest peas of Feb. 20. come to table." In his documentation of the arrival of peas, strawberries, and lettuces, one senses a kind of suppressed excitement. His garden entries, which continued through 1824 with only a few missing years, are the most certain primary sources we have concerning the table of Jefferson at Monticello. We have reams of material on the food and cookery of his day in Virginia, much of it recorded by him. There are endless accounts of household provisions and numerous culinary observations—even ten recipes in his own hand, along with more observations and recipes interspersed in his Garden and Farm Books. All of these sources combine to provide insight into the food served on the Monticello table.

Too many pop historians write that early Americans eschewed vegetables. Some of us know better. Jefferson's meticulous observations on sales of vegetables at the Washington Public Market during the years 1801-1809 are particularly valuable. His gardening records at Monticello are often dismissed as the hobby of a gentleman farmer, but it is difficult to dismiss public market records. If people bought vegetables, they probably did not feed them to rabbits. Between the evidence of these market records, purchases of produce from Monticello's enslaved community, and Jefferson's own

Surviving "receipts" associated with Monticello come from a variety of sources, such as when Jefferson recorded a recipe for wine jellies (opposite), or when his granddaughter Septimia Anne Randolph Meikelham attributed recipes to Monticello, such as waffles and crumpets, in her cooking manuscript (above).

KAREN HESS is editor of *The Virginia House-wife* and author of *Thomas Jefferson's Table: The Culinary Legacy of Monticello* (forthcoming). This essay is adapted from a talk given at Monticello on August 10, 1993.

VIRGINIA HOUSE-WIFE.

METHOD IS THE SOUL OF MANAGEMENT.

WASHINGTON:

PRINTED BY DAVIS AND FORCE, (FRANKLIN'S HEAD,)
PENNSYLVANIA AVENUE.
1824.

Mary Randolph was known to the Jefferson family as "Sister" or "Aunt" Randolph, and the families exchanged visits regularly. The Virginia House-wife, *first published by Randolph in 1824, is one of the most influential early American cookbooks and likely serves as a window into cuisine at Monticello.*

Garden Book, it is clear that vegetables played a prominent role at Monticello's table.

There was nothing about food that did not engage Jefferson's intellect, from the precise proportions of salt in curing pork to the best way of making coffee, all in his own hand. We also have manuscript collections, penned by his own granddaughters, reportedly copied from the notebook of their mother Martha Jefferson Randolph, who served as hostess and mistress of his household. These documents, many of which are in the keeping of the University of Virginia, are invaluable, but can in no way be described as primary material regarding Monticello. Recipes strongly associated with Jefferson are to be found pell-mell among recipes dating from decades after his death in 1826, some as late as the 1890s. Even those designated "Monticello" are all recopied, subject to the usual errors of transcription. In short, these must be evaluated with great care.

We also have *The Virginia House-wife,* written in 1824 by Mrs. Mary Randolph, a kinswoman of Jefferson's, who in addition was Martha Jefferson Randolph's sister-in-law by reason of Martha's marriage to Mary's brother. David Meade Randolph, Mary's husband, also a cousin of Jefferson's, became a bitter political enemy of his early in Jefferson's first term of presidency, yet nevertheless Mary Randolph sent Jefferson a copy of her book, which he elegantly acknowledged. More than fifty recipes from the book were entered into the manuscript collections, some of them with the specific mention of Monticello, so that we may infer that the work was used during Jefferson's lifetime. Also, Jefferson entered her proportions for curing pork in his Farm Book, attributing them to her. In the other direction, Mary Randolph's recipe for Bell Fritters is virtually identical to that which Jefferson's family collections attributed to Lemaire, Jefferson's maitre d'hôtel at the President's House. This is true right down to frying them "of a fine amber color" in her instructions, to "of a light amber color" in his. She may have gotten the recipe decades earlier, but she did not attribute it. *The Virginia House-wife* is not primary evidence in terms of Monticello, but I believe that it reflects fairly accurately day-to-day cuisine here. They were, after all, all Randolphs, Jefferson included, and there were a great many ties of longstanding.

Recipes from other works are also cited in the collections, most notably *Dictionnaire Portatif de Cuisine* (Paris, 1772) and *A New System of Domestic Cookery* by Maria Eliza Rundell (London, c. 1806). A copy of *The Art of Cookery* by Mrs. Hannah Glasse (the 1767 edition) was found in the Monticello inventory, so we may infer that it also was in use.

In his day, Jefferson was attacked by the fiery Patrick Henry as having "abjured his native vittles in favor of French cuisine."[1] Certainly Jefferson admired French cuisine and wine, going so far as to have slave cooks specially trained for service at Monticello and ordering scandalous amounts of very fine French wines. But he was not alone in his admiration, nor was he the first American to be smitten by French genius in the kitchen, contrary to much that has been written. The French were here long before Jefferson's time, even in Virginia, and *they* are responsible for strong French traces in traditional Virginia cookery, a fact not always taken into account by either food historians or Patrick Henry.

In pawing over his papers and other materials, I am left with the impression that Jefferson actually had very simple tastes in food. He was clearly possessed of a highly discriminating palate, but everything I find leads me to believe that he was more excited over the first new peas of spring than the most elaborate dish. He wrote that "vegetables constitute my principle dict," for example.[2] One might say that he appreciated the elegance of simplicity, a quality that characterizes the finest French cuisine, especially

that of the eighteenth century. Certainly when protocol demanded it, Jefferson put on a fine show. A famous stunt of serving ice cream baked in pastry at a

state dinner seems to have created a sensation, but it was just that—a stunt. As I look over the recipes that with certainty can be associated with Jefferson as a private citizen, I find no dazzlers. Out of over one hundred and fifty such recipes, I see "to make apple dumplings," "observations on soup," "okra soup," "catfish soup," "beef à la mode," "to stew beef," "breast of mutton," "broiled shad," "pancakes," "lemon pudding," "bread pudding," "sweet potato pudding," "to make cream cheese," "ice cream," "blanc manger," and "Petit's method of making coffee"—that is, homey dishes like soups, stews, and creams.

Note that a number of the dishes are pure Virginia dishes, such as the catfish. The fact is that in spite of an English warp, the cuisine of patrician Virginia shared a number of characteristics with that on the same level in eighteenth century France. And of course a number of dishes with French

Although French copper cookware was uncommon in early American kitchens, its presence at Monticello was a sign of Jefferson's intention to outfit a kitchen for the preparation of French-influenced cuisine.

Are there missing recipes from the Monticello manuscripts?

AS MUCH AS THE FAMILY'S collections of recipes and other sources tell us about the Monticello table, there are gaps. In part, this can be explained by the passage of time: Jefferson's daughter Martha Randolph apparently compiled a collection of recipes used at Monticello (including those, she noted, "which you will find no where else"), but this entire manuscript is unlocated.[3] Similarly, her daughter Virginia Trist's collection of "receipts" includes a table of contents promising sections on cakes and sauces, but over the years, those pages have disappeared. Vegetables, given Jefferson's apparent fondness for them, are strikingly underrepresented, and early recipes for bread in the family manuscripts are almost nonexistent, despite visitors' descriptions of bread on the table.

Yet the loss of written recipes may not be the only explanation for the absence or scarcity of dishes in a given category. Then, as today, cooks consulted recipes only as needed. Routine cooking of such staples as bread, vegetables, or a simple roasted chicken were rarely recorded in part because of the simple lack of need to do so, whereas the Christmas pudding, made only once a year, might fade from memory if not written down. The family served chocolate as a beverage so often that they nicknamed its silver service vessel the "duck"—and yet no recipe appears in the collections, perhaps because the family members could not envision a day when a recipe would be required.

In light of these gaps, the recipes in this book have been augmented by such evidence as the harvests noted in Jefferson's Garden Book and Farm Book, food purchases documented in family account books, and descriptions of meals in letters and diaries. For more information on this process, see "A Note on the Recipes," page 89.

— B.L.C.

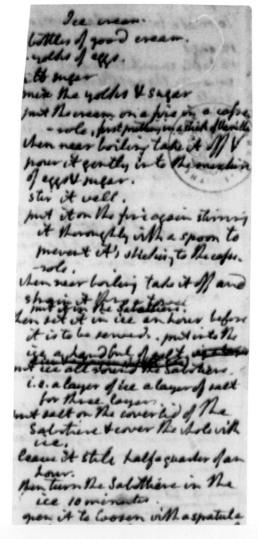

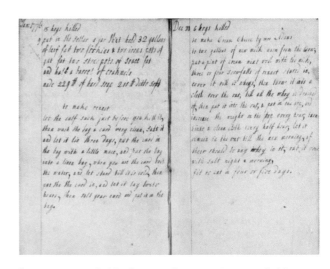

Ice cream is probably the most famous recipe recorded by Jefferson (left). Other recipes appear in family account books, such as the one maintained by his wife Martha Wayles Skelton Jefferson (above).

names had entered Virginia by way of England—beef à la mode, blanc manger, and so on, in addition to actual French influences noted earlier.

Another key aspect of Virginia cooking is the African influence. I have written that the near-mythic reputation of southern cookery can be attributed to the African presence. Black slave women did the cooking, and no matter how conscientiously they may have followed the recipes that were read to them by their mistresses, certain transformations took place. The Chinese so accurately call this "wok presence." That is, their hands had known other products, their noses other fragrances, and this was bound to affect the cookery for the better. In addition, products and dishes introduced from Africa or the slave trade are those that came to characterize southern cookery as differentiated from northern cookery. I speak of products such as okra, black-eyed peas, and red peas, which are from Africa; as well as eggplant and benne, or sesame seed, which came by way of Africa, among others. In Virginia cuisine, this African influence was a caress, creating a remarkably successful and sophisticated cuisine that reflected many influences. The slave cooks at Monticello may have been so well trained that French dishes may not have been appreciably altered, but the African presence was cardinal in the

Virginia dishes. For example, the recipe manuscripts contain several versions of okra soup, which is actually an African dish.

I close as I started, with Jefferson's gardening entries. Gardening was his most enduring passion, and you cannot hope to understand the cuisine of Monticello without studying those entries. Most obviously, they are a partial record of what vegetables were actually served there. More importantly, perhaps, they mark the season in a way that has been long forgotten by Americans. I am always moved when Jefferson notes that a specific vegetable comes "to table." That is what it is all about.

Okra soup—essentially gumbo—was common enough on the Monticello table that some of the recipes for it in the family collections are simply titled "soup." The use of okra and rice are some of the signs of African influence on Monticello's cuisine.

Dining at Monticello: The "Feast of Reason"

THOMAS JEFFERSON'S TABLE, "genteely and plentifully spread" with a great array of foods and his "immense and costly variety of French and Italian wines," impressed his visitors and no doubt played a large part in establishing Monticello's culinary distinction.[1] The ceremony of dining and the cosmopolitan menu helped to establish Jefferson as a member of an international community of educated and worldly people. But in addition to cultivating the palates of family, friends, and visitors, the twice-daily meals were a purposeful social experience designed both to entertain and to edify. With Jefferson as host, the Dining Room was a stage for engaged discussion, or as his granddaughter recalled, Monticello was "completely the feast of reason."[2]

The decoration of the unusual Dining Room, with its artwork-lined walls and books on the mantel, caught the attention of Monticello's guests. The young Bostonian Francis Calley Gray, for example, remembered seeing in the room "many books of all kinds, Livy, Orosius…."[3] Jefferson habitually read while he waited for his family to assemble for meals, and he and "his daughter used to sit and read, after tea in the cool or winter evenings" in two armchairs with a candle stand between them near the fireplace.[4] Still, the bookish atmosphere did not appeal to everyone. Judith Walker Rives wrote in her memoirs that some neighbors joked that "whenever Mr. Jefferson had any distinguished visitors of the bon vivant order, he always had them invited to Farmington, as furnishing rather a higher specimen of Virginia good cheer than they found at Monticello."[5]

Pictures packed the walls of the Dining Room as they did the Entrance Hall and Parlor and likely sparked discourse as family and guests enjoyed breakfast and

The Monticello Tea Room, set for dinner with tablecloths and napkins like this one (above) monogrammed with the initials of Martha Jefferson Randolph.

SUSAN STEIN is Curator at Monticello and author of *The Worlds of Thomas Jefferson at Monticello.*

The Dining Room featured not only American and European tablewares, but also a wide variety of art, from copies of Old Masters paintings to portraits and architectural drawings.

dinner. For the most part, copies of old master paintings, acquired by Jefferson in France, hung on the uppermost tier. Of the nine pictures Jefferson identified in his *Catalogue of Paintings*, c. 1810, only his copy of Raphael's *Holy Family* survives. The twelve or more images on the lower tier highlighted Jefferson's keen interest in America's architecture and landscape. Two engravings of Niagara Falls appeared, along with paintings of Natural Bridge and Harper's Ferry. Three architectural drawings by Robert Mills hung here, as well, featuring St. Paul's Church in lower Manhattan, Benjamin Latrobe's

Bank of Pennsylvania, and the west front of Monticello. Most other items were also American in focus, including depictions of the President's House, George Washington's Mount Vernon, and *A View of New Orleans Taken from the Plantation of Marigny*.

The adjoining Tea Room, which Jefferson described as his "most honorable suite," contained plaster busts of men Jefferson admired—Franklin, Washington, Lafayette, and John Paul Jones—all by Jean-Antoine Houdon. Here also were nearly two dozen representations, many of them miniature portraits, showing historical and political

WHO DINED AT MONTICELLO?

PETER FOSSETT, SON OF one of Monticello's cooks, remembered that "streams of visitors" came to Monticello, describing life there as a "merry go round of hospitalities."[28] More specifically, Martha Jefferson Randolph recalled that the record number of overnight guests at her father's house was fifty. Following Jefferson's retirement from the presidency in 1809, the number of guests rose dramatically at Monticello, but even without guests, the large household included his daughter Martha Randolph's family and a procession of relatives who stayed for weeks or months. As the retired President Jefferson wrote when encouraging Congressman Elbridge Gerry to visit Monticello, "a numerous family will hail you with a hearty country welcome."[29]

Monticello overseer Edmund Bacon speculated that many of Monticello's visitors aimed to avoid the expense of staying at taverns; other guests came to see the "sage of Monticello" and his "museum." Whatever their reasons, dinner guests came from as near as Jefferson's own neighborhood and as far away as Europe. Statesmen, scientists, soldiers, and socialites made the trek, from the Chevalier de Chastellux in 1782 to Jefferson's old friend and Revolutionary War hero, the Marquis de Lafayette, in 1824.[30] A Monticello resident compiled a more complete list of visitors: "We had persons from abroad, from all the States of the Union, from every part of the State.... People of wealth, fashion, men in office, professional men military and civil, lawyers, doctors, Protestant clergymen, Catholic priests, members of Congress, foreign ministers, missionaries, Indian agents, tourists, travellers, artists, strangers, friends."[31]

Two guests stayed so frequently at Monticello that rooms were named after them. The North Octagonal Room was dubbed "Mr. Madison's Room," and the North Square Room became known as the "Abbé Correia's Room." The Abbé José Correia da Serra, a Portuguese botanist, man of letters, and co-founder of the Academy of Science in Lisbon, visited Monticello seven times between 1812 and 1820. James and Dolley Madison were longtime friends of Jefferson and frequently made the trip from nearby Orange, Virginia, creating with Jefferson's neighbor James Monroe "a society to our taste."[32]

Despite the challenges of managing the domestic arrangements for all these guests, Martha Randolph appears to have extended hospitality even beyond her visitors' departure. Anna Maria Thornton wrote that after leaving Monticello, her party ate a picnic of "Mrs. Randolph's ham, chicken, bread, and punch[,] which with a bottle of wine she had put into the carriage without our knowledge."[33]

— B.L.C.

James and Dolley Madison (both rendered here by Thomas Sully in 1804) visited Monticello so regularly that the North Octagonal Room became known as "Mr. Madison's Room."

Upon his arrival in Paris, Jefferson promptly acquired silver spoons and forks, which he later transported back to the United States. Jefferson's granddaughter Ellen Coolidge recalled, "He ate with a silver fork when other people used steel."

figures from the Old and New Worlds.

Just as Jefferson's art collection reflected his wide-ranging interests in European and American subjects, Monticello's Dining Room also suggests a similar cultural amalgamation in the preparation and service of food. Margaret Bayard Smith visited Monticello on several occasions, commenting that "here indeed was the mode of living in general [of] a Virginian planter" but also noting a "European elegance."[6] Daniel Webster concurred; he visited Monticello in 1824 and observed that "Dinner is served in half Virginian, half French style, in good taste and abundance."[7]

The dining experience combined French and American traditions. Judging by contemporary accounts, dining at Monticello was rather less formal than one might suppose, differing from prevailing American social customs. Jefferson, who was familiar with comfortable, more casual Parisian dinner parties, devised a way of serving people that required fewer servants. A revolving serving door with shelves was installed in the small passage near the Dining Room.

A second course of dishes or the first course's soiled plates could be placed on the shelves; with a spin of the door, the contents moved in or out of the room.

Jefferson also used dumbwaiters, or sets of shelves on casters, placed between the diners for their convenience. At the President's House Margaret Bayard Smith wrote that when Jefferson "wished to enjoy a free and unrestricted flow of conversation, the number of persons at the table never exceeded four, and by each individual was placed a dumbwaiter, containing everything necessary for the progress of the dinner from beginning to end, so as to make the attendance of servants entirely unnecessary."[8] At Monticello, the tops of the dumbwaiters provided extra space for serving dishes, wine bottles, and perhaps a *seau crénelé*, a porcelain vessel for rinsing and chilling wine glasses. The lower shelves could hold clean (or dirty) plates and utensils. Jefferson's granddaughter Ellen Coolidge recalled, "He would have his plate changed several times during dinner; a habit not observed, in those days, by courtly gentlemen generally. I remember my cousin Dabney Terrell, who had lived in Europe many years, once said to me, 'Yours is the only table in the county where I dare ask for a clean plate.'"[9]

Dinner, intended to impress guests, was served in two courses in the mid to late afternoon. "At half past three the great bell rings," guest George Ticknor wrote, "and those who are disposed resort to the drawing-room, and the rest go the dining-room at the second call of the bell, which is at four o'clock."[10] Granddaughter Septimia Anne Randolph Meikleham recollected, "Half an hour before this meal Mr. Jefferson and Mrs. Randolph would go to the drawing room where the family and guests assembled for dinner.… [A]t 3 Oclock the bell announced dinner, and the old Butler—Burwell [Colbert]—opened the door into the dining room. Mr. Jefferson considered punctuality a virtue."[11]

Guests entered the Dining Room to find the serving dishes for the main or first course already placed symmetrically around the table.[12] Diners could choose among numerous offerings of roasted poultry, meats, fish, soup, and vegetables. Although few vegetable recipes survive in the family

A set of cruets, French serving dishes, and a stack of clean plates grace the shelves of dumbwaiters in the Tea Room. Placed near the table, the dumbwaiters enabled diners to reach what they wanted without assistance from waiters.

recipe collections, Daniel Webster noticed that Jefferson "enjoys his dinner well, taking with his meat large portions of vegetables."[13] Isaac Jefferson, an enslaved smith, later recalled the wide variety of foods his mother and others prepared at Monticello when he noted there were "from eight to thirty-two covers for dinner."[14] Guests observed that "the table liquors were beer and cider," some of it brewed and pressed at Monticello.[15]

Following the first course, plates and the top tablecloth were removed, and servants symmetrically arranged the second course of cakes, biscuits, custards, puddings, and jellies. After the second table cloth was removed, sweetmeats, nuts, and fruit were accompa-

nied by wine. Some of the sweetmeats and nuts were served in a glass epergne, a kind of tree with small baskets placed on its branches. George Ticknor commented, "The dinner was always choice, and served in the French style; but no wine was set on the table till the cloth was removed."[16] Jefferson, who consumed no hard liquors, enjoyed a glass or two of wine following the meal.

"After dinner," a granddaughter recollected, "Mr. Jefferson and Mrs. Randolph remained with their guests for the rest of the afternoon & evening accept [sic] for a short time when Mr. Jefferson retired to his own rooms."[17] Mrs. Randolph and her daughters "sat until about six, then retired, but returned with the tea-tray a little before seven, and spent the evening with the gentlemen."[18]

In the morning a bell summoned family and guests "at fifteen minutes after eight … and at nine, the second [bell] … assembled us in the breakfast room."[19] At breakfast, Jefferson enjoyed "tea and coffee, bread always fresh from the oven, of which he does not seem afraid, with sometimes a light accompaniment of cold meat," Daniel Webster wrote.[20] Margaret Bayard Smith remembered that the "breakfast table was as large as our dinner table; instead of a cloth, a folded napkin lay under each plate; wc had tea, coffee, excellent muffins, hot wheat and corn bread, cold ham and butter."[21] Francis Calley Gray wrote that after the meal he

chatted with the ladies for about an hour before joining Jefferson to examine the catalogue of his library.

The furnishings of the Dining Room and Tea Room demonstrated Jefferson's access to a variety of goods from American cities as well as London, the China trade, and especially Paris. At least one of the Virginia-made dining tables used in the Dining Room held a large French plateau, a mirrored tray with a gallery, designed to reflect light. On it were likely placed a pair of English silver-plated candelabras and a number of biscuit (unglazed soft paste porcelain) figurines about twelve inches high, of which two survive, *Venus with Cupid* and *Hope with Cupid*.[22] The candelabras might have been one of the four pairs of silver-plated Corinthian column candlesticks John Trumbull bought for Jefferson in London in 1789. Jefferson wrote Trumbull that he thought "no form is so handsome as that of the column."[23]

This preference for classical forms appears in Jefferson's own designs for silver. In France, the Parisian silversmith Claude-Nicolas Delanoy rendered Jefferson's de-

Daniel Webster recalled that "breakfast is tea and coffee, bread always fresh from the oven…, with sometimes a light accompaniment of cold meat." Jefferson drew several designs for coffee urns, including this one likely patterned after a silver urn (above) that he purchased in Paris.

sign for a pair of footed silver goblets with vermeil bowls, featuring a distinctively plain architectural form. Jefferson also drew plans for coffee urns in Paris, but only one silver urn survives. It came to America with Jefferson's French household goods in 1790, packed in one of the eighty-six crates of paintings, mattresses, furniture, china, flatware, cookwares, and more that outfitted Jefferson's fashionable residence.

ABOVE: *This* seau crénelé, *or vessel for rinsing and cooling wine glasses, was made at the royal French porcelain factory at Sèvres for the use of Louis XVI at Versailles. How Jefferson obtained this and a sugar bowl from the same service is unknown.*

OPPOSITE: *Monticello Tea Room. Guest Margaret Bayard Smith recalled, "We sat till near sun down at the table, where the dessert was succeeded by agreeable and instructive conversation in which every one seemed to wish and expect Mr. J. to take the chief part."*

While still in France, Jefferson saw an excavated Roman bronze askos, or pouring vessel, and had a wooden model made of it. More than a decade later, during Jefferson's presidency, Philadelphia craftsmen Anthony Simmons and Samuel Alexander rendered the form in silver. Despite the urn's classical origins, the family treated it familiarly, calling it "the duck—the silver chocolate-pot."[24]

Perhaps the most famous of Jefferson's tablewares were eight silver tumblers made with vermeil interiors, described by a relative as the "silver drinking cups he was wont to use."[25] Made in part from silver bequeathed from George Wythe, Jefferson's mentor, they are known today as the Jefferson or Wythe-Jefferson cups. A smaller French tumbler Jefferson owned served as a model for Richmond silversmith John Letelier.

Jefferson's tableware included an ample supply of French and Chinese export porcelain that he acquired while living in Paris and shipped home to the United States, with porcelain plates alone numbering 120. He also owned at least two pieces—a *seau crénelé* and sugar bowl—of a service decorated with a cornflower garland made especially for Louis XVI. Jefferson's daughter also referred to queensware, or creamware, a more common English ceramic. Her letters make clear that through daily use and periodic mishaps, tablewares were at risk, and by 1808, coffee cups and shallow plates were "amongst the deficiencies of the house."[26]

Surrounded by these accoutrements of dining, art works, and books, Daniel Webster found Jefferson's conversation "easy and natural.... The topics... at present, may be said to be science and letters, and especially the University of Virginia, which is coming into existence almost entirely from his exertions.... When we were with him, his favorite subjects were Greek and Anglo-Saxon, historical recollections of the times and events of the Revolution, and of his residence in France."[27] The "feast" at Monticello was as much a feast of ideas as it was a culinary banquet.

Jefferson and Wine: A "Necessary of Life"

ALTHOUGH BORN ON THE VIRGINIA FRONTIER and starting with very provincial tastes in wine, Thomas Jefferson became the most knowledgeable wine connoisseur of his age, and his tastes in wine covered the world: France, Germany, Italy, Cyprus, Hungary, Madeira, Portugal, Spain, and, of course, America.

Jefferson's interest in wine developed early, as indicated by his 1769 wine inventory of his home at Shadwell: eighty-three bottles of rum, fifteen bottles of Madeira, four bottles of "Lisbon wine for common use," and fifty-four bottles of cider.[1] This inventory is in keeping with the tastes of his countrymen in the British colonies, and it differs radically from the wine inventories he maintained following his travels in Europe. In 1773, Jefferson gave another indication of his early interest in wine culture when he financially supported Italian Philip Mazzei's plan to cultivate European grapes at a vineyard adjacent to Monticello. Although the project failed, Mazzei's hope that "the best wine in the world will be made here" was not lost on Jefferson, who later grew vines at Monticello and supported the efforts of other New World winemakers.[2]

Following the Revolutionary War, a new life began for Jefferson when Congress sent him to Paris to serve as trade commissioner with John Adams and Benjamin Franklin, who was serving as the first American minister to France. On July 5, 1784, Jefferson set sail from Boston with his oldest daughter, Martha, and four dozen bottles of Hock (a white German Rhine wine). Within less than a year of Jefferson's arrival, Franklin returned home, and Congress appointed Jefferson to succeed him as minister. During Jefferson's five years in France, he gained an incredible vinicultural education and shifted his attention from Madeira, Lisbon, and other wines

Monticello Tea Room. Guests recalled Jefferson's "immense and costly variety of French and Italian wines," indicated by his 1817 chart of wine tariffs (above). Jefferson noted that the "classification and prices are on my own knowledge."

JAMES M. GABLER is author of *Passions: the Wines and Travels of Thomas Jefferson.*

81

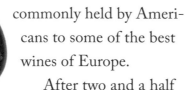

TOP: *French wine-bottle seal, marked "St. Julien L. Laguerenne Médoc," found near Building "o," a Mulberry Row slave cabin first built ca. 1770 and occupied until at least 1800. Possibly from a 1792 Jefferson request for 504 bottles of 1788 Médoc.*

ABOVE: *English wine bottle (ca. 1810) found in a sub-floor pit beneath Building "t," a Mulberry Row slave cabin built in 1793 and occupied until Jefferson's death in 1826.*

OPPOSITE: *Monticello Dining Room. Concealed in either side of the fireplace, wine dumbwaiters— elevators operated by pulleys— could lower and raise a wine bottle from the cellar directly below.*

commonly held by Americans to some of the best wines of Europe.

After two and a half years in France, Jefferson decided to learn firsthand about the wines he loved and set out on a spring tour through southern France. His journey took him to the vineyards of Burgundy, Côte Rôtie, Hermitage, and Provence, over the Alps into northern Italy, along the French and Italian Rivieras, through Languedoc, into Bordeaux country, and up the Loire Valley with visits to the great Roman antiquities of Gaul. Returning to Paris on June 10, he regarded his trip a personal triumph, remarking, "I never passed three months and a half more delightfully."[3]

Jefferson's tasting notes from this trip remain valuable to contemporary wine drinkers, for they constitute the first detailed modern accounts of wine in English and cover many important French wines such as Chambertin, Clos de Vougeot, Montrachet, and Goutte d'Or from Burgundy; Chateaux Lafite, Margaux, Latour, Haut-Brion, Yquem, and Carbonnieux from Bordeaux; Côte Rôtie and Hermitage from the Rhone Valley, and Champagne. The notes also include Chianti and Montepulciano from Italy, as well as Madeira and Sherry. Traveling through the French countryside,

Jefferson met vignerons, workers, and wine merchants, and he learned that only by purchasing directly from the vineyard owners could he avoid the deception of middlemen blending inferior wines into his selected purchases. Consequently, he began ordering directly from the winemaker, in effect receiving his wines chateau-bottled, a method that did not become standardized in Bordeaux until the 1930s.

A year later, with a comprehensive background of France's viticulture locked in his encyclopedic mind, Jefferson traveled down the Rhine to learn about German wines. Although he did not visit the Moselle, he was advised that the best Moselle wines were made near Koblenz on the mountain of Brownberg. He rated Wehlen second, Graach and Piesport third, Zelting fourth, and Bernkastel fifth.[4] From personal visits to the Rheingau vineyards, he felt that it was "only from Rudesheim to Hocheim, that the wines of the very first quality are made…. and even in this canton, it is only Hocheim, Johansberg, and Rudesheim that are considered as of the very first quality."[5] Although present-day wine experts might quibble over the precise rankings of the wines from these famous vineyards, all will concede that the vineyards Jefferson singled out for praise still produce wines of remarkable quality.

Hurrying home to Paris, he stopped

in Epernay, in Champagne. He classified Champagne's wines as mousseaux (sparkling) and non-mousseaux (still), noting that "the mousseaux or sparkling is dearest because most in demand for exportation, but the non-mousseaux is most esteemed by every real connoisseur," a preference he shared.[6] Years later, his champagne choices were particularly praised by guests, as when one wrote, "His wine was truly the best I ever drank, particularly his champaign—It is delicious indeed."[7]

When Jefferson became president in 1801, the roads leading to the raw, new capital on the Potomac were dirt. In 1803, one senator described the city vividly: "All we lack here are good houses, wine cellars, decent food, learned men, attractive women and other such trifles…."[8] With no hotels or restaurants, Congress and visitors lodged at boarding houses grouped around the still-unfinished Capitol building. In a community starved for amenities, Jefferson accepted the social leadership expected of him, and presidential dinners took precedence over everything. Jefferson's dinners, including fine wines, were an expedient manner of meeting informally with his political friends and foes, and he used these almost-nightly gatherings as a form of legislative lobbying. Serving the best wines, Jefferson preferred Madame Rauzan's Margaux (Chateau Rauzan Ségla),

WAS WINE MADE AT MONTICELLO?

THOMAS JEFFERSON HAS BEEN described as America's "first distinguished viticulturist," and "the greatest patron of wine and winegrowing that this country has yet had."[14] Although he aspired to make a Monticello-grown wine, there is no evidence that he either did or didn't produce a successful vintage. The continual replanting of the vineyards, however, suggests a losing struggle with grape cultivation. But Jefferson was not alone. The successful cultivation in eastern North America of *Vitis vinifera*, the classic European wine species, was virtually impossible until the development of modern pesticides. Native grapes were more effectively grown, yet they produced wine of questionable quality.

The two vineyards, northeast (nine thousand square feet) and southwest (sixteen thousand square feet), were ideally sited for grape-growing in the heart of the South Orchard below the garden wall. In 1807, Jefferson documented the planting of 287 rooted vines and cuttings of twenty-four European grape varieties, the most ambitious of seven experiments.[15] Many of these *vinifera* cultivars had never been grown in North America. Such a varietal rainbow, many of them table grapes, represents the vineyard of a plant collector, an experimenter rather than a serious wine maker. The 1807 plan for the northeast vineyard was restored in 1985, the southwest, in 1992. Documentary evidence suggests that Jefferson's vines were "espaliered," or trained over a permanent structure, so the modern recreation includes a fence-like system built according to an eighteenth-century treatise on grape growing.[16] Jefferson's European varieties were also grafted on the more resilient native rootstock to encourage hardiness and pest resistance.

Although Jefferson's own efforts to produce wine seem to have failed, today wine bottled from Sangiovese grapes grown in the southwest vineyard is sold in the Monticello Museum Shop.

— P.J.H.

The Monticello wine cellar, located directly underneath the Dining Room. Although Jefferson aspired to make wine at Monticello, the historical record is unclear as to whether he succeeded.

Chateau Yquem from Sauternes, Chambertin among Burgundies, white Hermitage, Champagne, and Frontigan. Unlike today, the household and entertainment funds did not come out of the public coffers, but from his annual presidential salary of $25,000. He spared no expense for his dinners: food totaled over $6,000 one year, and wine was $7,597 the first term.

After two presidential terms, Jefferson returned to Monticello. His daily discipline began with correspondence in the morning, followed by riding among his farms, visiting plantation shops, and walking in his gardens until the main meal of the day at three or four o'clock in the afternoon. Entertaining, however, was still an important part of his routine, with dinners served daily for a wide circle of extended family and a vast array of visitors. After the cloth was removed from

Monticello vineyard. These grapes, collected from the wild near a Maryland vineyard in 1985, seem to possess the qualities of the lost Alexandria grape, which produced a wine Jefferson said was "worthy of the best vineyards in France."

the table following the second course, wine was served.

Old age did not dim Jefferson's ardor for drinking and serving wine, but his reduced income necessitated a change in his wine tastes to the lesser-known wines from southern France and Italy. From France his choices included cask wines from Roussillon and Muscat de Rivesaltes and red wines from Languedoc, Provence, Limoux, and Ledanon, regions that today are known for producing "value" wines. From Italy he imported Chianti, Poncina, Artimino, and his favorite, Montepulciano.

As he approached his seventy-sixth birthday, his retirement routine had changed little and his health remained excellent, which he attributed in part to the daily consumption of wine. In 1815, he wrote to a Portuguese wine merchant, "Wine from long habit has become an indispensable for my health, which is now suffering by it's disuse."[9] Comparing his daily habits to those of Philadelphia Doctor Benjamin Rush, he notes, "I double, however, the Doctor's glass and a half of wine, and even treble it with a friend; but halve its effects by drinking the weak wines only. The ardent spirits I cannot drink, nor do I use ardent spirits in any form."[10]

Clearly, wine was for Jefferson a life-long passion; he called it a "necessary of life."[11] His involvement with wine, however, went far beyond just drinking it. Interested in viticulture, he made notes on German and Italian grape growing and examined the details relative to the most celebrated wines of France. He planted vineyards at Monticello and experimented with grape growing in his Paris garden on the Champs-Elysées using vine cuttings from such famous vineyards as

Chambertin, Clos de Vougeot, Montrachet, Hochheim, and Rudesheim. In addition, he encouraged Philip Mazzei, John Adlum, and others in their vine-growing efforts. His wine advice to merchants and friends opened channels for the importation of wine into the United States from France, Italy, Portugal, and Spain. To further encourage importation, he effectively lobbied for a reduction in U.S. wine tariffs while serving as secretary of state and president, as well as later in retirement. He served as a wine adviser to Presidents Washington, Madison, and Monroe: all but five lines of his congratulatory note to the newly elected Monroe focused on wine recommendations for presidential occasions.

Throughout his life, Jefferson was a passionate advocate of wine as the beverage of temperance and health, arguing that "No nation is drunken where wine is cheap; and none sober, where the dearness of wine substitutes ardent spirits as the common beverage."[12] He fervently believed that "we could, in the United States, make as great a variety of wines as are made in Europe, not exactly of the same kinds, but doubtless as good," an understanding that expressed his vision for the future of wine in America.[13] A procession of wine pioneers have carried Jefferson's vision into America's vineyards and wine cellars and made it an exciting reality.

The Recipes

A Note on the Recipes

THE RECIPES IN THIS collection come from several sources relating to Thomas Jefferson's family, beginning with some penned by Jefferson himself.[1] Other records, correspondence, and items such as Jefferson's menu notes from the President's House provide an important glimpse into his famed hospitality.[2]

Another critical source of guidance and recipes are account books, in which family members recorded daily household purchases, along with the occasional recipe. Jefferson's wife (Martha Wayles Skelton Jefferson), daughter (Martha Jefferson Randolph), and granddaughters (Anne Cary Randolph and Mary Jefferson Randolph) kept these journals.[3]

Jefferson's granddaughters (Septimia Anne Randolph Meikleham and Virginia Randolph Trist) and great-granddaughter (Martha Jefferson Trist Burke) formally gathered recipes in three surviving manuscript collections. A fourth recipe manuscript, traditionally labeled the "Cookbook of Martha Jefferson Randolph," was in actuality recorded by a number of undetermined individuals, possibly including Martha Randolph.[4] We refer to recipes from this collection as "previously misattributed to Martha Jefferson Randolph." None of these four manuscripts limit themselves to Jefferson's years at Monticello, the period on which this book focuses. Alongside recipes with a clear connection to Monticello, the women also copied later recipes, including some from cookbooks published long after Jefferson's death or featuring ingredients that were unknown during his lifetime.

Sorting through this jumble would be challenging at best; thankfully, our task was aided by the scholarship of Karen Hess, a culinary historian and author of *Mr. Jefferson's Table: The Culinary Legacy of Monticello* (forthcoming), in which she examines the great breadth of documents related to Monticello's food history. In addition to transcribing almost every known recipe connected with the Jefferson family, she has also annotated each entry, including an analysis of its likely (or unlikely) association with Monticello. Beyond assisting us with decisions about which recipes to include, her commentary was invaluable in developing the recipes for modern cooks. Mrs. Hess was always close at hand with her personal library and vast knowledge of historical cookery, and we are grateful for her support of this project.

In some cases, recipe selections were straightforward. Recipes written by or mailed to Thomas Jefferson are favored. Most recipes recorded in family manuscripts that can reasonably be dated to years before Jefferson's death are included, particularly those attributed to Monticello, Martha Jefferson Randolph, James Hemings (an enslaved cook at Monticello), or Etienne Lemaire (maitre d'hôtel at the President's House during Jefferson's administration). Many of the recipes in the family manuscripts are credited to Mary Randolph, a relative of the family and author of *The Virginia House-wife* (1824). For reasons discussed on pages 66 and 68, the most important and representative of these recipes are included. In addition, since the Jefferson women

revealed a lack of culinary expertise as they copied their recipes, many of the entries in the family collection are problematic. Where necessary, we have turned to *The Virginia House-wife* or other period cookbooks to add missing steps or ingredients or otherwise "fix" a recipe.

There are a few other notes about the recipes to keep in mind. We have made every effort to achieve "doable authenticity." These recipes are entirely in keeping with the original "receipts," using ingredients and techniques that closely align with eighteenth century practice yet adding clarity and, often, twenty-first century technology. Some recipes closely related to Monticello do not appear in this book, including Martha Wayles Skelton Jefferson's recipe to make rennet, beginning as it does with "let the calf suck just before you kill it." Similarly, tansey pudding is not included owing to the rarity of the herb today, and wafer-like waffles were omitted because they require a special, archaic iron that is largely inaccessible to readers. With limited space, we wanted to maximize accessibility, inviting as many people as possible to participate in the celebrated cuisine of Monticello.

—**Beth L. Cheuk,** *coordinator*
—**Damon Lee Fowler,** *recipe developer*

(Note: Unless otherwise noted, Damon Fowler wrote all the commentary in the following pages.)

"Our breakfast table was as large as our dinner table; ... we had tea, coffee, excellent muffins, hot wheat and corn bread, cold ham and butter," recalled visitor Margaret Bayard Smith.[5] The "excellent muffins" are likely a reference to those shown on the plate, which also appear in family correspondence and recollections (see pages 91 and 93).

Monticello Muffins

Makes about 16 muffins

HISTORICAL NOTES: *Muffins were so loved within the Jefferson family that Jefferson himself requested the recipe while living at the President's House, as did his granddaughter Ellen after she moved to Boston. Today we call them "English" muffins to distinguish them from our present-day cupcake-like muffins, which were unknown in Jefferson's day. My interpretation is based mainly on the description given by Mrs. Meikleham, supplemented by* The Virginia House-wife. *The corn flour or meal used for shaping the muffins here is not mentioned in the period recipes, but aligns with traditional practice. Rice flour works even better, but it was probably not used at Monticello. See page 96 for a discussion of flour. The cooks at Monticello probably used an iron griddle to cook the muffins, but a coated aluminum griddle will work fine. The griddle is not greased, as would be necessary for a battercake or crumpet.*

¼ teaspoon active dry yeast, or ½ ounce compressed fresh yeast

2 cups water, at room temperature

20 ounces (about 4 cups) unbleached all-purpose flour, including ¼ cup whole-wheat pastry flour

1 rounded teaspoon salt

rice or corn flour, or fine white cornmeal, as needed

unsalted butter, for serving

1. Dissolve the yeast in the water in a small bowl and let it proof for 10 minutes. Whisk or stir together the flour and salt in a large bowl. Make a well in the center and pour in the yeasted water, gradually stirring the flour into it. Aggressively stir the dough until it is cohesive and smooth (it will be almost too stiff to stir but too slack to knead by hand). Cover with plastic wrap, or a double-folded damp towel, and set aside to rise until almost doubled, about 3 hours. The dough can also be covered with plastic wrap and allowed to rise overnight in the refrigerator.

2. Lightly dust a work surface with rice or corn flour or cornmeal. If the dough has been refrigerated, let it stand at room temperature for several minutes until it is warmed almost to room temperature. Beat the dough down with a wooden spoon and sprinkle the top with a little corn flour or meal. With lightly floured hands, scoop up small handfuls of dough, shaping each one into a round, flat disc, about ½ inch thick and 2½ inches in diameter. Put them on the flour-dusted surface spaced at least 1 inch apart, and let them rest for 15 to 30 minutes.

3. Heat a griddle or wide shallow skillet over medium-low heat. With a spatula, transfer as many muffins as will fit to the griddle with at least 1 inch around them. Cook slowly until the bottoms are lightly browned, about 8 to 10 minutes. Turn, lightly pressing with the spatula, and cook until uniformly browned and set, but still moist at the centers, about 8 minutes longer. Serve hot with butter.

Cornbread

Makes about 12 muffins

HISTORICAL NOTES: *Cornbread appears in a visitor's description of breakfast at Monticello, Jefferson's notes allude to raising corn for bread, and Martha Jefferson Randolph referred to the family being "fond" of Indian, or corn, meal.[6] Yet the only cornbread recipe in the family manuscripts, recorded by a great-granddaughter of Jefferson, has no obvious connection to Monticello. This is Mary Randolph's recipe, and almost certainly one of the breads served on the Jefferson table. Today we know these as corn muffins, but these are leavened with yeast rather than the soda and baking powder usual in cornbread. The resulting crumb is delicate and, for my taste, far more delicious. I recommend placing the muffin tins on a baking stone, which imitates the brick floor of the domed brick oven. The enslaved community at Monticello received cornmeal as part of their distributions, and hoecake, an elemental griddle cake of meal and water, is consequently a likely staple of their diet.*

1½ cups whole milk

¼ (scant) teaspoon active dry yeast

1 tablespoon lukewarm water

2 large eggs

1 teaspoon salt

2 ounces (4 tablespoons) unsalted butter

10 ounces (2 cups) fine stone-ground white cornmeal

1. Scald the milk over medium heat and let it cool to 110 degrees. Dissolve the yeast in the water and let it proof 10 minutes. Break the eggs into a separate bowl and beat until smooth, and then beat in the milk, yeast, and salt.

2. Rub the butter into the cornmeal with your fingertips until it is evenly distributed and resembles fine crumbs. Make a well in the center, pour in the liquid ingredients, and quickly stir until the batter is fairly smooth (a few small lumps won't matter). Cover and set in a warm place until slightly risen and thick with small air bubbles, at least 1 hour and as long as 2 hours.

3. Position a rack in the upper third of the oven and preheat the oven to 400 degrees. Butter a 12-cup standard muffin pan and divide the batter among the cups, filling each about three-quarters full. Bake until puffed, golden brown, and set, about 35 minutes. The bread will begin to separate from the edges of the pan when it is done.

JEFFERSON'S great-granddaughter, Ellen Wayles Harrison, recalled a family story concerning a breakfast at Monticello when Dolley Madison was a guest. Jefferson's grandson Benjamin Franklin Randolph appears to have taught Mrs. Madison a lesson about eating muffins (page 91): "On one occasion little Benjamin Franklin ... seated next to Mrs. M., found himself unequal to the management of his muffin. Mrs. Madison's aid being invoked, she took the knife to cut it, but a little hand was laid on hers, and an earnest voice exclaimed, 'No! No! That is not the way!' 'Well, how then Master Ben?' 'Why, you must tear him open, and put butter inside and stick holes in his back! And then pat him and squeeze him and the juice will run out!' Mrs. Madison, much amused, followed his directions. Any lover of the English muffin will appreciate their wisdom!"[7]

To Make Bread

One 10-inch round loaf, or about 12 small rolls

HISTORICAL NOTES: *For the daily bread of Monticello, and, indeed, all the gentry of colonial and early federal Virginia, we look to Mary Randolph's* The Virginia House-wife. *As Karen Hess notes, this was the daily bread of the English upper classes from at least the fourteenth century through the early days of American colonization, all the way up to the advent of iron ranges and steel-roller milling. Even though the Jefferson family has no recorded recipe for wheat bread, this process was so standard as to be rarely written out, and only this loaf will give reasonably authentic results in recipes calling for bread and bread crumbs. Those who are not after historical accuracy could substitute an artisanal baker's cottage loaf and still be in the same ballpark.*

¼ teaspoon active dry yeast, or ½ ounce compressed fresh yeast
1½ cups water, at room temperature
20 ounces (about 4 cups) unbleached all-purpose flour (including ¼ cup whole-wheat pastry flour)
2 teaspoons salt

1. Dissolve the yeast in the water in a medium bowl and allow to proof until creamy and foamy, about 10 minutes. Beat in about 1½ cups of the flour to form a smooth batter (also called a sponge).

2. Put half of the remaining flour in a large bowl. Pour in the sponge and cover with all but 1 cup of the remaining flour. Sprinkle the salt over the top and cover with a damp towel or plastic wrap. Let it rise until doubled, about 2 to 4 hours (depending on the temperature of the room).

3. Stir the flour into the sponge by hand or with an electric mixer fitted with the dough hook attachment. Turn it out onto a lightly floured work surface and knead in the remaining flour, adding it as needed until the dough is no longer sticky. Continue kneading until the dough is elastic and smooth (it should spring back into shape when pressed with a finger), about 8 minutes.

4. Gather the dough into a ball, pinching it together at the bottom, and lightly flour the surface. Wipe out the bowl and return the dough to it. Cover with a double-folded damp towel or plastic wrap and let rise until doubled, 4 to 6 hours (again, depending on the temperature of the room). (The dough can also rise overnight in a cool room or refrigerator.)

5. Punch down the dough and put it on a lightly floured work surface. Knead lightly for 1 to 2 minutes until smooth. Gather it into one large ball, or divide it into about 12 equal balls. Place the single loaf on a lightly floured baker's peel (see opposite page) or an un-rimmed baking sheet. Arrange the rolls on a lightly greased baking sheet. Cover with a damp towel and let rise until almost doubled.

6. Meanwhile, position a rack in the lower third of the oven, put a baking stone on it, and set a metal pie or cake pan on the floor of the oven. Preheat the oven to 450 degrees for at least 30 minutes. If baking the bread in rolls, skip to step 8.

7. To bake the single loaf, slash the top with a sharp knife or razor blade in a "tick-tack-toe" pattern. Put the peel on the baking stone and, with a quick jerk, remove the peel, leaving the loaf on the stone. Quickly, but carefully, throw ¼ cup water into the pie or cake pan and immediately close the oven. Bake for 15 minutes, reduce the heat to 400 degrees, and continue to bake for another 15 minutes. If the bread appears to be browning too quickly, reduce the temperature to 350 degrees. Bake for about 15 minutes more, or until the bread is golden brown and sounds hollow when tapped on the bottom. Cool on a wire rack.

8. To bake rolls, slash the tops with a sharp knife or razor blade in a circle or cross pattern. Put the baking sheet directly on the baking stone, throw ¼ cup water into the pie or cake pan, and immediately close the oven. Bake for about 20 minutes, or until the rolls are golden brown and sound hollow when tapped. If they appear to be browning too quickly, reduce the heat to 400 degrees. Cool the rolls on a wire rack.

MAKING EIGHTEENTH CENTURY BREAD TODAY

TO IMITATE THE TEXTURE of bread baked in a domed brick oven, the modern baker will need the right flour (see page 96) and some special equipment: a pizza baking stone or clean terra cotta tiles laid end to end on a rimmed baking sheet, and a baker's peel (a large wooden paddle)—usually sold in kits with pizza stones. Adding a little supplemental steam (as described in steps 7 and 8) creates bread of reasonable authenticity. The only thing the modern cook will not be able to reproduce is the subtle suggestion of smoke inherent in a wood-fired brick oven. Mary Randolph clearly baked the bread in rolls, in those days the nicest way to do it, but Monticello's inventory also featured a bread toaster designed for slices from a larger loaf.

The brick oven at Monticello (at left). A wood fire was built inside the domed interior and exhausted through the flue located at the opening to the oven. After the oven reached the correct operating temperature, the fire was cleared out, the food item placed inside, and a wooden door placed in the antechamber to block off the flue and prevent heat from escaping.

How is flour different today?

VIRGINIANS IN JEFFERSON'S DAY used soft-wheat flour, milled from winter wheat, as had their European ancestors before them. Soft-wheat flour has a low gluten content, but its gluten is of a very high quality and is tolerant of the slow fermentation process that Mary Randolph used. Unbleached pastry flour or a Southern brand of unbleached "all-purpose" flour milled from soft winter wheat will give reasonably good results.

I suggest a mixture of flours that will be reasonably similar to that used at Monticello. It is still "white" but the whole-wheat pastry flour puts back some of the flavor and texture that is squeezed out of flour that has not been stone-milled. I cannot speak for its absolute authenticity, since to get near the absolutes, the cook would have to use stone-milled, hand-bolted soft-wheat flour, and would spread it and warm it in a warming oven to control the moisture content. Those who are not as concerned for authenticity can use a national brand of un-bleached all-purpose flour, which is a blend of both soft and hard wheat. In either case, for all commercially milled flour I recommend including 1 ounce (about ¼ cup) whole-wheat pastry flour to give the flour flavor and body. Most natural food grocers sell it. To have success with these proportions, not to mention producing something near the daily bread of Monticello, the reader should *not* use *bread flour*: made from hard red summer wheat, it weighs heavier, and has a much higher gluten content and absorption rate than soft-wheat flour. If in doubt, try this test: soft-wheat flour will actually feel soft and velvety and will hold its shape when squeezed in your fist. Hard-wheat flour has a course, mealy texture and will not hold its shape when squeezed.

Jefferson's manufacturing mill, completed in 1807, processed local wheat into flour, which was then shipped down the Rivanna River to market in Richmond. Jefferson leased out this mill, here illustrated in a magazine from 1853.

Crumpets

Makes about 2 dozen

HISTORICAL NOTES: *These griddlecakes were common in old Southern cookbooks, and the recipe attributed to Monticello in Mrs. Meikleham's manuscript is typical. It's a little sketchy on technique, so I have turned to Mrs. Randolph for the necessary details of griddle-baking. Crumpets are yeast-leavened griddlecakes characterized by a honeycomb of air holes that develop in the top as they bake on the griddle. They are traditionally not turned, and are baked in old-fashioned muffin rings, so that the batter, while somewhat thin, bakes up in a uniform round about as thick as a modern pancake. For equipment, a wide, shallow-rimmed griddle will work. Cast iron is preferable but coated heavy aluminum will suffice, though it will produce crumpets of slightly different texture and color. Muffin rings are available from many kitchenware stores, but one could also use large (2¼-to-2½-inch diameter) biscuit cutters without handles.*

¼ teaspoon active dry yeast, or ½-ounce cake compressed fresh yeast

¼ cup water

1⅓ cups whole milk

10 ounces (about 2 cups) unbleached all-purpose flour

½ teaspoon salt

1 large egg

unsalted butter, chilled and sliced wafer thin, for serving

1. Stir the yeast in the water and let it proof for 10 minutes. Scald the milk in a small heavy-bottomed saucepan over medium heat and let it cool to 110 degrees. Whisk or sift together the flour and salt in a large mixing bowl. In a separate bowl, beat the egg lightly and beat in the milk and yeast. Gradually beat the liquids into the flour. The batter will be moderately thin. Cover it with a damp double-folded towel (or plastic wrap) and set in a warm place until risen (batter will not "double" as dough will) and filled with small air bubbles, about 3 hours.

2. Position a rack in the center of the oven, put a baking sheet on it, and preheat the oven to 150 to 170 degrees (the warm setting). Heat a griddle or wide heavy-bottomed skillet over medium-low heat. Butter 4 muffin rings and lightly brush the griddle or skillet with melted butter. Put the rings into the pan and carefully pour in enough batter to fill each ring ¼-inch deep. Cook slowly until the tops appear dry and honeycombed with air holes and the bottoms are evenly browned, about 6 to 8 minutes. Crumpets should not be turned.

3. As they are done, put them on the baking sheet in the oven to keep warm while the remaining batter is cooked. Stack them on a warm plate with wafer-thin slices of butter between them and serve hot.

The prominence of soup on Jefferson's table is apparent in a letter from Jefferson's granddaughter Ellen Wayles Randolph Coolidge. After marrying and moving to Boston, she wrote to her mother at Monticello, requesting favorite recipes: " I wish to tax each of the girls the writing of an occasional receipt for me on a small slip of paper which can be put in a letter. those I am most in need of are 1st soup. 2. vermicelli soup. 3. coffee. 4. muffins. 5. a charlotte. 6. gingerbread such as Edy makes. 7. rice cakes for breakfast. 8. drop biscuit. & several others which I cannot call to mind."[8] Soups are the first two that did come to mind. Vermicelli soup appears on page 103, and "soup" likely refers either to Beef Soup Monticello (opposite page), or Okra Soup (page 106).

Beef Soup Monticello

Serves 8

HISTORICAL NOTES: *Both Septimia Anne Randolph Meikleham and her sister Virginia Randolph Trist recorded similar recipes for "Beef Soup" or "Soup Monticello." My interpretation follows mostly Mrs. Trist's rendition, with bits and pieces and serving details supplied by Mary Randolph, and the technique for the broth taken from Jefferson's recording of classic French practice that he titled simply "Observations on Soups"—which was subsequently copied by his granddaughters in their manuscripts. As for equipment, the soup would certainly have been cooked in the stew holes at Monticello, either in a lined copper or iron soup kettle, though the initial drawing of the broth was begun on an open fire. A heavy-bottomed soup kettle of lined copper or stainless steel will answer for modern cooks.*

- 2 tablespoons unsalted butter
- 3 pounds beef shanks, boned, rinsed, and marrow removed (for another use)
  salt
  whole black pepper in a pepper mill
- 2 large sprigs each fresh parsley and thyme, tied in a bundle with twine
- 1 large white onion, peeled and chopped (about 2 cups)
- 12 cups water
- 3 large carrots, peeled and diced (about 2 cups)
- 2 medium turnips, peeled and diced (about 1½ cups)
- 2 medium parsnips, peeled and diced (about 1½ cups)
- 1 small green cabbage, cored and thinly sliced into 1-inch strips (about 3 cups)
- 3 large ribs celery, peeled and diced (about 1½ cups)
- 2 cups Toasted Croutons (page 100, step 6)

1. Melt the butter in a large heavy-bottomed soup pot over medium-low heat. Add the shank meat, season with salt and several grindings of pepper, and toss in the herb bundle. Strew the onion over the top, cover, and reduce the heat to the lowest possible setting, cooking at a bare simmer until the juices are fully extracted and reduced almost to a glaze, about 2 hours.

2. Pour in the water, increase the heat to medium, and bring it to a simmer, skimming any scum as it rises. Add the carrots, turnips, parsnips, and cabbage, let it come back to a simmer, and reduce the heat to medium low. Cook at a bare simmer, again skimming any scum as it rises, until the meat and vegetables are very tender, about 2 hours, or until the broth is reduced by about one-third, adding the celery after 1½ hours.

3. Remove and discard the herbs, remove the meat, and let it cool enough to handle. Cut it into bite-size pieces, cover, and refrigerate until just before finishing the soup. Let the broth cool and skim away the fat (or chill the soup until the fat hardens, about 4 hours or overnight, lift it off the top, and discard it).

4. Put the meat back in the soup, bring to a simmer over medium heat, and simmer for about 5 minutes. Arrange the meat in a warm soup tureen and ladle the soup over the top. Serve with Toasted Croutons.

White Bean Soup

Serves 8 to 12

HISTORICAL NOTES: *As with Beef Soup Monticello, this recipe appears in the Meikleham and Trist manuscripts, entitled "White Bean Soup" or just "Bean Soup." Described by both sisters as "a receipt brought by [their uncle] Gouverneur Morris from France," this recipe is indeed a classic French bean soup, likely gleaned by Morris during his years in Europe. Despite its European heritage, this soup became Southern practice for two centuries, although few modern Southern cooks would make it without an onion in the pot. As for equipment, the purée was originally accomplished by rubbing the solids through a perforated colander; a modern food mill does exactly the same thing with far less effort. Those who cannot manage hand rubbing could resort to a stick blender (preferred), a cup blender, or a food processor on the understanding that the purée will not have the same body and texture.*

1½	pounds (4 cups) dried navy, great Northern, or cannellini beans
4	quarts water
	salt
2	large carrots, trimmed, peeled, and diced
2	small turnips, trimmed, peeled, and diced
1	medium parsnip, trimmed, peeled, and diced
3	large ribs celery with leafy green tops, chopped
2 - 3	tablespoons unsalted butter
4	slices bread, ½ inch thick (see To Make Bread, page 94)

1. The night before or 6 to 8 hours ahead, sort the beans, removing any small stones and discarding any beans that are deformed or discolored, and wash well. Drain and put them in a large bowl that will hold twice their volume and cover with cold water by at least 2 inches. Soak for 6 to 8 hours or overnight.

2. Drain the beans and put them in a large heavy-bottomed pot or 6-quart Dutch oven. Cover with the 4 quarts of water and bring slowly to a simmer over medium heat, skimming any scum as it rises to the surface. Simmer gently until the beans are tender, about 1 hour. Replenish the liquid with additional simmering water as needed. Season generously with salt.

3. Add the carrots and turnips and simmer until tender, about 15 minutes. Add the parsnip and simmer until the vegetables are quite soft, about 15 to 30 minutes longer.

4. Purée the soup through a wire strainer or a food mill (a blender may be used, but will not produce an authentic texture—see Historical Notes), and return to the pot. If it is too thick, thin it with additional simmering water.

5. Just before serving, return the soup to a simmer, stir in the celery, and simmer gently, stirring occasionally, until the celery pieces are tender, about 15 minutes.

6. Butter the bread slices and grill-toast them in a skillet over medium heat, turning frequently, until golden brown. Using a serrated knife, cut them into bite-size pieces and put them in the bottom of a warm soup tureen or divide among warm bowls. Ladle the soup over them and serve at once.

Rabbit (or Chicken) Soup

Serves 6

HISTORICAL NOTES: *From Isaac Jefferson, once enslaved at Monticello, we know rabbits were raised and eaten there.[9] For this classic soup, I have mostly followed Mary Randolph's recipe for Hare Soup in* The Virginia House-wife, *which is more nicely detailed than Martha Randolph's recipe as recorded in Mrs. Trist's manuscript. I've used Mary Randolph's ingredients, adding thyme and using salt pork instead of anchovies. The manuscript calls for parboiling, but it is unnecessary with commercially raised rabbit and would make our commercially raised chickens so bland as to not be worth bothering. The stew can be made a day ahead of time up through step 3. In fact, like most stews, it is better made ahead, and is easier to degrease when it is cold and the fat is congealed on the top. Shortly before serving, finish it with the thickening and wine in steps 3 and 4.*

2 large rabbits, skinned, or two young chickens (2 to 3 pounds each), cut up as for frying

½ teaspoon whole cloves

1 whole blade mace

salt

whole black pepper in a pepper mill

small pinch ground cayenne pepper

4 ounces lean salt pork or country ham, thickly sliced

2 large white onions, peeled and thinly sliced

2 large sprigs each fresh parsley and thyme, tied in a bundle with kitchen twine

8 cups boiling water

2 tablespoons unsalted butter

1 tablespoon Browned Flour (page 111)

¼ cup claret (red Bordeaux wine) or Madeira

2 tablespoons chopped fresh parsley

1. Rinse the rabbits or chicken under cold running water, pat dry, and put them in a single layer in the bottom of a large heavy-bottomed pot or Dutch oven. Grind the cloves and mace with a mortar and pestle or in a spice mill. Season the meat with salt, several grindings of pepper, cayenne pepper, and half of the spices. Cover with some of the pork or ham and half of the onions. Repeat with the remaining ingredients and toss in the herb bundle.

2. Pour in the boiling water and bring to a boil over medium heat, skimming any scum that rises. Cover loosely and reduce the heat to low. Simmer until the meat is very tender and the broth is somewhat reduced, about 2 hours.

3. Knead the butter and flour together in a small bowl. Remove and discard the herb bundle and pork or ham and skim any fat from the surface. Stir in the butter and flour mixture a little bit at a time and simmer until the broth has thickened, about 3 or 4 minutes more.

4. Stir in the wine and simmer for about 5 minutes more. Garnish with chopped parsley.

Nouilly à maccaroni (Noodles)

Makes about 1 pound of noodles

HISTORICAL NOTES: *This is one of the recipes that has survived in Jefferson's own hand, cut in scale by half and augmented by traditional Italian recipes for details on mixing and kneading. The only way to work the proportions is by feel, since the moisture content of the eggs will vary from batch to batch. Flour is the usual variable, but since the recipe was specific about the amount of flour, I've made milk the variable. For the details of shaping and cutting, I've consulted Mary Randolph. Jefferson's directions imply that noodles were meant to be round, like spaghetti, but Mrs. Randolph's noodles clearly were flat and were even twisted into a corkscrew. To use the noodles in soup, as they would mostly have been eaten at Monticello, see Vermicelli Soup (opposite page); to dress them as macaroni, see Baked Macaroni (page 145). The noodles may also be cooked plain and sauced as you would any fresh pasta, though they were probably not eaten that way at Monticello.*

1 pound (3¼ to 3½ cups) unbleached all-purpose flour
1 teaspoon salt
3 large eggs
¼ cup whole milk (approximately)

1. Mound the flour on a smooth work surface, sprinkle with salt, and form a well in the center. Break the eggs into a bowl and lightly beat them with 2 tablespoons of the milk. Pour this into the well in the flour and gradually stir in the surrounding flour with a fork. Add more milk by spoonfuls as needed to make the dough smooth and pliable but not sticky. Knead the dough until it is very smooth, about 7 minutes. Form it into a ball and lightly dust it with flour. Cover with a damp towel and let it rest for 15 to 30 minutes

2. Divide the dough into quarters. Working with one piece at a time (keeping the remaining dough covered with the towel) lightly dust the dough with flour and roll with a rolling pin or pasta machine until very thin (about 1/16 inch thick).

3. Lightly dust the dough with flour, roll it lengthwise into a cylinder, and slice it crosswise with a very sharp knife into narrow noodles, slightly less than ¼ inch wide (the cutting can also be done with the cutting roller of the pasta machine). Noodles intended for soup are cut into short lengths—from ¼ inch square to as long as 2 inches. Spread them on kitchen towels and repeat with the remaining dough.

4. The noodles may be cooked immediately or completely dried and stored for later use. To dry them, coil handfuls of noodles into loose nest shapes, and set them on linen towels to dry completely—about 6 hours or overnight. Make sure they are completely dried before storing or they will mold, and store them in an airtight container.

Vermicelli Soup

Serves 4

HISTORICAL NOTES: *Vermicelli Soup is among the recipes requested by Jefferson's granddaughter Ellen Coolidge, and its presence on the Monticello table is further suggested by Jefferson's directions about how to use noodles in soups. Even so, no family recipe survives, so this interpretation is based on Mary Randolph's and other period recipes.*

5   cups clear broth from Beef Soup (page 99), or beef, veal, or chicken broth

2   quarts water

1   tablespoon salt

¼   pound *Nouilly à maccaroni*, cut into pieces ¼ inch wide and ¼ to 2 inches long

1.   Bring the broth to a simmer over medium heat. Meanwhile, bring 2 quarts water to a rolling boil over high heat.

2.   Add the salt to the water, let it return to a boil, and add the noodles, stirring with a fork or wooden spoon to prevent sticking. Cook until tender, about 2 minutes if the noodles are fresh, 4 to 6 if dried. Drain thoroughly.

3.   Stir the noodles into the simmering broth, let it return to a simmer, and serve immediately.

A NOTE ON EQUIPMENT FOR PASTA

For authentic equipment, the reader wants a long cylindrical wooden rolling pin, often sold today as "French" or sometimes as "pasta" rolling pins. A pasta machine (the rolling device, not the electric mixing machine that extrudes the dough through a die) will answer almost as well and give authentic enough results. For more on Jefferson and pasta, including his quest for a pasta mold, see page 144.

Catfish Soup

Serves 8

HISTORICAL NOTES: *This handsome soup is in essence a classic chowder, thickened with egg yolks in the old European manner. Mrs. Trist's manuscript varies only in detail from Mary Randolph's recipe in* The Virginia House-wife. *Both call for white, deep-water catfish—but readers will not be able to make a distinction unless they catch their own, since catfish are sold skinned and are rarely identified by type. The intention is freshwater fish; although the farm-raised fresh-water catfish that are so widely available today will work fine, they are not likely to be as strongly flavored. One caution is that readers should resist the temptation to use fillets; the finest flavor and richness of broth is to be had from whole, bone-in fish. Although almost all of the many fish purchases documented in Martha Randolph's account book simply say "fish," the journal does specify "5 cat fish from Madison" Hemings, for 50 cents.[10]*

- 3 pounds whole catfish (about 2 large), skinned, gutted, and cut into about 8 pieces
- 1 large white onion, peeled and finely chopped
- ½ cup chopped fresh parsley
  - salt
  - whole black pepper in a pepper mill
  - pinch ground cayenne pepper
- 12 ounces lean salt pork, country ham, or prosciutto, thickly sliced
- 8 cups boiling water
- 1 tablespoon unsalted butter, softened
- 2 tablespoons all-purpose flour
- 4 large egg yolks
- 1 cup half-and-half

1. Put the fish pieces in a large soup pot. Spread the onion and parsley over them and season generously with salt, several grindings of pepper, and cayenne pepper. Add the salt pork or ham, pour the boiling water over it, and bring to a simmer over medium-high heat. Reduce the heat to medium low, cover, and cook at a slow simmer until the onions are tender and the fish is fully cooked, about 20 to 30 minutes.

2. Remove and discard the pork. Take up the fish. It may be left whole, as originally served, or boned, if necessary, but kept in large pieces. Cover and keep warm.

3. Bring the broth back to a simmer over medium heat. Mix together the butter and flour in a medium bowl and beat in the egg yolks. Heat the half-and-half to nearly boiling and slowly beat into the egg yolk mixture. Gradually stir this into the broth and simmer, stirring constantly, until thickened, about 4 minutes. Taste and adjust the seasonings.

4. Transfer the fish to a warm soup tureen, or divide it among warm soup plates, and ladle the soup over it.

Oyster Soup

Serves 8

HISTORICAL NOTES: *A version of this recipe, attributed to Martha Randolph, is found in Mrs. Trist's manuscript; however, I have mostly followed Mary Randolph's rendition, since it is more lucid than Mrs. Trist's recording. In the original recipes, the first quantity of oysters was boiled for broth and discarded. The presentation oysters were then added and poached just until they were plumped and their gills curled. This was a common technique at the time, though it seems wildly extravagant today. But oysters were not as dear then as they are now and, after all, the Randolphs were gentry. To make the dish more affordable for modern cooks, I've compromised by using oyster liquor that yields much the same results. Many fishmongers who sell shucked oysters in bulk will give away or sell the surplus liquor; failing that, readers may use the strained liquor from the oysters supplemented with fish stock.*

2 pints shucked oysters, with liquor
2 cups oyster liquor or fish stock
4 ounces lean salt pork or country ham, thickly sliced
1 medium white onion, peeled and chopped
3 large sprigs fresh parsley
1 large sprig fresh thyme
  whole black pepper in a pepper mill
1 rounded tablespoon all-purpose flour
1 cup heavy cream
4 large egg yolks
  salt

1. Set a wire-mesh sieve over a bowl, pour in the oysters, and drain for 30 minutes. Cover and refrigerate the oysters.

2. Measure the strained liquor and put it with the additional oyster liquor or fish stock in a heavy-bottomed 4-quart pot. Add enough water to make 12 cups of liquid, and put in the salt pork or ham, onion, parsley, and thyme. Bring it to a boil over medium-high heat, skimming the scum as it rises. Reduce the heat to medium, season lightly with a grinding of pepper, and simmer until the liquid is reduced to 8 cups, about 45 minutes to 1 hour.

3. Strain the broth, discarding the solids, return it to the pot, and bring it back to a simmer over medium heat. Put the flour in a small bowl and gradually beat in the cream with a whisk or fork until smooth. Beat in the egg yolks.

4. When the broth is simmering, add the oysters, bring it back to a simmer, and cook just until the gills begin to curl, about 2 minutes. Slowly stir in the cream and egg yolks and cook, stirring, until the soup is lightly thickened and the oysters are plump, about 2 minutes longer. Remove it from the heat, taste, and add salt and additional pepper as needed. Pour the soup into a warm tureen, or divide it among warm individual soup plates.

Okra Soup

Serves 18

HISTORICAL NOTES: *This gumbo (pictured on page 69) was attributed to Martha Randolph in her daughter Virginia Randolph Trist's manuscript.* *Six other gumbo or okra soup recipes appear in the family manuscripts, one simply entitled "Soup," suggesting that it was almost commonplace. In addition, I've added a few details from Mary Randolph's version. This soup—with African origins— survives today in virtually every Southern cook's repertory as "vegetable soup." Only Mary Randolph's recipe gives us the nice detail of blanching the salt pork to remove the excess salt. To do this, rinse the salt pork under cold running water. Bring at least 1 quart of water to a rolling boil over medium-high heat. Add the pork and bring it back to the boiling point. Lower the heat to a steady simmer and cook about 5 minutes. Drain, and if the pork was especially salty, wipe it with a clean towel.*

4 quarts water

1 pound young okra (each 2 to 3 inches long), trimmed and sliced

1 large white onion, peeled and finely chopped

2 cups fresh lima beans, or 1 package (10 ounces) frozen lima beans, thawed

salt

whole black pepper in a pepper mill

1 chicken (3½ pounds), cut up as for frying, setting aside the back and neck for another use

4 ounces salt pork, sliced about ¼ inch thick and blanched (see Historical Notes)

2 large sprigs each fresh parsley and thyme, tied together in a bundle with kitchen twine

1 pound (about 3 medium) pattypan or yellow summer squash, trimmed and diced

5 medium tomatoes, blanched, peeled, cored, and diced (about 2 cups)

2 tablespoons unsalted butter

1 rounded tablespoon unbleached all-purpose flour

3 cups cooked white rice

1. Bring the water to a simmer in a large saucepan or Dutch oven. Stir in the okra and onion and return to a simmer. Reduce the heat as low as possible and cook at a bare simmer for 1 hour. Add the lima beans and simmer for another 30 minutes, or until the beans are just tender.

2. Season liberally with salt and a few grindings of pepper and add the chicken, salt pork, herb bundle, and squash. Raise the heat briefly to return to a simmer, lower it once more, and cook at a bare simmer until the chicken is fully cooked, about 1 hour. Add the tomatoes and continue simmering for another hour. Remove from the heat and discard the salt pork and herb bundle. The soup can be made ahead and cooled, covered, and refrigerated. When chilled (about 6 hours or overnight), remove and discard any fat that surfaces. Otherwise, let it cool until all the fat settles to the top, and skim it off.

3. When ready to serve the soup, return it to a simmer over medium heat. Knead together the butter and flour in a small bowl and stir it into the soup, simmering until lightly thickened, about 4 minutes. Serve it in warmed bowls with a whole piece of chicken in each bowl and about ¼ cup of white rice spooned into the center of each serving.

Pepper Vinegar

Makes about 2 cups

HISTORICAL NOTES: *Jefferson obtained seed of the Texas Bird Pepper in 1812 and 1813 from Captain Samuel Brown, along with a suggestion to use it in pepper vinegar.*[11] *Lacking a detailed recipe, I turn again to Mary Randolph. Although her method varies from modern practice, the pickling vinegar from commercially made pickled hot peppers is actually a reasonable substitute. In addition to the small bird peppers, Monticello's gardens also featured long cayenne peppers, but readers may also substitute twice as many jalapeño or serrano peppers. While this vinegar simmers, make sure the kitchen is well ventilated, using an exhaust fan and an open window, and don't stand over the pot: the fumes are quite strong and can be painful. The vinegar makes a fine accompaniment for Okra Soup (opposite page).*

8 large fresh red cayenne chili peppers (each at least 3 inches long)
3 cups red or white wine vinegar

1. Stem and split the peppers in half lengthwise, reserving the seeds. Put the peppers, seeds, and vinegar in a medium saucepan and bring to a boil over medium-high heat. Reduce the heat to medium and simmer until the liquid is reduced to 2 cups.

2. Strain the vinegar and pour into sterilized screw-capped bottles or pint canning jars (see Note).

Cap with clean lids and store in a cool, dark cupboard or in the refrigerator. The vinegar will keep indefinitely, and for at least 1 year.

• • •

Note: To sterilize jars, submerge them in boiling water and boil for at least five minutes.

VIRGINIA 'GUMBO'

This okra soup is in effect "gumbo" as it was made in Virginia, and marks the strong early creolization (that is, Africanization) of the cooking of the Virginia gentry, right down to the directions to serve it with rice—a significant whiff of West African cookery. Such soups are derived from classic African "long-pot" cooking, and the simmer must be kept slow and imperceptible.

Cymlings, or pattypan squash, are not universally available. Substitutions include mature yellow crookneck squash and yellow—not green—zucchini. Frozen limas will suffice without much compromise. For strict authenticity, this soup can only be made seasonally with fresh okra and truly vine-ripened tomatoes. The chicken should be a small one, preferably an all-natural, grain-fed bird, weighing in at no more than 3 pounds, and ideally less.

Visiting Jefferson's retreat home, Poplar Forest, with her grandfather, Ellen Coolidge wrote to her mother back at Monticello: "We have received great kindness and attention from our neighbours, particularly Mrs Walker, who is constantly sending us little presents … sometimes, fruit of different kinds, melons, apples, ripe peaches &c, then again vegetables, and on one occasion cake and … sweet meats. you will laugh to hear that lamb has become such a rarity, that we were greatly pleased to receive from the same kind old lady, a quarter of one, very fat and tender." [12]

Mutton Chops

Serves 4 to 6

HISTORICAL NOTES: *Ellen's comment (opposite page) shows the primacy of mutton and lamb at Monticello: "you will laugh to hear that lamb has become such a rarity." Although Mrs. Trist's manuscript lists "Boiled Mutton Chops," she made a scribal error, writing "boiled" for "broiled"—an easy, if hair-raising, mistake. "Broiling" was the equivalent of modern grilling: the food was cooked on a lightly greased gridiron set over live coals. Mutton, alas, is a rarity nowadays, but fortunately what passes for "lamb" in American markets is closer to mutton than true lamb, and American lamb rib chops do handsomely for the recipe. "Frenching" the chops—that is, scraping all the meat, cartilage, and fat from the long rib bone, leaving only the meaty "eye"—is a nice touch. Care should be taken not to trim too much fat from the eye; over-trimming can make grilled meat dry.*

8 mutton or lamb rib chops (at least ¾ to 1 inch thick)
    salt
    whole black pepper in a pepper mill
½ cup water
¼ cup Mushroom Catsup (page 131)
2 tablespoons unsalted butter, cut into bits
½ cup freshly grated horseradish

1. Prepare a grill with hardwood coals. When the coals have burned to a medium-hot fire, rub the grill rack with a cloth dipped in lard or bacon drippings and position it about 4 to 6 inches above the coals.

2. Season the chops with salt and several grindings of pepper and grill them, turning once, until cooked to the doneness of choice, about 3 to 4 minutes per side for medium rare. Remove them to a warm platter and set aside to keep warm.

3. Bring the water to a simmer in a small saucepan. Add the Mushroom Catsup, additional salt if needed, and simmer for about 1 minute more. Remove from the heat, whisk in the butter, and pour it over the chops. Sprinkle a little horseradish over them, and spoon the remaining horseradish around the edges of the platter.

• • •

Note: Readers who are not concerned for authenticity or who are unable to grill-broil may use the oven broiler, though it won't have the distinctive flavor of wood-coal grilling. Position a rack about 6 inches below the broiler and preheat it for 20 minutes. Rub the broiling pan rack with lard or drippings and lay the chops on it. Lightly brush them with melted butter (necessary for oven broiling) and season with salt and pepper. Broil, turning once, until done to taste, about 3 to 4 minutes per side for medium rare.

Beef à la Mode

Serves 8 to 10

HISTORICAL NOTES: *Mrs. Trist credited this recipe to Etienne Lemaire, Jefferson's butler at the President's House. To it, I've added details from* The Virginia House-wife *and a later recipe from the family collections. The method of baking rather than simmering over direct heat comes from Mary Randolph, along with her wonderfully heady dose of garlic, thyme, and Mushroom Catsup. She indicates that this may be served cold with salad, so if readers wish to experiment, the broth will jell into aspic and can be clarified using the method for Beef à la Daube Lemaire (page 112). The cooking pot should be close-fitting and lidded. For the larding, it's possible to push the fat through the meat using a thin-bladed boning knife, but the task is easiest with the aid of a larding needle— a long, hollow needle with a clamping gripper at the end to hold the fat. They are widely available at cookware stores.*

- 1 teaspoon whole cloves
- 1 teaspoon whole allspice berries
- 1 teaspoon whole black peppercorns
- whole nutmeg in a grater
- ground cayenne pepper
- ½ cup minced fresh parsley, plus 1 tablespoon, for garnish
- 8 ounces salt-cured pork fat back, cut into ¼-inch-square strips a little longer than the beef is thick
- 3½ pounds beef eye round
- salt
- 1 tablespoon chopped fresh thyme, or 1 teaspoon dried
- 4 large or 6 medium cloves garlic, peeled and minced
- 3 large white onions, peeled and chopped
- 2 large or 3 medium carrots, peeled and chopped
- 4 ounces lean salt pork, sliced into ¼-inch-thick pieces
- ¼ cup brandy
- 2 cups white wine
- 1 tablespoon Browned Flour (opposite page)
- 2 tablespoons unsalted butter
- 1 tablespoon Mushroom Catsup (page 131)

1. Grind the cloves, allspice, and pepper to a powder with a mortar and pestle or in an electric spice mill. Grate in 2 teaspoons of nutmeg and add a generous pinch of cayenne pepper. Mix the spices and the ½ cup of parsley in a wide shallow bowl. Roll the fat back in the spices and put them on a wax-paper-lined baking sheet. Freeze until firm, about 30 minutes.

2. Rinse and dry the beef. With a long narrow-bladed boning knife, poke all the way through the meat, leaving the blade in place. Take a strip of chilled fat and clamp it onto a larding needle. Slide the needle along the blade of the filet knife until it protrudes from the other side. Carefully pull the needle through, threading the fat into the meat, and remove the knife. Loosen the needle and repeat at 1-inch intervals until the meat is well larded. All the fat may not be needed.

3. Rub the meat with the remaining spices, a little salt, the thyme, and garlic (keeping in mind that the fatback is already adding seasoning). Spread the onions and carrots over the bottom of a heavy-bottomed Dutch oven or enameled iron casserole dish that will hold all the meat in a fairly close fit. Put the beef on top of them and lay the salt pork and any remaining seasoned fat back over it. Pour in the brandy and wine and cover tightly.

(Continued on next page)

Beef à la Mode
(continued)

4. Position a rack in the center of the oven and preheat the oven to 300 degrees. Bake until fork-tender, about 4 hours. Remove the meat to a platter, discarding the salt pork, and let it rest for at least 15 minutes before carving.

5. Carefully skim the fat and strain the vegetables from the broth and bring it back to a simmer over medium heat. Knead together the Browned Flour and butter until smooth. Add it in bits to the simmering broth, stirring constantly, and stir in the Mushroom Catsup. Simmer the gravy until lightly thickened, about 4 minutes.

6. Thinly slice the beef across the grain and arrange it, slightly overlapping, on a serving platter. Drizzle with gravy, sprinkle with the remaining tablespoon of parsley, and serve with gravy passed separately.

Browned Flour

Makes 1 cup

HISTORICAL NOTES: *This flour was indispensable in kitchens of the early Republic and remained common in Southern cooking well into the twentieth century. It is similar to a Creole brown roux, except that the flour is toasted in a dry pan instead of hot fat. In that regard, it is much more versatile. It was used for almost any brown sauce or pan gravy and is crucial for a number of the Jefferson family recipes. Any heavy-bottomed pan will do, but a cast iron skillet works best.*

1 cup all-purpose flour

1. Put the flour in a well-seasoned cast iron or nonstick skillet over medium heat. Cook, stirring almost constantly, until it begins to color. Reduce the heat to medium low and cook, stirring frequently, until it is an even rich medium brown and develops a pleasantly nutty aroma, about 30 minutes. If it begins to smell or appear at all burned, immediately transfer the flour to a large, shallow bowl and stir until cooled.

2. Take it off the heat and spread it on a plate or wide shallow bowl to cool. Spoon the flour into a glass jar, seal with a tight lid, and store in a cool dark cupboard.

Beef à la Daube Lemaire

Serves 8 to 10

HISTORICAL NOTES: *Jefferson copied this recipe himself, attributing it to Etienne Lemaire. I've mostly followed his rendition, with a few details supplied in recipes recorded by Mrs. Trist and Mary Randolph. Readers should note the difference between lean salt pork and fat back (salt-cured pork fat), since both are called for here. This must be made a day ahead to allow time for the clarifying and jelling of the aspic. The equipment is the same as that for Beef à la Mode, except that it uses a direct heat method (stewing) as opposed to baking, so the pot should of course be flameproof. Most likely cooks at Monticello used tin-lined copper or an iron kettle; an enameled iron casserole would substitute handsomely, as would a heavy-bottomed stainless-steel-lined Dutch oven. Larding needles are discussed in the Historical Notes for Beef à la Mode (page 110).*

1 teaspoon whole cloves
1 teaspoon whole allspice berries
1 teaspoon whole black peppercorns
  whole nutmeg in a grater
  generous pinch ground cayenne pepper
¼ cup minced fresh parsley
8 ounces salt-cured fat back, sliced into long ¼-inch-thick strips a little longer than the beef is thick
3½ pounds boneless beef eye or top round
  salt
1 large white onion, peeled and diced
2 large carrots, peeled and diced
1 pound beef shank (bone-in), cut into ½-inch-thick slices
2 tablespoons chopped fresh thyme, or 2 teaspoons dried
4 ounces (2 to 3 slices) lean salt pork
  whites and shells of 4 large eggs
  chopped fresh parsley, for garnish

1. Begin a day ahead. Grind the cloves, allspice, and pepper to a powder using a mortar and pestle or an electric spice mill. Grate in 2 teaspoons of nutmeg and add the cayenne pepper. Mix the spices with the parsley in a wide shallow bowl. Roll the fat back in the spices and put them on a wax-paper-lined baking sheet. Freeze until firm, about 30 minutes.

2. Rinse and dry the beef. With a long thin narrow-bladed boning knife, poke all the way through the meat, leaving the blade in place. Take a strip of chilled fat back and clamp it onto a larding needle. Slide the needle along the blade of the filet knife until it protrudes from the other side. Carefully pull the needle all the way through, threading the pork into the meat, and remove the knife. Loosen the needle and repeat at 1-inch intervals until the meat is well larded. All the fat back may not be needed. Rub the meat with the remaining spice mixture and a little salt, keeping in mind that the seasoned fat back will also flavor the meat.

3. Spread the onion and carrots over the bottom of a deep heavy-bottomed Dutch oven that is just large enough to hold all the meat snugly in a close fit. Put the meat on top of the vegetables, surround it with the slices of beef shank, and sprinkle with thyme. Lay any remaining seasoned fat back and salt pork slices over the meat and add enough water to just cover.

(Continued on next page)

Beef à la Daube Lemaire
(continued)

4. Put the pot over medium heat, cover loosely, and bring slowly to a simmer, carefully skimming any scum as it rises to the surface. Reduce the heat and cook at a bare simmer until the meat is tender, about 3 hours. Remove it to a platter, let it cool, and then cover it loosely. Raise the heat to medium and continue simmering the broth until reduced by one-third. Strain and let it cool. Refrigerate both the meat and broth until well chilled, about 4 hours.

5. Carefully remove and discard the solidified fat from the broth and put the jellied broth in a large saucepan. If it has not sufficiently jelled, return it to a simmer and cook until reduced by about one-quarter. Let cool. If sufficiently jelled, warm it over medium-low heat until barely melted. Whisk the egg whites until frothy. Crush the eggshells and mix them into the whites. Stir this into the broth and slowly bring to a simmer. Simmer gently until the eggs solidify and rise to the top. Gently push their mass aside and take a spoonful of broth with a bright metal spoon to make sure it is sparkling clear. Set a strainer lined with clean cotton muslin into a shallow pan and carefully ladle the broth into it, letting it drip through. Cool once more until it begins to thicken but not yet jell.

6. Thinly slice the beef across the grain and arrange it, overlapping slightly, on a platter. Spoon some of the broth over the beef, cover, and chill until it jells. Spoon on a second layer of broth and chill until jelled. Meanwhile, pour the remaining broth into a shallow 9-inch-square pan and chill until solid. Break up the jelly by raking it with a fork or knife and use it to garnish the edges of the platter. Just before serving, sprinkle with chopped parsley.

When Thomas Jefferson married the young widow Martha Wayles Skelton in 1772, she brought to their household a number of items acquired during her first marriage, including this silver ladle made in London.

Bouilli

Serves 8 to 10

HISTORICAL NOTES: *Jefferson's granddaughter Ellen Coolidge recalled, "He liked boiled Beef, Bouilli, better than roast." She felt that this preference, coupled with others that were "contrary to the custom of his countrymen," appeared to "his enemies as so many proofs of his being under french influence and conspiring with Bonaparte."[3] To supplement the two manuscript sources for Bouilli—one previously misattributed to Martha Randolph and one by Mrs. Trist— I've looked to a later version in Mrs. Trist's manuscript and to Mary Randolph. The early manuscript recipes don't mention garlic, leeks, or herbs, but it's inconceivable that the French-trained cooks at Monticello would not have used them. This must cook at a barely perceptible simmer, as described below, with the surface of the water barely "shimmering." The accompanying Veal Glace (opposite page) and Sauce Hachée (page 116) are part of the original recipe. Save the broth: it's an ambrosial base for onion or beef barley soup.*

3½ pounds beef rump roast or brisket

1 teaspoon whole black peppercorns

½ teaspoon whole cloves

salt

2 large sprigs each fresh parsley and thyme, tied into a bundle with kitchen twine

8 small white onions, peeled and left whole, or 4 medium onions, peeled and quartered

4 medium carrots, peeled and cut into 1-inch-long pieces

4 medium turnips, peeled and quartered

6 ribs celery with leafy greens, cut into 1-inch-long pieces

4 large or 6 small cloves garlic, lightly crushed, peeled, and left whole

4 small leeks

Veal Glace (recipe follows)

Sauce Hachée (recipe follows)

1. Rinse the meat under cold running water. Put it in a deep close-fitting Dutch oven that will comfortably hold it and all the vegetables and cover with cold water. Bring it slowly to a boil over medium heat, skimming the scum as it rises.

2. Tie the peppercorns and cloves into a bundle made with a small square of cheesecloth and kitchen twine. When bubbles begin to surface around the edges of the pot, season liberally with salt, put in the bundles of spices and herbs, and add the onions, carrots, turnips, celery, and garlic cloves. Let it return to a simmer, reduce the heat to low, and cook at a bare simmer (the top of the water should just shimmer) until the meat is tender, about 4½ to 5 hours.

3. When the meat has been cooking for 4 hours, trim the root ends of the leeks and remove the tough outer leaves. Cut off most of the greens, leaving the leeks about 6 inches long, and split them in half lengthwise. Thoroughly wash away the grit from between their layers under cold running water and add the leeks to the pot. Let it come back to a simmer and cook until the beef and leeks are tender, about 30 minutes to 1 hour. (The leeks may be removed if they get tender before the beef is quite done.)

4. Take up the meat to a serving platter and let it rest for 15 minutes. Remove and discard the herb and spice bundles. Lift the vegetables out of the broth and arrange them on the platter around the beef or in a separate serving bowl. Pour the Veal Glace over the beef and serve, carving it at the table, with the sauce passed separately.

Veal Glace

Makes about 1 cup

HISTORICAL NOTES: *Meat glazes, syrupy reductions of stock made mostly from veal, are more a part of elegant haute cuisine than home cooking, since only the kitchens of restaurants and wealthy households had the necessary staff and separately made stocks for making them. In this case it is used exactly like an egg glaze in baking— to give an elegant, glossy finish to boiled meat. Since all the manuscript versions of Bouilli contain a method for veal glacé within them, it was surely a part of Lemaire's original directions, though—like the rest of the recipe—it has been somewhat corrupted in repeated copying.*

1 tablespoon unsalted butter

1½ pounds veal shank, cut into 1-inch-thick slices
whole black pepper in a pepper mill

2 ounces (about 2 ¼-inch-thick slices) lean salt pork or country ham

1 sprig each fresh parsley and thyme, tied in a bundle with kitchen twine

1 small white onion, peeled and thinly sliced

1 carrot, peeled and thinly sliced

1. Put the butter in a small heavy-bottomed saucepan and melt it over medium-low heat. Put in the veal and sprinkle it with several grindings of pepper. Lay the salt pork or ham and herb bundle over it and scatter the onion and carrot on top of them. Cover tightly and reduce the heat as low as possible. Cook slowly until juices have been fully extracted from the veal and vegetables, about 1 hour.

2. Strain the broth and return it to the pan. Bring it back to a simmer over medium-low heat and simmer until it is considerably reduced and almost syrupy, about 1 hour longer.

Sauce Hachée

Makes about 1¼ cups

HISTORICAL NOTES: *This recipe straddles the gap between what was known as sauce hachée in the eighteenth and in the nineteenth centuries. It's adapted both from the rather sketchy version within the Bouilli of Mrs. Trist's manuscript, and from the* Dictionnaire Portatif de Cuisine, *an eighteenth-century French cookbook known to have been in Jefferson's library, from which Mrs. Trist copied out other recipes, including one calling for this sauce. I've included the anchovy, gherkin, and capers from her rendition, as they came to characterize a sauce hachée in the nineteenth century; the* Dictionnaire, *presenting the older version, does not mention them. Classically, the puréeing was done with a tamis, or drum sieve, but a food mill fitted with its finest disk will accomplish much the same thing. A blender will not substitute as it does far too good a job.*

- 4 medium brown (crimini or baby bella) mushrooms
- 1 ounce (about a ¼-inch-thick, 2-inch-square slice) country ham
- 2 ounces (4 tablespoons) unsalted butter, softened
- 1 penny-size slice garlic
- 1 large sprig parsley
- 1 medium scallion or green onion, trimmed
- 3 whole cloves
- 1 cup broth from Bouilli (page 114), or beef broth (such as from Beef Soup, page 99)
- 2 teaspoons Browned Flour (page 111)
- 1 whole salt-cured anchovy, or 2 oil-packed anchovy fillets
- 1 tablespoon chopped French-style sour pickled gherkins (about 2 small)
- 1 tablespoon nonpareil capers

1. Wipe the mushrooms clean with a dry cloth and chop them. Put the ham in a small heavy-bottomed saucepan, cover, and place over low heat. Let it come slowly to a simmer and cook until the juices thrown off are thick and beginning to color.

2. Add 2 tablespoons of the butter, the mushrooms, garlic, parsley, scallion, and cloves. Cover and simmer slowly for 20 minutes or until the juices are fully extracted.

3. Remove and discard the ham, parsley, and cloves and skim off the excess fat. Purée through a wire sieve or a food mill fitted with the finest disk. Return it to the pan, add the broth, and bring it to a simmer over medium-low heat. Simmer for 15 minutes.

4. Knead the Browned Flour into the remaining butter. If using a whole anchovy, rinse well, split, and bone it; if using fillets, rinse well and brush away any bones. Chop fine.

5. Stir the anchovy, gherkins, and capers into the sauce. Return it to a simmer and stir in the butter and flour. Simmer, stirring constantly, until thickened, about 2 minutes. Remove it from the heat and pour it into a warm sauceboat.

Forcemeat Balls

Makes 1 pound, or about eighteen 1-inch balls

HISTORICAL NOTES: *Forcemeat balls, essentially sausages without casings, were popular garnishes until around the mid-nineteenth century and appear both as an entry in Mrs. Trist's manuscript and as an ingredient in other family recipes. For improved clarity and for numerous missing details, I turn to Mary Randolph, whose recipe in terms of flavoring is very similar. It almost certainly came from the same source, perhaps Monticello, to which Mrs. Trist attributes her recipe. The lemon peel is a nice touch, once common in sausage recipes. Originally cooks chopped forcemeat fine by hand and then beat it almost to a pulpy paste in a mortar. It's grueling work and even I am not interested in doing it for authenticity's sake. Unhappily, the food processor makes the forcemeat rather too mushy, so I've opted for ground meat and fat kneaded together by hand.*

8 ounces lean ground veal

8 ounces beef suet, finely chopped or ground

2 teaspoons chopped fresh marjoram, or 1 teaspoon dried and crumbled

2 teaspoons chopped fresh thyme, or ½ teaspoon dried and crumbled

2 teaspoons chopped fresh sage, or ½ teaspoon dried and crumbled

1 tablespoon chopped fresh parsley

½ teaspoon freshly ground mace or freshly grated nutmeg

grated zest of ½ lemon

salt

whole black pepper in a pepper mill

1 large egg yolk

lard or peanut oil, for frying

¼ cup all purpose flour, for dredging

1. Put the veal and suet in a mixing bowl and knead until evenly mixed. Knead in the herbs, mace or nutmeg, lemon zest, a large pinch of salt, several generous grindings of pepper, and the egg yolk.

2. Put enough lard or oil into a skillet to cover the bottom by ¼ inch and heat it over medium-high heat until it is hot but not quite smoking (about 375 degrees).

3. Put the flour in a shallow bowl or plate. With hands moistened in cold water, roll the meat into 1-inch-diameter balls. Roll the forcemeat balls in the flour, shake off the excess, and slip enough of them into the fat to fill the pan without crowding. Fry, turning frequently, until richly brown and cooked through, about 8 minutes.

• • •

Note: Forcemeat balls may be poached instead of fried, especially if they are to be used in white sauce. Omit the lard and flour and bring 1½ quarts water to a boil in a 3-quart saucepan over medium heat. Slip enough forcemeat balls into the pan to fill it in one layer, and simmer until they are just cooked through, about 8 to 10 minutes.

Veal Cutlets

Serves 4

HISTORICAL NOTES: *Mrs.
Trist attributes this recipe in her
manuscript to* The Virginia House-
wife, *and not specifically Monticello,
but it is very much of the period and
was almost certainly served on the
Jefferson table. That Mary Randolph
added the recipe in a later edition of
her book is suggestive. It seems odd
to modern palettes: though breaded
and fried, the cutlets are afterwards
stewed in aromatic broth until fork
tender. Cutlets crisp-fried in the
classic Milanese or Viennese tradition
appear much later—at least, in
America. Dishes of this sort turned up
on the breakfast table in those days;
breakfasts were much more substantial
meals than ours are. Forcemeat Balls
(page 117) are included as a garnish in
the original recipe; I include them as
optional here.*

1½ pounds veal round cutlets, cut across the grain into ½-inch-thick pieces

salt

whole black pepper in a pepper mill

2 ounces salt pork, sliced ¼ inch thick

1 clove garlic, lightly crushed and peeled

2 large sprigs each fresh parsley and thyme, tied in a bundle with kitchen twine

1 cup dry bread crumbs

¼ cup chopped fresh parsley

½ - 1 teaspoon freshly grated nutmeg

1 large egg, lightly beaten

lard or peanut oil, for frying

¼ cup Madeira or dry sherry

¼ cup Mushroom Catsup (page 131)

2 ounces (4 tablespoons) unsalted butter

1 tablespoon Browned Flour (page 111)

Forcemeat Balls, optional (page 117)

1. Put the veal in a saucepan that will hold it in one close-fitting layer. Sprinkle it lightly with salt and a few grindings of pepper. Lay the salt pork over it and add the garlic, herb bundle, and enough water to cover by 1 inch. Bring to a simmer over medium heat and simmer for 15 minutes. Lift the veal out of the pan and spread it on a plate to cool. Let the cooking liquid continue simmering until it is reduced to 2 cups. Strain and reserve it.

2. Toss together the bread crumbs and parsley and season with salt, pepper, and nutmeg to taste. Dip a basting or pastry brush into the beaten egg and brush it over one side of the veal. One at a time, put each piece of veal on the crumbs, egg side down, and press the crumbs into it. Place it crumbed side up on a plate and let stand for 15 minutes, then turn and brush the second side with egg and coat it with crumbs in the same manner. Let stand 15 minutes longer.

3. Put enough lard or oil in a wide skillet to cover the bottom by ¼ inch. Heat it over medium-high heat until it is hot but not quite smoking (about 375 degrees). Fit a wire rack over a rimmed baking sheet and set it near the skillet. Fry the cutlets, turning once, until golden on all sides, about 3 minutes per side. Lift the cutlets out of the pan, letting the excess fat drip back into the pan, and then put them on the wire rack to finish draining. With a wire skimmer or slotted spoon, lift out any crumbs that have fallen into the fat during the frying and drain them on absorbent paper. Add the Forcemeat Balls, if using, and fry until they are uniformly golden, about 8 minutes. Lift out and drain them on absorbent paper.

**Veal Cutlets
(continued)**

4. Pour off the fat from the skillet and wipe it out. Pour in the reduced cooking liquid, Madeira or sherry, and Mushroom Catsup. Bring it to a simmer over medium heat. Knead the butter and Browned Flour together and stir it into the sauce. Simmer, stirring frequently, until it is lightly thickened, then add the veal and reserved fried crumbs, and put in the Forcemeat Balls around the edges. Cover and let it return to a simmer. Reduce the heat to medium low and simmer until the veal is fork tender, about 30 minutes. Transfer the cutlets to a warm serving platter, lay the Forcemeat Balls around the edges, and pour the sauce over them.

Meat At Monticello

Probably the biggest challenge to modern cooks who would recapture the flavors of Monticello's table is animal food: red meat, game, poultry, pork, and fish. Beef, mutton and lamb, until well into the twentieth century, were entirely grass-fed. Grain is not a natural part of the diet of grazing animals, and does neither the animal nor its flesh any good, contrary to popular wisdom. In animals that have been allowed to forage and to mature in their natural course without commercial force-feeding, the flavor and texture are more complex. The meat is also more individual, and requires a little more care and attention than the relatively uniform cuts from cereal-fed animals. While grain-fed meat can certainly be used in these recipes, those who would come closer to the authentic flavors and textures of Monticello's table will do well to seek out local producers of grass-fed beef, veal, mutton, and lamb, as well as poultry and pork that have been allowed to forage (so-called "free-range").

For lamb and mutton, Jefferson singled out the Barbary broadtail (now Tunis) sheep for praise, shown here in a detail of an 1810 engraving.

Stuffed Cabbage

Serves 4 to 6

HISTORICAL NOTES: *This is one of the recipes copied out by Jefferson himself, originally entitled "A Cabbage Pudding." Cooked whole and wrapped in a cloth, it does resemble the boiled puddings of the day. I have added illuminating details from Mary Randolph's rendition, mixing some of the heart of the cabbage with the stuffing and serving it "whole with a little melted butter in the dish." Since Jefferson only listed "sweet herbs," I've chosen the herbs usually used with beef in the period. Originally, the beef was finely chopped by hand, not ground, but readers who are not as concerned for authenticity may substitute ground beef. At Monticello, they would most likely have used a tin-lined copper or iron pot—and may have cooked it on the stew stove. For home cooks today, a heavy-bottomed stewing pan or Dutch oven will answer. It's a lovely recipe, and not as complicated as it looks.*

1 large green cabbage (about 2 pounds)

8 ounces very lean beef sirloin, finely chopped

8 ounces beef suet, finely chopped

1 small white onion, peeled and minced

1 tablespoon chopped fresh parsley

1 tablespoon chopped fresh herbs, such as thyme, marjoram, or summer savory, or 2 teaspoons crumbled dried herbs

¼ cup dry bread crumbs

3 large egg yolks, lightly beaten

salt

whole black pepper in a pepper mill

2 tablespoons unsalted butter

1. Bring a large pot of water to a boil. Remove the outer green leaves of the cabbage, saving several if they are unblemished, and wash well under cold water. Slip the cabbage and any reserved outer leaves into the pot, return it to a boil, and cook until the outer leaves soften and can be pulled back easily, about 15 minutes.

2. Lift the cabbage out of the water and drain in a colander, leaving the water in the pot. Carefully pull back two or three rows of leaves, but leave them attached to the stem. Cut a large cross through the center, going all the way to the stem, but taking care not to puncture any of the outer leaves. Bend back the outer layers of the center and cut out the rest of it, leaving the outer leaves attached at the base.

3. Finely chop the center portion of the cabbage and toss in a large bowl with the beef, suet, and onion. Stir in the herbs, bread crumbs, and egg yolks and season liberally with salt and several grindings of pepper.

4. Spread a 14-inch-square piece of double-folded cheesecloth flat and place the cabbage in the center. Gently pull back the leaves and pack the stuffing into the center, being careful not to break the outer leaves. Fold the leaves back over the stuffing and wrap any reserved leaves around it so that the cabbage appears whole. Fold the cloth over the cabbage, wrap it with twine, and knot it securely.

5. Bring the cooking liquid back to a boil. Carefully lower the cabbage into it, return to a boil, and lower the heat to a gentle simmer. Simmer until the filling is fully cooked and the cabbage is tender, about 2 hours.

6. Lift the cabbage from the pot, draining well, and remove the cloth. Transfer it to a warm serving platter and rub it with butter. Serve whole, cutting it into individual wedges at the table.

WRONGLY ANTICIPATING *retirement from politics in 1792, Jefferson wrote his daughter Martha Jefferson Randolph, "The ensuing year will be the longest of my life and the last of such hateful labors; the next we will sow our cabbages to-gether." Although Jefferson would not retire from public service until 1809, cabbages were periodically planted before then in the Monticello gardens. The Garden Book documents the planting of twenty-nine varieties of the vegetable in the Monticello Kitchen Garden, but cabbage was also one of the vegetables most frequently purchased from Monticello's enslaved community for use at the family table.*

— *P.J.H.*

JEFFERSON APPEARS *to have cultivated tomatoes as early as 1781, when he wrote in his* Notes on the State of Virginia: *"The gardens yield musk melons, water melons, tomatas, okra, pomegranates, figs, and the esculent plants of Europe."[14] Note that Jefferson does not single out tomatoes as unusual objects in Virginia gardens, and in other parts of the country, the fruit was also available. Jefferson's records during his presidency (1801-1809) show that the vegetable markets in Washington offered tomatoes, and Philadelphia nurseryman Bernard McMahon provided cultivation instructions for the fruit in his* American Gardener's Kalendar *(1809). Even so, in parts of Virginia, tomatoes were suspect or uncommon, and Jefferson apparently created some consternation when he publicly ate a tomato in Lynchburg.[15]*

—MONTICELLO RESEARCH DEPARTMENT

Olla

Serves 4 to 6

HISTORICAL NOTES: *This meat-and-vegetable stew is Spanish in origin and derives its name from the terra cotta casserole in which it originally cooked. Several variations of the recipe appear in the manuscript previously misattributed to Martha Randolph, and* The Virginia House-wife *contains a more complete version. The vegetables vary in each of the four manuscript recipes, reinforcing Mary Randolph's assertion that the cook may use "any kind of vegetables you like." It's likely that all these recipes had the same source—Mary Randolph's sister, Harriet Randolph Hackley, who learned the dish while her husband was an ambassador. Mary Randolph calls for a rich mélange of meats—beef, mutton, and chicken in addition to pork—but I've followed the family manuscript, which, while it implies use of another meat, specifies only one in each of its variations. In short, the reader can practically run wild and still be within historical context.*

- 2 pounds lean pork shoulder or loin
- salt
- whole black pepper in a pepper mill
- 1 medium white onion, peeled and finely chopped
- ¼ pound salt pork or country ham, thickly sliced
- 1 pound tomatoes (about 3 medium), blanched, peeled, seeded, and chopped
- 2 large sprigs fresh mint, plus 1 tablespoon chopped, for garnish
- 2 large sprigs fresh parsley
- water
- 1 cup fresh or frozen lima beans (optional)
- 2 medium pattypan or winter squash, scrubbed, peeled if necessary, and diced (optional)
- 2 medium, firm apples, such as Winesap or Granny Smith
- 1 pound sweet potatoes (about 2 medium), peeled and thickly sliced
- 1 cup fresh young green beans, broken into 1-inch pieces
- ½ cup white rice

1. Rinse the pork under cold running water, pat dry, and rub it on all sides with salt and several grindings of pepper. Scatter some of the onion over the bottom of a heavy-bottomed Dutch oven or flameproof casserole dish, put in the pork, scatter the remaining onion over it, and lay the salt pork or ham over and around it.

2. Put in the tomatoes and sprinkle them lightly with salt and several liberal grindings of pepper. Add the mint and parsley sprigs and pour enough water into the pot to cover the meat halfway. Loosely cover and bring it slowly to a simmer over medium heat. Reduce the heat to low and simmer gently, turning the meat occasionally, for 2 to 2½ hours, or until it is fork-tender.

3. Add the lima beans and squash, if using, and simmer 15 minutes. Peel and quarter the apples and add them to the pot along with the sweet potatoes and green beans. Bring it back to a simmer and cook until all the vegetables are tender, about 20 minutes longer.

4. Remove the meat from the Dutch oven and let it rest for at least 15 minutes before carving. Meanwhile, stir in the rice and simmer until it is tender, about 14 minutes. Slice the meat and arrange it on a warm platter. Surround it with the rice and vegetables and sprinkle with chopped mint.

Roast Duck with Onion Sauce

Serves 4 to 6

HISTORICAL NOTES: *Mrs. Trist copied this recipe directly out of* The Virginia House-wife, *but it surely reflects the way duck would have been roasted at Monticello. Many enslaved families raised poultry for sale at Monticello, and the frequency of roasted fowl on Jefferson's table is better evidenced by these purchases than the few surviving family recipes. The sage and onion seasoning for the duck and separately cooked onion sauce are suave, subtle, and truly elegant. Readers with a rotisserie would do well to use it, keeping a pan of water below the bird to catch the dripping fat, which should be drawn off regularly. The original recipe called for lemon catsup, a condiment similar to the brine from lemons preserved in salt, which I suggest as an alternative. A little fresh lemon juice, while not as intensely flavored, can also be substituted. Readers after strict authenticity can make the catsup easily following the recipe in* The Virginia House-wife.

1   6- to 6½-pound duck
      salt
      whole black pepper in a pepper mill
1   medium onion, peeled and thinly sliced
5 - 6 large fresh sage leaves, thinly sliced
1   tablespoon lard or unsalted butter, melted
3   tablespoons all-purpose flour (approximately)
1   blade mace, or ½ teaspoon freshly grated nutmeg
1   teaspoon whole peppercorns
1   tablespoon Mushroom Catsup (page 131)
1   teaspoon juice of salt-preserved lemons, or 2 teaspoons fresh lemon juice
2   cups water
      Onion Sauce (opposite page)

1. Position a rack in the center of the oven and preheat the oven to 500 degrees. Remove and reserve the neck and giblets from the duck. Wash the duckling well under cold running water, drain, and pat dry. Rub it inside and out with salt and several grindings of pepper and fill the cavity with the onion and sage. Brush the outside well with melted lard or butter and dust it lightly with 1 to 1½ tablespoons of the flour. Put the duck on a rack in a roasting pan.

2. Put the neck and giblets in a saucepan with the mace or nutmeg, whole peppercorns, Mushroom Catsup, and preserved or fresh lemon juice. Add the water and bring it to a simmer over medium heat. Simmer, stirring occasionally, for at least 30 minutes (longer will improve it). If the liver is with the giblets, take it out after 10 minutes or it will make the broth bitter. Raise the heat to medium high, boil until it is reduced to ½ cup, and then strain and reserve.

3. Roast the duckling until the outside is seared and beginning to color, about 20 minutes. Reduce the heat to 400 degrees, turn it to one side, and roast 20 minutes longer. Turn to the other side, baste with pan juices, and draw off the excess fat from the roasting pan (best done with a bulb baster). Roast 20 minutes, reduce the heat to 375 degrees, and turn it breast side down. Again draw off the excess fat, baste well, and roast until done to taste, about 20 minutes more, drawing off the excess fat as it accumulates. (Using a meat thermometer inserted into the thickest part of the thigh, cook to 140 to 145 degrees for medium rare, or 165 degrees for medium well.) Turn the bird breast side up, baste one last time, dust lightly with the remaining 1 to 1½ tablespoons flour, and let roast 10 to 15 minutes longer.

4. Remove the duckling to a platter and let it rest 15 minutes. Reheat the broth, pour it over the duck, and serve with Onion Sauce passed separately.

• • •

Note: For rotisserie roasting, keep the temperature high, never less than 400 degrees. For those without a rotisserie, the turning is easy enough to manage with a good pair of tongs and a carving fork stuck into the cavity from the open end, but the duck can also be turned breast down after twenty minutes and roasted in that position until the last 15 minutes.

Onion Sauce

Makes about 1¾ cups

HISTORICAL NOTES: *This handsome recipe follows the roast duck recipe in* The Virginia House-wife. *It's a "sauce" on the order of applesauce— thick and substantial, yet subtle and delicious.*

1 pound white onions, peeled and left whole
2 ounces (4 tablespoons) unsalted butter, softened
¼ cup heavy cream
   salt

1. Put the onions in a large pot and cover them by at least 1 inch with cold water. Bring to a boil over medium-high heat, reduce the heat to medium low, and simmer until they are about half done (slightly tender). Drain, cover with fresh cold water, and simmer again until the onions are very tender. Drain them well, let cool enough to handle, and finely chop.

2. Heat the onions and butter in a large saucepan over medium-low heat, stirring until the butter is melted. Add the cream, season with salt to taste, and bring to a simmer, cooking about 3 to 4 minutes. Serve in a warm serving bowl.

Tree, or Egyptian, onions were planted in the Monticello gardens on April 11, 1809. This unique type of onion produces edible (and plantable) bulbs above, as well as below, the ground.

Chicken Fricassee

Serves 4

HISTORICAL NOTES: *Mrs. Trist attributes this recipe, originally entitled "A White Fricassee," to her mother, Martha Randolph, so it is unfortunate that it is a little problematic. Aside from directing an extravagant waste of the cooking broth, it sacrifices flavor left and right for the sake of pristine whiteness, and the sauce is really no whiter than it would be if accomplished well. I've therefore looked both to Mary Randolph's rendition of it in* The Virginia House-wife *(1828 edition) and to a later family recipe for chicken fricassee. Both are superior in all respects to the Trist manuscript's version and probably are more reflective of what the cooks actually did at Monticello. The back, neck, and giblets may be reserved to make broth.*

1 small chicken (no more than 3 pounds)
   salt
2 cups whole milk
8 ounces small white mushrooms
1 cup heavy cream
½ teaspoon ground mace (preferably freshly ground)
½ - 1 teaspoon freshly grated nutmeg
2 ounces (4 tablespoons) unsalted butter
2 tablespoons all-purpose flour
¼ cup dry white wine

1. Disjoint the chicken as for frying, chopping the breast in half and then into halves again. Set aside the back, neck, and giblets for broth. Put the chicken into a deep skillet or sauté pan that will hold it all in one close-fitting layer and pour boiling water over it until completely covered. Cover and soak 15 minutes. Strain and reserve the liquid and rinse the chicken under cold running water.

2. Wipe out the pan and return the chicken to it. Sprinkle lightly with salt and pour the milk and enough of the reserved liquid over it to cover it completely, discarding the rest of the soaking liquid. Bring to a simmer over medium-low heat, cover the pan, and reduce the heat to a bare simmer. Cook until the chicken is tender, about 30 minutes.

3. While the chicken is cooking, wipe the mushrooms clean with a dry cloth. If the mushrooms are small, leave them whole; if large, thickly slice them.

4. Remove the chicken from the pan, cover, and keep warm. Strain the broth, wipe out the pan, and return 2 cups of the cooking broth to it. Stir in the cream, mace, and nutmeg, season with salt to taste, and bring it back to a simmer over medium heat. Meanwhile, knead together the butter and flour. Stir it by bits into the liquid and simmer until lightly thickened.

5. Add the mushrooms and chicken and bring back to a simmer. Stir in the wine and cook until the mushrooms are just cooked through and the chicken is hot again, about 8 minutes. Remove the chicken to a warm deep-rimmed serving platter, pour the sauce and mushrooms over it, and serve hot.

Baked Virginia Ham

Serves about 25 to 30

HISTORICAL NOTES: *In her recipe attributed to Monticello, Mrs. Trist describes the way that the celebrated Virginia hams have been cooked since the very beginning, concluding with a cautionary note: "it is best not to boil it until the meat begins to string." As Mrs. Hess notes in her commentary, Mrs. Trist is trying to say that the ham must not actually boil, but cook at a gentle, poaching simmer. Modern recipes generally call for long soak periods, and readers who are not accustomed to the intensity of aged dry-cured hams might want to soak the ham for at least 24 hours and change the soaking water twice during that period. However, such treatment will not produce a ham as intensely flavorful as would have been enjoyed at Monticello. Carve these hams in small, wafer-thin slices—as some old recipes put it, so thin that one could almost read a newspaper through it.*

1 country-style (dry-cured) Virginia ham (11 to 13 pounds)
1 cup dry bread crumbs

1. Scrub the ham with a stiff brush under cold running water to remove as much mold as possible. Put the ham in a large tub or basin, cover completely with cold water, and soak for 8 to 24 hours, changing the water once. Drain and scrub the ham a second time to remove any remaining mold.

2. Put the ham in a large deep pot that will hold it flat. Add enough cold water to completely cover the ham by 1 inch and bring to a simmer over medium-low heat, skimming any scum as it rises to the surface.

    Reduce the heat to a barely perceptible simmer (no bubbles should actually break the surface) and simmer for 4 hours. Turn off the heat and cool the ham in the cooking liquid.

4. Position a rack in the center of the oven and preheat the oven to 375 degrees. Remove the ham from the cooking liquid, drain, and pat dry. Using a sharp knife, remove the skin (rind) and some of the fat, leaving a thick layer of fat on the surface. Score the fat in a crisscross pattern and put the ham in a roasting pan, fat side up. Sprinkle all sides evenly with bread crumbs, pressing lightly into the fat.

5. Bake the ham, uncovered, until the crumbs are toasted and brown, about 45 minutes to 1 hour. Remove the ham from the pan and let it rest for 15 minutes.

    To carve the ham, slice a deep vertical cut just above the shank joint and begin slicing toward the cut at an oblique angle into wafer thin slices.

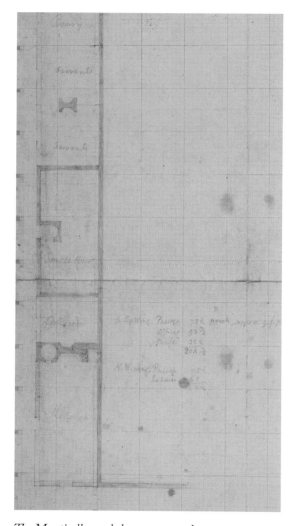

The Monticello smokehouse processed an enormous amount of meat. Unlike most freestanding smokehouses of the day, Monticello's was incorporated into the service wing of the house (above). It also featured an unusual vestibule that allowed workers to tend the fire in an exterior fireplace, which vented into the smokehouse proper and allowed the meat to be secured at all times.

Creamed Cod

Serves 4

HISTORICAL NOTES: *In her commentary on Mrs. Trist's manuscript, Karen Hess suggests that this recipe, attributed to Monticello, may have come from Ellen Randolph Coolidge. Coolidge lived in Boston and, against her better judgment, supplied her grandfather with the ingredients and instructions for cooking cod's tongues and sounds (see opposite page). As Mrs. Hess aptly notes, the fish should never be allowed to actually boil: the poaching liquid must shimmer in much the same way as for ham. The scribe is on the mark to prefer real cream to a cream sauce made with flour-thickened milk. This would probably have been served over toast, buttered and cut on the diagonal, which was usual. The bread should be something hearty like the recipe supplied on page 94, and it would be more authentic if browned under an oven broiler instead of in a modern toaster.*

1 pound dried salt cod (*baccalà*)
2 cups heavy cream
2 tablespoons unsalted butter
  salt
  whole white pepper in a pepper mill
½ - 1 teaspoon freshly grated nutmeg
1 hard-cooked egg, white and yolk separated
8 buttered toast points

1. Rinse the cod well under cold running water and put it in a wide stainless steel or glass bowl. Pour boiling water over the fish until it is completely covered by at least 2 inches. Let it soak until the water is barely warm, about an hour, drain, and again cover with boiling water. Let it soak until lukewarm. Taste the cod and if it is still too salty, drain, cover with boiling water, and soak a third time.

2. Drain the fish well and put it in a large pot. Cover with water by at least 1 inch and bring it to a simmer over medium-low heat. Loosely cover, reduce the heat to a bare simmer, and gently poach until tender, about 45 minutes. Drain thoroughly and flake the cod.

3. Bring the cream and butter to a simmer in a wide shallow pan over medium heat. Cook, stirring occasionally, until slightly reduced and thickened. Add the fish and bring it back to a simmer. Taste and add salt, if needed, a grinding of white pepper, and nutmeg to taste. Reduce the heat to medium low and simmer gently for 10 minutes. Chop and add the egg white and simmer until heated through.

4. Pour the fish into a warm serving dish, force the yolk through a wire strainer and sprinkle it over the top. Serve with toast points.

A KEG OF 'TONGUES AND SOUNDS'

ANOTHER USE OF COD that Jefferson especially enjoyed was a dish made from its tongues and sounds (air bladder). A keg of "tongues and sounds" was frequently on his orders sent to Richmond, and he took advantage of friends and family living in the Boston area to supply this "great delicacy." The tongues and sounds he received from friend and political colleague, Jacob Crowinshield, came with the advice to, "... let the sounds & tongues remain in water at least a day before eating to take off the fatt [sic]. But those not intended for immediate use should be kept in the pickle." Jefferson suggested his granddaughter in Boston, Ellen Randolph Coolidge, send a recipe along with twenty to thirty pounds of tongues and sounds. Ellen responded that tongues and sounds "are scarcely ever brought upon table in Boston" but "... the principal care is to freshen them as much as possible by washing and soaking and they are oftenest boiled plain and served with a sauce." Jefferson took no notice that Bostonians lacked enthusiasm for this dish and pronounced the tongues and sounds "highly approved" at Monticello.[16]

Jefferson annually ordered twelve barrels of herring and one barrel of shad from a supplier in Richmond. Much if not all of the herring would have been distributed to hired and enslaved workmen, but no doubt he intended the shad for his own use. He pronounced shad superior to carp and tried to obtain it fresh locally when in season, as in the spring of 1812 when he sent a young Monticello slave, James, to a neighbor's with the request that, "if ... he can be admitted to join in hauling the seyne & come in for a share of shad so as to bring us some, I will thank you...." Years earlier while serving as vice president and living in Philadelphia, he would make note of when the first shad appeared in the city's market.[17] Jefferson makes no reference to the shad's roe, which is so prized today. In fact, an aide at the British legation noted that few American congressmen appreciated the fish roe he attempted to serve them but rather, "spit it out unceremoniously as a thing excessively nasty."[18] Perhaps the American palate had not yet become accustomed to caviar; however, a recipe for shad survives in Jefferson's granddaughter Virginia Trist's manuscript book (see page 130).

— G.B.W.

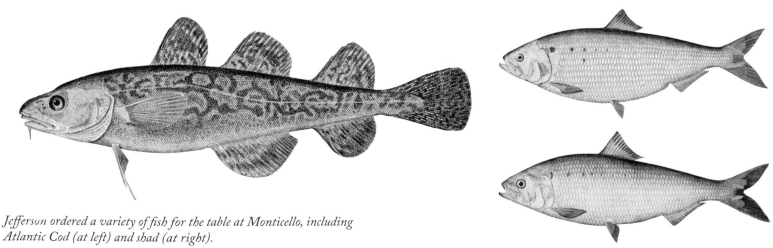

Jefferson ordered a variety of fish for the table at Monticello, including Atlantic Cod (at left) and shad (at right).

Broiled Shad

Serves 2 as a main dish, or 4 as a fish course

HISTORICAL NOTES: *This is Mary Randolph's simple and handsome recipe, copied out word for word by Mrs. Trist in her manuscript. As with the mutton chops (page 109), broiling here was the equivalent of modern grilling, best done today with a hinged grilling basket. Although Mrs. Randolph doesn't say whether to fully bone the fish, I have taken the liberty of doing so for even cooking and presentation. Because shad is extremely bony, in today's markets it is mostly sold already filleted. If you buy fillets and don't have a grilling basket, use the alternate instructions for oven broiling, as the fillets are difficult to manage without the structure of skin and bone. Readers after strict authenticity should use whole fish and butterfly it themselves or have it butterflied by the fishmonger. The fish should not be skinned.*

1 whole shad (1½ to 2 pounds), gutted, head removed, and cleaned
2 tablespoons unsalted butter, softened
  salt
  whole black pepper in a pepper mill
  Butter Sauce (page 141)

1. Butterfly the fish (or have the fishmonger do so) as follows: split it down the belly side with a boning knife. Carefully separate one side from the backbone, lay it flat, and remove the backbone entirely, leaving the two sides attached at the back fin. Do not skin it. Rub all sides lightly with butter and lay it skin side down on a baking sheet. Sprinkle lightly with salt and a few grindings of pepper and let it stand for 15 to 30 minutes.

2. Prepare a grill with enough hardwood coals to cover the bottom. Ignite and let them burn until they are glowing red, beginning to ash over, and a hand can be held 2 inches above the coals for only 3 or 4 seconds (a medium-hot fire).

3. Rub the grill's rack or a grilling basket, if using, with butter. Position the grill rack 4 to 6 inches above the coals. If using a grilling basket, put the fish into it and clamp it shut. Place the fish skin side down on the grill and broil until the top is opaque, about 4 minutes, carefully turn, and broil until cooked through and lightly browned, about 3 minutes longer. Transfer it to a serving platter, lightly drizzle with Butter Sauce, and serve with the remaining sauce passed separately.

• • •

Note: The fish can also be broiled under the oven broiler. While in no way authentic, the advantage in oven broiling is that the fish doesn't need turning, a particular advantage with fillets. Preheat the broiler for at least 20 minutes. Rub a rimmed baking sheet with butter, lay the fish on it skin side down, and broil until cooked through.

Mushroom Catsup

Makes about 2½ to 3 cups

HISTORICAL NOTES: *Historically, catsups were not at first made with tomatoes, and many old recipes call for a variety of flavored catsups. Recipes in the Jefferson family collection use mushroom catsup, but since no directions are given, I've turned to* The Virginia House-wife. *I've cut Mary Randolph's quantities in half and have added dried mushrooms to compensate for the use of bland cultivated mushrooms. Thin homespun cotton was probably used for straining the juice from the mushrooms; a double-folded cheesecloth probably comes closest to approximating it. Use a tight-weave muslin, however, for filtering the dried mushroom's soaking water so that it will trap the sand that is usually clinging to them. Refrigerate the catsup unless it is sealed by processing in a water-bath. For the time-pressed, specialty condiment companies sometimes offer mushroom catsup, and I've included a quicker substitute (see Note).*

1 ounce dried porcini or cèpes mushrooms

1 cup boiling water

2 pounds crimini or baby bella mushrooms

1 tablespoon salt, plus more as needed

4 large cloves garlic, peeled and smashed (left whole)

2 teaspoons ground cloves

1. Put the dried mushrooms in a small bowl, pour the boiling water over them, and soak for 15 to 30 minutes, until softened. Gently wipe the fresh mushrooms with a dry cloth to remove any dirt and grit. Working in batches, lightly sprinkle about one-third of the mushrooms at a time with salt and crush them with a mortar and pestle or shred them in a food processor fitted with a steel blade.

2. Lift the dried mushrooms from the soaking water, dipping them several times to remove any sand or grit that may be clinging to them, and put them in a large saucepan. Strain the soaking liquid through clean muslin or a coffee filter into the pan. Add the crushed or shredded mushrooms, cover loosely, and bring to a simmer over medium heat. Cook until they are completely softened and have released most of their juices, about 20 minutes.

3. Line a large strainer with a double layer of cheesecloth and set it over a large bowl. Pour the mushrooms into the strainer, pressing with a spoon or spatula until most of their juice is extracted. Gather the cloth into a bundle and squeeze out as much juice as possible. They should yield about 5 cups of liquid. Wipe out the saucepan and return the juice to it. Add the garlic and cloves and simmer until reduced by almost half. Taste and adjust the salt as needed. Strain the catsup into bottles or jars, sealing them with clean lids, or, for an authentic touch, seal the bottles with corks and refrigerate. It will keep indefinitely.

• • •

Note: For a quick substitute for mushroom catsup, bring 2 cups of water to a boil. Put 1 ounce of dried mushrooms in a stainless steel pan and pour the water over them. Add a lightly crushed clove of garlic, ½ teaspoon of salt, and 3 or 4 whole cloves. Bring to a simmer over medium heat and simmer until reduced by half. Taste and adjust the salt, then strain it through a fine mesh strainer lined with muslin or a coffee filter. Store it in a clean half-pint jar.

On *April 16, 1810,
Thomas Jefferson wrote
from Monticello to his
namesake grandson, "We
are out of sallad-oil, and
you know it is a necessary
of life here. Can any be
had in Richmond?"*[19]
*Jefferson described the oil
procured by his grandson
as "very good," yet he
typically imported olive
oil from France. The salad
shown here is made from
a late autumn harvest of
the Monticello gardens,
including nasturtium,
spinach, French sorrel,
and three types of
lettuce—Tennis-ball,
Brown Dutch, and spotted
Alleppo.*

To Dress Salad

Serves 6

HISTORICAL NOTES: *Although salads are well documented at Monticello, the only two recipes for dressings in the family manuscripts appear to postdate Jefferson's death by some thirty years. Given that Jefferson favored imported olive oil and wine vinegar, the classic French vinaigrette seems a likely staple at Monticello's table, prepared tableside with oil and vinegar brought to the table in handsome cruet sets. (One such set so captured Jefferson's attention in Germany that he sketched the clever design in his notes, and a set associated with the Trist family is part of the Monticello collection today.) The basic formula has not significantly changed. The proportions are of necessity approximate: they depend on the strength of the vinegar, the quality of the oil, and the delicacy of the salad greens, but the reader can confidently start with 1 part vinegar to 3 parts oil, adding more oil as needed to taste.*

- 2 tablespoons wine vinegar or tarragon wine vinegar
- salt
- whole black pepper in a pepper mill
- 6 - 8 tablespoons extra virgin olive oil
- 6 cups mixed salad greens, such as seasonal lettuce, spinach, endive, radicchio, and cress (see page 56)
- fresh herbs, such as sweet basil, marjoram, mint, and summer savory, to taste
- 6 small scallions, trimmed

1. Put the vinegar, a small pinch of salt, and several generous grindings of pepper in a salad bowl and beat with a fork until the salt is dissolved.

2. Gradually beat in about 6 tablespoons of olive oil, a little at a time, in a steady thin stream, beating constantly until emulsified. Taste and adjust the salt, pepper, and oil as needed.

3. Add the greens and herbs to the dressing and toss lightly to coat. Taste and adjust the seasonings again, toss, and arrange the scallions around the edges of the bowl.

Braised Artichokes with Fine Herbs

Serves 4

HISTORICAL NOTES: *In Jefferson's menu notes from the President's House we find mention of this handsome dish,* artichaux étouffés aux fines herbes et beurre, *braised artichokes with herbs and butter (*étouffé *literally meaning "smothered").[20] It is a French classic that survives in the cooking of French Creole New Orleans. I include as a variation at the end another French classic,* artichaux à la lyonnaise, *in Jefferson's menu notes as* artichaux, sauce roux aux oignons *(braised artichokes with brown onion sauce). Both were certainly served at the President's House, and Edith Fossett or Fanny Hern could well have brought knowledge of the recipe back to the kitchen at Monticello to prepare the artichokes grown in the vegetable garden.*

1   lemon, halved
4   medium artichokes
     salt
6   tablespoons unsalted butter
½   cup veal or chicken broth or water
¼   cup finely chopped fresh sweet herbs, such as parsley and chervil

1. Fill a large basin halfway with cold water and squeeze the juice of half the lemon into it. Peel and trim the artichoke stem with a sharp paring knife, rub well with the remaining lemon half, and pull off the large, tough outer leaves. After 2 layers, place a thumb at the base of each leaf and pull down: it will snap at the fleshy, edible part, pulling away most of the tough fiber. Rub periodically with lemon. When the pale, inner surfaces of the center cone of leaves is exposed about two-thirds of the way up, cut off the dark green top and rub the cut with lemon. Trim away any tough dark green fibers that remain around the base with a sharp paring knife, again rubbing with lemon. Cut it into quarters and cut out the choke. Drop the trimmed and quartered artichokes into the acidulated water.

2. Put 2 quarts of water into a 4-quart pot, bring it to a rolling boil over high heat, and add a small handful of salt. Drain and add the artichokes to the pot, and cover the pot until it begins boiling again. Uncover and cook until half done and still bright green, about 6 to 8 minutes. Drain and refresh them under cold running water.

3. Melt the butter over medium-high heat in a skillet or sauté pan that will hold the artichokes in one layer. Add them and toss until hot. Reduce the heat to medium and add the broth or water. Cover and braise, gently shaking the pan occasionally, until tender, about 20 minutes. Uncover, continue cooking until the excess liquid has evaporated, and toss with the herbs. Serve warm.

• • •

Artichokes in Brown Onion Sauce: Omit the herbs and broth or water and reduce the butter to 2 tablespoons. Have ready one recipe of Brown Onion Sauce (page 142). Prepare the artichokes through step 3, substituting the sauce for the broth or water, and braise until they are tender (omit the evaporating at the end of the step). Garnish with 1 tablespoon of chopped parsley.

Fried Asparagus

Serves 4

HISTORICAL NOTES: *Jefferson's papers mention frying asparagus in such a way as to suggest it was commonplace at Monticello.[21] No instructions survive in the family manuscripts, so we must turn to period recipes. In most, only the tips are fried, leaving the stems for another use. Since that's an extravagance which few modern cooks will want to indulge, I include the entire spear here. Peeling the tough parts of the stem renders the entire stalk delicate and edible and makes it fry evenly. The blanching step, common to the period, makes it possible to fry quickly so that the vegetable spends very little time in the pan and absorbs less fat. I've adapted the batter from a formula jotted down by Jefferson in his menu notes for the President's House. Though included in a dessert list, and apparently meant for dessert fritters, the batter would have differed little from one for vegetable fritters.*

1 **pound asparagus**
  salt
5 **ounces (about 1 cup) unbleached all-purpose flour**
1 **small egg**
1 **cup cold water**
2 **ounces (4 tablespoons) unsalted butter, melted**
  lard or peanut oil, for frying

1. Rinse and trim the asparagus. Peel the tough part of the stem with a vegetable peeler and cut the asparagus into 1½-inch-long pieces. Half fill a 2-quart pan with water and bring it to a boil over high heat. Add a small handful of salt and, when the water returns to a boil, slip in the asparagus. Cook until bright green and crisp-tender, about 4 minutes. Drain and refresh it under cold running water.

2. Whisk or sift together the flour and 1 teaspoon of salt in a medium mixing bowl and make a well in the center. In a separate bowl, whisk together the egg, water, and butter until smooth and then pour it into the center of the flour. Gradually whisk the flour into the liquid, beating until smooth. Set aside for at least 15 minutes.

3. Preheat the oven to 150 to 170 degrees (the warm setting). Put enough lard in a deep skillet or heavy-bottomed pot to cover the bottom by 1 inch but to come no more than halfway up the sides. Heat it over medium-high heat until hot but not quite smoking (375 degrees). Fit a wire rack over a rimmed baking sheet and set it near the skillet.

4. Drop the asparagus into the batter a few pieces at a time, stirring to coat, and lift them out with tongs or a fork, allowing the excess batter to flow back into the bowl. Slip them into the hot fat and repeat until the pan is full but not crowded. Fry, stirring occasionally, until uniformly golden, about 3 to 4 minutes. Lift the asparagus out of the fat with a wire skimmer, allowing the excess fat to flow back into the pan, and put them on the wire rack. Keep them in the warm oven while frying the remaining asparagus. Salt generously and serve piping hot.

Asparagus with Herb Vinaigrette

Serves 4

HISTORICAL NOTES: *In a letter to his son-in-law, Jefferson alludes to asparagus dressed "in the French way."[22] This is the standard, classic recipe for asparagus with vinaigrette that goes back at least two centuries and survives almost intact to this day, though, beginning in the late nineteenth century, modern recipes were often slightly sweetened. The first part is Mary Randolph's basic recipe for cooked asparagus and the vinaigrette is much the same as the one given elsewhere for salad (page 133). Since some period recipes suggest that it be made with lemon juice for asparagus, I give it here as an option. As for the herbs, tarragon, thyme, marjoram, and basil are all fine with asparagus and appeared in the Monticello gardens.*

1½   pounds asparagus

    salt

2   tablespoons wine, tarragon, or other herbed wine vinegar, or lemon juice

    whole black pepper in a pepper mill

6 - 8   tablespoons extra virgin olive oil

2   tablespoons chopped fresh herbs, such as parsley and tarragon

1. Rinse the asparagus well under cold running water. Peel the tough parts of the stems and tie them into two equal bundles with kitchen twine or 1-inch-wide strips of cotton fabric. Bring 3 quarts of water to a rolling boil, add a small handful of salt, and when it begins boiling again, slip the asparagus into the pot. Cook until it is just tender and still bright green, about 15 minutes (when tied together it will take a little longer).

2. Meanwhile, prepare a basin of ice water. When the asparagus is done, drain thoroughly and plunge it into the ice water. When it is completely cooled, drain, pat dry, and arrange on a serving platter.

3. Put the vinegar or lemon juice in a bowl with a small pinch of salt and several liberal grindings of pepper. Beat with a fork or whisk until the salt dissolves.

4. Gradually beat in the oil a little at a time in a steady thin stream, beating constantly until it is emulsified. Start with 6 tablespoons, then taste and add salt, pepper, and oil, as needed. Beat in 1 tablespoon of the herbs. (The vinaigrette may be made ahead. If it separates, beat it again until emulsified and smooth.)

5. About 15 minutes before serving, pour the vinaigrette over the asparagus, and let it marinate. Just before serving, sprinkle with the remaining herbs.

JEFFERSON AND 'SALLAD' OILS

WHILE IN EUROPE, JEFFERSON fully investigated olive oil and pronounced the oil of Aix in southern France to be the finest in the world. In the 1770s he attempted cultivation of the olive tree at Monticello after obtaining seeds and cuttings from an Italian neighbor but realized that it would not flourish in Virginia's climate. However, believing that it would be an excellent crop for South Carolina and Georgia, he shipped from France as many as five hundred trees to the Agricultural Society in Charleston. He later expressed disappointment that the project was not given "the enthusiasm necessary to give it success."[23] Jefferson annually imported olive oil for use at Monticello and saw "sallad-oil" as "necesary of life," noting "what a number of vegetables are rendered eatable by the aid of a little oil."[24]

There was only one other oil he felt comparable, that of the sesame plant (or what he termed "benni," "beni," or "beny"). After receiving a sample bottle of sesame oil, he wrote, "I did not believe that there existed so perfect a substitute for olive oil." He conducted a test to gather other opinions: "I tried it at table with many companies & their guesses between two dishes of salad dressing, the one with olive oil, the other with that of Beni, shewed the quality of the latter in favor." He saw it as a possible substitute for lard and butter and suggested the seed could be eaten "parched for a dessert, or used in substance in soups, puddings, etc."[25]

He enthusiastically sent seeds and instructions to Monticello and engaged neighbors in the experiment as well. But after three years he had to admit, "Our cultivation of Benni has not yet had entire success." Early frost, difficulty in separating the seed from the pod, as well as difficulty in extracting the oil made for disappointing results. From one bushel of seed he was able to obtain only one gallon of oil, not the three gallons anticipated. While gardeners continued to sow "Benni" at Monticello, Jefferson never dropped olive oil from his grocery orders.[26]

— G.B.W.

ABOVE: *Jefferson recorded harvesting asparagus twenty-two times at Monticello and described eating it "dressed in the French way"— presumably in a vinaigrette.*

LEFT: *Sesame growing at Monticello. Jefferson acclaimed the species "among the most valuable acquisitions our country has ever made," and credited its American introduction to African-American slaves.*

French Beans

1 pound very thin young green beans (preferably haricot verts)
salt
Butter Sauce (page 141)

HISTORICAL NOTES: *Although Jefferson recorded a variety of beans grown in the gardens at Monticello, including "long haricots," no family recipe for the classic green bean survives. Fortunately, for vegetables cooked in the French style that Jefferson preferred, we need look no further than this gorgeous and careful recipe from* The Virginia House-wife. *True haricots verts are the ideal beans to use, but any immature green bean will do. Mary Randolph's is the classic French method, ideally illustrated by her stern objection to splitting the beans lengthwise, as was common in many period English versions. She doesn't specify, but most vegetables simply boiled in salted water were tossed in butter or served with Butter Sauce. Another delicious French way of serving them is in vinaigrette (page 136), or better—as Jefferson mentioned—simply tossed with salt, pepper, and a little olive oil.*

1. Fill a large bowl with cold water. Snap off the stem ends of the beans, pulling off the strings (if there are any). Then snap off the pointed tips, making make sure that all the strings have been removed. Drop each bean as it is trimmed into the cold water. If not perfectly fresh, let them soak for 15 to 30 minutes.

2. Bring 2 quarts of water to a boil in a 3-quart pot over high heat. Add a small handful of salt. Drain the beans and slip them into the boiling water. Let it come back to a boil and cook until they are just tender but still firm and bright green, about 8 to 10 minutes, depending on size and freshness.

3. Drain quickly but thoroughly and pour them into a warm serving bowl, or arrange in even rows on a small platter. Pour a little Butter Sauce over them and serve hot with the remaining sauce passed separately.

• • •

Alternative Serving Suggestions: The Butter Sauce can be omitted and still be historically accurate. Instead, toss the beans while hot with 2 tablespoons of butter or olive oil, or chill them by plunging them straight from the pot into ice water and serve with Herb Vinaigrette (page 136).

White Beans with Brown Onion Sauce

Serves 6

HISTORICAL NOTES: *Jefferson titled this recipe simply "dried beans." Despite that rather plebian name, it is actually a delicate and lovely recipe, and the same or a similar preparation appears as "White Beans, Brown Onion Sauce" on Jefferson's notes of dishes served at the President's House. Jefferson calls for boiling the beans "till done but not mashed," and I've turned to Mary Randolph for elaboration on that process. Period cookbooks do not mention presoaking dried beans to re-hydrate them before cooking, and modern chemistry says that there is no real reason to do this. Parboiling and changing the water would only take away flavor, which in this dish should come to the fore, so I have not used it. The critical thing for beans that are not presoaked is to bring them to a boil slowly; otherwise they swell too quickly and the skins begin to split.*

1 pound (about 2½ cups) dried white beans, such as great Northern
2 tablespoons unsalted butter
½ medium white onion, peeled and minced
1 rounded teaspoon Browned Flour (page 111)
2 cups beef broth, or cooking liquid from the beans (or slightly more)
salt
whole black pepper in a pepper mill

1. Sort through the beans to remove small stones or any that are blemished. Wash them well, drain, and place in a medium pot with enough water to cover by 2 inches. Bring the beans slowly to a boil over medium heat, skimming any scum as it rises. Reduce the heat and simmer until the beans are tender, about 1½ to 2 hours. Continue to add hot water as needed to keep the beans completely covered.

2. To make the sauce, melt the butter in a large pot over medium-high heat. Add the onion and sauté, stirring frequently, until deep gold in color. Stir in the flour and cook until bubbly and smooth, about 30 seconds more. Gradually stir in 1 cup of broth (or bean cooking liquid), and cook, stirring constantly, until the sauce is thickened and smooth, about 4 minutes.

3. Drain the beans, reserving the cooking liquid, and stir them into the sauce. Add enough additional broth (or cooking liquid) to just cover the beans, and bring it back to a simmer. Season generously with salt and several grindings of pepper, simmer for about 5 minutes, and serve hot.

Cabbage with Butter Sauce

Serves 4

> 1 small green cabbage (1 to 1½ pounds)
> salt
> Butter Sauce (opposite page)

Butter Sauce (opposite page)

HISTORICAL NOTES: *In his menu notes from the President's House, Jefferson listed both cabbage and carrots served with butter sauce; for these, we turn to Mary Randolph. Her treatment matches period French cooking and also reflects standard American practice for her time. For the cabbage, I note that other period recipes suggest serving the vegetable in wedges standing point-up. This required careful attention in the kitchen: overcooked cabbage wedges will not hold their shape standing vertically. As for the carrots, Mary Randolph prescribes cooking them whole and unpeeled, and then rubbing them with a cloth to remove the outer skin. To preserve the flavor and texture intended by her method, but without the ordeal of skinning hot carrots with a towel, I offer a cooking method that is much easier to control. Since the cooking juices are minimal and included in the sauce, the end result is much the same.*

1. Pull off the tough outer leaves of the cabbage and discard them. Trim the stem end just enough so it sits flat and rinse it well under cool running water. If the cabbage is smaller than 6 inches across, leave it whole. If larger, cut it into quarters.

2. Bring 2 quarts of water to a boil in a 3½- to 4-quart pot. Add a small handful of salt, let it come back to a boil, and slip in the cabbage. Skim off any scum that rises as it returns to a boil. Boil briskly until tender, but still holding together, about 20 minutes for a whole cabbage, 10 to 15 minutes if quartered.

3. Drain thoroughly and transfer to a warm serving bowl, stem side down if whole, or with the wedges arranged points up like flower petals. Pour a little Butter Sauce over the cabbage and serve hot, passing the remaining sauce separately.

Carrots in Butter Sauce

Serves 4

> 16 very small baby carrots or 6 medium carrots
> salt
> Butter Sauce (opposite page, not made ahead; see step 3 below for preparation)

1. Scrub the carrots well under cold running water and drain. Trim and lightly peel them. Leave the small carrots whole. If using large carrots, cut them into quarters and then 2-inch-long pieces. Put them in a sauté pan or saucepan that will hold them in one layer and almost cover with water. Sprinkle very lightly with salt.

2. Cover the pan and bring it to a boil over medium-high heat. Reduce the heat to medium-low and cook, gently shaking the pan occasionally, until the carrots are tender, about 10 minutes. Lift them out of the pan with a slotted spoon and transfer them to a warm serving bowl. Cover and keep warm.

3. Boil the cooking liquid until it is reduced to 2 tablespoons and make the Butter Sauce in the pan, using the reduced liquid in place of the water called for. Pour the sauce over the carrots, toss gently until coated, and serve immediately.

Butter Sauce

Makes ½ cup

2 tablespoons water
    large pinch salt
4 ounces (1 stick) unsalted butter, chilled and cut into bits

1. Put the water in a small heavy-bottomed saucepan, add the salt, and bring it to a simmer over very low heat. When it begins bubbling, toss in a couple bits of butter and whisk until barely melted. Continue whisking in a few bits at a time until all are incorporated and the butter is the consistency of thick cream. If it begins to overheat and separate, immediately take it from the heat and whisk in a few bits of butter to cool it slightly.

2. As soon as all the butter is incorporated, remove the sauce from the heat and pour it into a warm sauceboat.

• • •

Flavoring Butter Sauce: Substitute a tablespoon of Mushroom Catsup (page 131) or Worcestershire Sauce (a near-substitute for Mrs. Randolph's Fish Sauce) for part of the water, or lemon juice for all of it. Omit salt when using either sauce. Mrs. Randolph swirled catsup into the sauce when finished, but for the buerre blanc technique, add it first. For a classic French wine flavoring, simmer a minced shallot in ¼ cup of wine until reduced by half, then strain it and use the wine in place of water. To flavor it with herbs, allow a large fistful of whole parsley, tarragon, or chervil. Blanch them in simmering water to cover, drain, squeeze dry, and mince fine. It should yield about ¼ cup. Whisk them into the butter at the end.

Cauliflower in Brown Onion Sauce

Serves 4 to 6

HISTORICAL NOTES: *In Jefferson's menu notes for the President's House he grouped together three vegetables to be served with brown onion sauce: white beans (page 139), artichokes, and cauliflower, suggesting that all three were prepared similarly. However, since Jefferson was no cook, he may have been mistaken. I don't find a period recipe for cauliflower cooked in this way, so this is an adaptation. I've broken the head into florets as period French recipes direct, though Mary Randolph's cauliflower is cooked whole. Possibly she was only concerned with presentation, but she may also have found the whole vegetable easier to handle. I derived this straightforward, simple sauce—which is similar to the French sauce lyonnaise—from the one that dresses Jefferson's dried white beans. Following Jefferson's menu notes, I've also given instructions about how to pair artichokes with the sauce (page 134).*

1 medium cauliflower (about 1½ pounds)
salt
Brown Onion Sauce (below)
1 tablespoon chopped fresh parsley

1. Rinse the cauliflower under cold running water and drain well. Trim and cut it into uniform-size florets. Fill a 3-quart pot halfway with water and bring it to a boil over high heat. Add a small handful of salt and, when it returns to a boil, add the cauliflower. Cover until it begins boiling again, uncover, and cook until the florets are about half done, about 4 to 6 minutes. Drain thoroughly and refresh them under cold running water.

2. Bring the Brown Onion Sauce to a simmer in a sauté pan or skillet over medium heat. Add the cauliflower, cover, and let it come back to a simmer. Reduce the heat to medium low and braise, gently shaking the pan occasionally, until the cauliflower is tender, about 10 minutes. Pour it into a warm serving bowl and garnish with chopped parsley.

Brown Onion Sauce

Makes about 2 cups

2 ounces (4 tablespoons) unsalted butter
1 small white onion, peeled and minced
1 tablespoon Browned Flour (page 111)
2 cups rich beef broth (see Beef Soup, page 99)
salt
whole black pepper in a pepper mill

1. Melt the butter in a small heavy-bottomed saucepan over medium heat. Add the onion and sauté, tossing occasionally, until it is golden, about 10 minutes. Stir in the Browned Flour and cook until bubbly, about 1 minute.

2. Slowly stir in the broth, a little at a time, bring to a simmer, stirring constantly, and cook until lightly thickened and smooth, about 4 minutes. Taste and add salt and pepper as needed. Serve in a warm sauceboat.

Roasted Corn

Serves 4 to 8

HISTORICAL NOTES: *This is perhaps the nicest way to prepare fresh corn, then or now, so simple and commonplace that it was rarely written down. In fact, the only way that we know it to have been eaten at Monticello is from Jefferson's casual mention of "rosten ears" in his Weather Memorandum Book.[27] The corn cooks in the husk, which not only seals in its natural moisture, but protects and enhances its delicate flavor in a way no other wrapping can. Originally ears were roasted buried in the hot, banked ashes of the kitchen hearth, but a modern oven does the job well enough. For those after more authentic flavor, I include an alternate grill-roasting method that imitates the subtle flavor of ash-roasting.*

8 ears fresh young corn
unsalted butter
salt
whole black pepper in a pepper mill

1. Position a rack in the center of the oven and preheat the oven to 400 degrees. Put the corn in a basin and add enough cold water to cover it. Soak for at least 10 minutes.

2. Drain the corn thoroughly and roast directly on the oven rack until the husks begin to brown and char at the edges and the kernels are just cooked through, about 20 minutes.

3. Using a thick kitchen towel, kitchen mitts, or insulated gloves, take the corn from the oven, pull off the husks (most of the silk will pull away with them), wipe off any silk that remains, and trim away any discolored or damaged spots. Rub lightly with butter and pile them into a warm serving bowl. Serve hot with butter, salt, and pepper passed separately.

• • •

Note: To come closer to the flavor of ash-roasted corn, prepare a charcoal grill with coals, let them burn until they are beginning to ash over, spread them, and position a grill rack about 8 inches above them. Roast the (soaked and drained) corn on the rack, turning occasionally, until the husks are charred and the corn is cooked through and tender, about 20 to 30 minutes.

A 'MOULD FOR MAKING MACCARONI'

THE PASTA OF ITALY (all of which Jefferson called "maccaroni") caught Jefferon's attention while he was in Europe. He took notes on the types of flour used, the amount of yeast, and how the dough was pressed, even drawing a diagram of a pasta machine.[28] When his secretary, William Short, toured Italy, Jefferson saw an opportunity for obtaining a "mould for making maccaroni." After a flurry of correspondence, the "mould" finally arrived in Paris—but only after Jefferson had left for the United States.[29] The mold followed Jefferson home to America, and for some years there is no mention of the device. As with many modern-day kitchen gadgets, its status appears to have tumbled from coveted to neglected: the mold's final mention is an appearance on a packing list of "superfluous" goods.[30]

Despite the pasta mold and Jefferson's handwritten recipe for *Nouilly à maccaroni* (page 102), Jefferson purchased macaroni throughout his presidency and retirement. When ordering groceries from the Richmond firm of Gordon, Trokes, and Company in 1809, he requested twenty pounds of macaroni and suggested they contact a supplier from New Jersey that he had used while in Washington: "I have formerly been supplied from Sartori's works at Trenton, who makes them well, and would be glad to supply you should the Richmond demand make it worth your while to keep them."[31] Apparently the Richmond demand was not great or Sartori had left the business, as Jefferson continued to receive pasta with his wine shipments from Marseilles until his death.

— G.B.W.

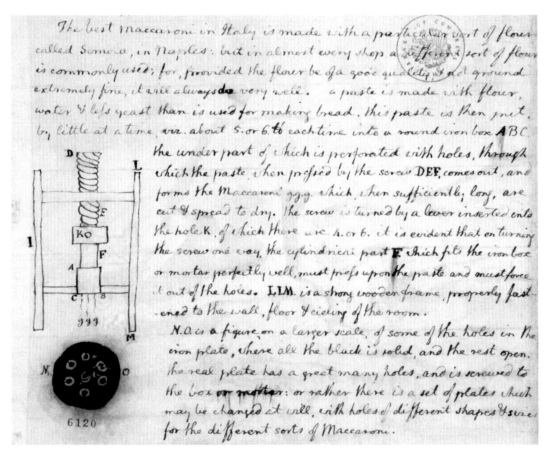

Jefferson's notes and drawing of a "Maccaroni Press." Jefferson notes that the plate at the bottom of the press could be changed to make "different sorts of Maccaroni."

Baked Macaroni with Cheese

Serves 6

HISTORICAL NOTES: *For baked macaroni as it was probably served at Monticello, I've turned to Mary Randolph's "Macaroni," essentially the same as Jefferson's great-granddaughter's manuscript recipe of the same name, so similar as to suggest that Mrs. Burke got the recipe from* The Virginia House-wife, *or that, equally as likely, Mary Randolph got it from Monticello. At the President's House, Federalist senator Manasseh Cutler ate "a pie called macaroni," which he mistook for a crust filled with onions (see page 15). It may well have been in pastry, or it might have been this recipe, which was fairly standard for Anglo-Southern kitchens of the period. This dish is not Italian by any stretch of the imagination and uses factory-made macaroni. The noodles recorded by Jefferson under the name Nouilly à maccaroni (page 102) may also be dressed in this way, even though they were intended mostly for soup.*

4 cups whole milk

4 cups water

1 pound tube-shaped macaroni, such as small penne
   salt

6 tablespoons unsalted butter, cut into small bits

8 ounces imported Parmesan cheese, or extra sharp Farmhouse Cheddar

1. Position a rack in the upper third of the oven and preheat the oven to 375 degrees. Stir together the milk and water in a large pot and bring to a boil. Add the macaroni, stirring well, and return to a boil. Reduce the heat and simmer, stirring occasionally, until the macaroni is tender (about 2 minutes for fresh, 4 to 6 minutes for fresh and dried, and 8 to 12 minutes for commercial pasta). Lightly drain it in a colander (it should still be a little wet) and return it to the pot. Season with salt to taste and toss well.

2. Lightly butter a 2-quart casserole dish and cover the bottom with one-third of the macaroni. Dot with one-third of the butter and shave one-third of the cheese over it using a vegetable peeler or mandolin. Repeat the layers twice more, finishing with a thick layer of cheese, and bake until golden brown, about 20 to 30 minutes.

Anne Cary Randolph's Peas

Serves 4 to 6

HISTORICAL NOTES: *This elegant dish (pictured, opposite page) is one of two culinary receipts in Anne Cary Randolph's account book, recorded while she lived at Monticello during Jefferson's presidency. Fortunately, the recipe is clear enough, except for its proportions, and the French recipes we know to have been in the Monticello collection provide those details. Cooks unaccustomed to egg liaisons should use particular care, since they easily curdle if overheated. The classic technique is to shake the pan once the egg liaison is added, but gentle stirring works fine. Finally, if truly fresh peas aren't available, frozen petits pois make a plausible substitute and may in fact be more flavorful than the "fresh" peas that we often get today.*

1 pound freshly shelled green peas

2 tablespoons unsalted butter

2 teaspoons all-purpose flour

1½ cups chicken broth or water (or slightly more)

1 small white onion, peeled and studded with 3 whole cloves

salt

2 teaspoons sugar

2 large egg yolks

2 tablespoons water

1. Rinse and drain the peas and put them in a medium saucepan. Add the butter and cook over medium heat, shaking the pan gently until the butter is melted. Cook, shaking the pan frequently, until the peas are bright green. Sprinkle in the flour and shake the pan or stir until it is incorporated and smooth.

2. Stir in enough broth or water to completely cover the peas and bring to a simmer. Add the onion and return to a simmer, stirring occasionally, until the peas are tender, about 20 minutes. Taste and add salt as needed.

3. Remove and discard the onion, stir in the sugar, and return to a simmer. Whisk together the egg yolks and water in a small bowl until smooth. Gradually beat a few spoonfuls of the hot broth into the egg yolks. Slowly add the yolk mixture to the peas, stirring constantly, and heat until the sauce begins to thicken, about 30 seconds. Immediately pour the peas into a warm bowl and serve at once.

JEFFERSON ENGAGED *in friendly competitions with his neighbors to determine who could bring the first English pea to the table in late spring, the winner then hosting a community dinner that included a feast on the winning dish (or teaspoon) of peas. One neighbor, George Divers, proudly regarded himself as the perennial, undisputed champion of the pea contest. According to family tradition, when one year Jefferson harvested the first neighborhood pea, the sage of Monticello refused to divulge his victory in fear of rocking the pride of his friend. Even if the story of Jefferson's selflessness is historically unproven, the larger story of the neighborhood contest clearly demonstrates recognition of food not only for its nutritional content, but as a means of social interaction.*

— P.J.H.

Fried Potatoes

Serves about 6

HISTORICAL NOTES: *Jefferson's menu notes from the President's House listed "potatoes, raw, in small slices, deep-fried"—in other words, French fries, perhaps the earliest American reference to the now-iconic food. Other than his notes, which amount to a sketchy recipe, no other mention survives in the family collection, so our source for detail must be Mrs. Randolph's The Virginia House-wife, as she surely understood the way things were done at Monticello. She specifies "large" mature potatoes and slices them thicker than is usual in most period French recipes. Modern cooks should note that "large" is relative: Mary Randolph never saw anything like the mammoth russet "baking" potatoes of our day. For strict authenticity, only lard will answer for the frying, or a combination of lard and bacon drippings. Those who are less concerned for strict authenticity or who are avoiding animal fats can use peanut oil and come within shooting distance of the original.*

2 pounds white potatoes
lard or peanut oil, for frying
salt

1. Prepare a large bowl of ice water. Peel the potatoes and, using a sharp knife, mandolin, or food processor fitted with a slicing disk attachment, slice the potatoes into rounds ¼ inch thick or thinner. Drop them into the cold water and soak for 30 minutes.

2. Position a rack in the center of the oven and preheat the oven to 150 to 170 degrees (the warm setting). Put enough lard or oil in a heavy-bottomed Dutch oven or deep skillet to cover the bottom by at least 1 inch but to come no more than halfway up the sides. Place over medium-high heat and heat until very hot but not quite smoking (about 365 to 375 degrees). Fit a wire rack over a large rimmed baking sheet and set it near the skillet.

3. Drain and thoroughly dry the potatoes on absorbent towels and slip them, a few at a time, into the fat until the pan is full but not crowded. Fry, stirring frequently to prevent them from sticking together and help them crisp, until they are crisp and golden brown. Remove the potatoes with tongs or a skimmer, allowing the fat to drain back into pot, and spread on the prepared rack. Put the rack in the warm oven while frying the remaining potatoes. When all of the potatoes are fried, sprinkle lightly with salt and serve hot.

• • •

To Make Mary Randolph's Potato Chips:
With a paring knife or vegetable peeler, shave the potatoes around like peeling a lemon into long, thin spirals or shave them into round chips with a mandolin or vegetable peeler. Blot carefully on absorbent towels and fry, a few at a time, as directed above, stirring frequently to prevent them from sticking to one another. Paper-thin chips cook more quickly than thick slices, so watch them carefully.

Mashed Potatoes

Serves 8

HISTORICAL NOTES: *Since this is a recipe that survives in Jefferson's own hand, I've used the cooking method dictated by that recipe, entitled "To Dress Potatoes." It is notably inferior to Mary Randolph's rendition, in which the potatoes are cooked in their skins and are peeled afterwards—a far more flavorful way of cooking them—and I encourage readers to experiment with her method. For clarity of detail in the purée and mashing steps, I've turned to her recipe. Both renditions are silent on heat but imply beating the butter and cream into the potatoes over low heat, which is of course the best way of doing it. At Monticello, cooks puréed the potatoes by mashing them through a colander with a wooden spoon; a food mill or potato ricer will make neater and shorter work of this with the same results.*

3 pounds small boiling potatoes, as much the same size as possible
salt
4 ounces (1 stick) unsalted butter
½ cup heavy cream
whole milk, as needed
¼ - ½ teaspoon freshly grated nutmeg

1. Scrub the potatoes well under cold running water. Peel and put them in a large pot. Add enough cold water to cover them by 1 inch and then lift out the potatoes.

2. Bring the water to a boil over medium-high heat, add a small handful of salt, and carefully slip the potatoes back into the pot. Bring it back to a boil, reduce the heat to medium low, and simmer until a fork pierces easily to the center.

3. Drain thoroughly, leaving the potatoes in the pot. Cover and leave in a warm spot for 10 to 15 minutes, then transfer the potatoes to a bowl.

4. Press the potatoes through a potato ricer, food mill, or colander back into the pot. Over low heat, beat in the butter and cream with a wooden spoon until fluffy and light. If they are too stiff, add a little milk and beat until warm and fluffy. Season lightly with nutmeg, taste, and adjust the salt and nutmeg. Spoon them into a warm serving bowl.

Smuggling rice out of Italy

WHILE SERVING HIS COUNTRY in France, Jefferson felt committed to fostering the export of American products, including rice. When Jefferson investigated the poor sale of Carolina rice on the French market, he learned that buyers spurned American rice because of its poor appearance, owing either to the variety grown or the method used to clean it.

This news—as well as letters from some gentlemen in South Carolina asking for samples of different varieties of rice—prompted Jefferson to undertake an ambitious journey to Italy. There he purchased the tool the Italians used to clean their rice, and, at the risk of the prevailing penalty of death, he smuggled some unhusked Piedmont rice out of the country, writing, "I could only bring off as much as my coat and surtout pockets would hold."[32] He also made arrangements for a larger supply to follow him later. These treasures eventually reached South Carolina, horrifying at least one rice planter, who feared that the contraband would "be the means of propagating an inferior species among us. For that reason I should be glad that you would not send us any more of it."[33]

After breaking the law and aggravating South Carolina rice growers, Jefferson learned that it was the *price* of American rice, rather than its appearance, which discouraged French buyers; in fact, Carolina rice was the most esteemed variety on the French market. He thereafter concentrated on encouraging American exporters to ship their rice directly to France instead of using British middlemen.

Jefferson then turned his attention to a different kind of rice—the dry or upland variety grown in parts of Africa and Asia. In the hopes of displacing the

"Harvesting the Rice," from an 1859 magazine illustration, depicts an activity prevalent on South Carolina's rice plantations.

"pestiferous culture of the wet rice," he inaugurated a global search for samples of the grain and eventually had some shipped to South Carolina and Georgia.[34] In later years, Jefferson was delighted to learn that the cultivation of upland rice for family use had spread throughout the hilly parts of Georgia.

On a more personal level, Jefferson recorded a recipe for preparing rice and cultivated upland rice for a time at Monticello. At Poplar Forest, Jefferson's granddaughter once gave some rice to a neighbor, noting that "some bottles of red wine, a few crackers, and a part of our nice south-Carolina rice, have served to shew her that our wills were good."[35]

—MONTICELLO RESEARCH DEPARTMENT

Glazed Turnips

Serves 4

HISTORICAL NOTES: *This is classic French cookery, but recorded many years after Jefferson's death by his great-granddaughter, Mrs. Burke. After such a passage of time, her memories of "turnips with sugar" are flawed at best. Happily, Mary Randolph, as usual, got it absolutely right in her lucid rendition of the same dish entitled "Ragout of Turnips." It is a splendid and delicious recipe. The turnips should be small, and of much the same size. Larger roots may be cut up and trimmed to small ovals or rounds so that they roll easily during the browning.*

12 very small turnips (about 2 pounds), as much the same size as possible
2 tablespoons unsalted butter
1 tablespoon sugar
1 cup rich veal or beef broth (see Beef Soup, page 99)
salt

1. Scrub the turnips under cold running water, drain well, and peel, trimming them into even ovals that will roll easily. Put the butter in a large skillet over medium-high heat. When it is just melted, put in the turnips and toss until well coated. Sprinkle with sugar and sauté, gently shaking the pan to roll them, until they are nicely and evenly browned, about 5 minutes.

2. Pour in the broth and bring it to a boil, again gently shaking the pan. Cover, reduce the heat to medium-low, and simmer gently until the turnips are just tender. Taste and add salt as needed and pour into a warm serving bowl.

WHERE ARE THE VEGETABLE RECIPES?

Though by many accounts (see page 5) Jefferson's diet consisted mostly of vegetables and fruits, the family manuscripts say little of vegetable cookery. This seeming paradox is easily explained when we understand that manuscript books recorded recipes in inverse proportion to their use. Cooks whose lives revolved around preparing the family meals did not need written instructions for routine daily cooking. Notes were necessary only for infrequently prepared dishes, and even then, recipes tended to be general and sketchy—little more than a list of ingredients to jog the cook's memory. As Martha Jefferson Randolph apologetically noted of her "receipts," they were written "for people who are adepts and not beginners who require to be told every thing."[36]

At least one visitor, Jane Blair Smith, remarked on the fruit and cakes served at Monticello, and Martha Jefferson Randolph wrote that she had recipes for "Many kinds of little cake usefull enough where there are many children visitors."[37] When these cakes, such as Savoy Biscuits (page 170) or Naples Biscuits (what we today know as lady fingers) remained leftover, cooks transformed them into Trifle.

Trifle

Serves 6

HISTORICAL NOTES: *Among the recipes that Mrs. Trist copied from* The Virginia House-wife *is Trifle, a classic way of using leftover cake that has survived into our day. The recipe calls for decorating the dish with "preserves of any kind, cut ... thin," which I take to be glacéed fruit or whole preserves such as brandied peaches. Mary Randolph's method for whipping cream was makeshift because she probably did not have a reliable whisk and may have even used two forks turned in on one another. The cream was beaten until froth formed on top, which was skimmed off as it appeared. The process is tedious and produces an unsubstantial topping that is hard to create with a good whisk because the cream begins to thicken and the froth stops forming. Therefore I've given directions for a full whip here, and, as cream whips much more elegantly by hand, I don't recommend a mixer.*

6 - 8 Savoy Biscuits (page 170)
½ cup white wine (approximately)
4 cups Boiled Custard (page 164), chilled
1 cup heavy cream
2 - 3 tablespoons sugar, or to taste
1 cup glacé fruit, thinly sliced or cut into decorative shapes

1. Line the bottom of an 8-cup trifle bowl or glass serving bowl with Savoy biscuits (if the biscuits are very thick, cut them in half crosswise). Sprinkle the biscuits with about 1/3 cup of the wine—just enough to moisten well but not make them soggy. Allow them to stand for a few minutes to fully absorb the wine. Spoon the custard evenly over the top (the dish should be no more than three-quarters full).

2. Stir no more than 2 to 3 tablespoons of wine into the cream (too much will cause the cream to curdle), sweeten with sugar to taste, and whip it by hand with a whisk until it forms soft peaks. Mound the cream over the custard. Just before serving decorate the top with the glacé fruit.

Meringues

Makes 3 dozen

HISTORICAL NOTES: *Jefferson recorded recipes for both Meringues and Macaroons (opposite page). I've cut this recipe in half, since a dozen large eggs would make an unmanageable amount of meringues for most modern households. Jefferson's version measures sugar by the "spoonful," and I've assumed that to be a heaping old kitchen spoon, or about 4 level tablespoons. This amount takes into account that grade-A large eggs are bigger than the eggs of their day and will need at least this much sugar for the proper structure. For meringues, professional bakers prefer superfine sugar and purists insist that hand-whipping is superior, but regular granulated sugar works fine and electric mixers don't significantly change the texture. In Jefferson's time, meringues were baked on pans lined with paper, just as today. These were likely to have been baked in Monticello's brick oven when it had cooled after the last of the bread had baked.*

6	large egg whites, at room temperature
12	ounces (1½ cups) sugar

1. Position a rack in the center of the oven and preheat the oven to 175 to 200 degrees. Line a large baking sheet with parchment paper.

2. Place the egg whites in a large bowl or the bowl of an electric mixer fitted with the whisk attachment and whisk by hand or beat on medium-high speed until frothy. Gradually add the sugar and beat until the meringue forms glossy, stiff peaks (over-whipping will produce a dry meringue).

3. Place a small amount of meringue in each corner of the baking sheet to secure the parchment paper. Spoon or pipe the meringue onto the parchment-lined baking sheet into 2-inch rounds, leaving about 1 inch between each one (they will slightly puff during baking). Bake for 45 minutes to 1 hour, or until the meringues are dry and crisp but still white.

4. Loosen the parchment from the pan and slide it carefully onto a wire cooling rack. When completely cooled, peel the meringues off the paper and store them in airtight tins.

• • •

Note: Meringues should only be attempted in dry weather. They are impossible on humid days, even in modern air-conditioned houses.

Macaroons

Makes about 4 dozen

HISTORICAL NOTES: *Jefferson's recipe is problematic; indeed, Mrs. Hess calls it "hopeless" since there are no amounts or proportions and the oven directions are all wrong. The basic method is all right, but even so it does not direct cooks to make a meringue from the egg whites. For a workable period recipe, I've turned as usual to Mary Randolph, who probably had the same source and knew what she was doing. Jefferson's recipe does not mention rosewater, but it was common in period recipes, including Mrs. Randolph's, and it adds a nice touch. The reader wants culinary rosewater, available at specialty grocers and kitchenware stores. To be authentic, the paste should be made from scratch with a mortar and pestle, but it is quite frankly grueling work. The food processor and commercial almond paste make short work of it. Both Jefferson and Mrs. Randolph direct that macaroons, like meringues, be baked on paper.*

1 pound almond paste

2 - 3 tablespoons rosewater

6 large egg whites

1 pound (2 cups) sugar, plus more, for dusting the macaroons

1. Position a rack in the center of the oven and preheat the oven to 325 degrees. Break up the almond paste and knead in the rosewater by the spoonful as needed to make it smooth. This can be done in the food processor fitted with a steel blade. Roughly break up the paste and put it in the processor bowl. Pulse until it is mealy and then pulse in the rosewater.

2. Beat the egg whites with a whisk, or at medium-high speed in the bowl of an electric mixer fitted with a whisk, until frothy. Gradually beat in the sugar and beat until the meringue is glossy and the consistency of marshmallow cream. Mix it into the almond paste a few tablespoons at a time, either with a spoon or by pulsing in the food processor. The paste should be soft but hold firm peaks when dropped from a spoon.

3. Drop the dough in rounded teaspoons onto parchment-lined baking sheets. Dust lightly with sugar and bake until puffed and lightly colored, about 25 minutes.

4. Cool the macaroons on the baking sheets and then carefully peel them off the parchment and store them in an airtight (preferably metal) container.

Crisp Gingerbread

Makes about 14 dozen wafers

HISTORICAL NOTES: *Included in Ellen Coolidge's request for recipes from Monticello after her move to Boston was "gingerbread such as Edy makes," a tribute to the skills of Edith Hern Fossett, who cooked at Monticello and the President's House. We cannot know whether she desired one of the surviving family gingerbread recipes or one from* The Virginia House-wife *(see Historical Notes, opposite page). This recipe follows mostly Mary Randolph, since it is an old-fashioned gingerbread. However, I've also used details on mixing, rolling, and baking from a family recipe called "Fanny's crisp ginger bread," a possible reference to another Monticello cook, Fanny Gillette Hern. Compared to the delicate crispness of cookies lightened with baking powder, these wafers are quite hard when freshly made, though both texture and flavor improve dramatically after two or three days' storage in an airtight tin. The dough would be rendered far more tender if the butter were increased by half or as much as doubled, as it was in Fanny's recipe.*

4 ounces (½ cup) turbinado (raw) sugar
20 ounces (about 4 cups) unbleached all-purpose flour
1 rounded tablespoon ground ginger
¼ teaspoon ground cloves
2 ounces (4 tablespoons) unsalted butter, melted
1⅓ cups unsulfured molasses

1. Position a rack in the center of the oven and preheat the oven to 325 degrees. Finely crush the sugar with a mortar and pestle or in a food processor fitted with the steel blade.

2. Whisk or sift together the sugar, flour, and spices and make a well in the center. Stir together the butter and molasses and pour them into the center of the dry ingredients, working them into the flour to form a smooth, fairly stiff dough. (This step can be done with a food processor fitted with the steel blade. Put the sugar, flour, and spices in the bowl of the processor and process until well blended. Pour in the butter and molasses and process until the dough forms a smooth ball.)

3. Divide the dough into 6 lumps. Lightly flour a work surface and roll out one lump until it is wafer thin, about 1/16 inch thick or less. Cut into 1¼-inch rounds or various shapes and transfer with a metal spatula to buttered baking sheets. Bake until the color lightens and they look dry, about 5 to 6 minutes. Cool on the pans and, when crisp, transfer to airtight tins. Repeat with the remaining dough. Store for at least 2 days before serving.

Drop Biscuits

Makes 6 dozen

HISTORICAL NOTES: *Another of the recipes that Ellen Randolph Coolidge requested of her family is "drop biscuits." She was not asking for a bread recipe, but used the word biscuit with its older meaning (which survives in Europe) to describe what we would call a cookie or cracker. Her mother mailed back "all my manuscript receipts except those which you will find in Sister R[andolph]'s book."[38] While the recipes mailed to Mrs. Coolidge have been lost and no other family recipe for Drop Biscuits survives, this confection, a delicate, crisp sweet wafer, was indeed one of the recipes included in Sister (Mary) Randolph's book,* The Virginia House-wife. *I've only cut the quantity and added a suggested flavoring that was usual for the period and almost certainly intended.*

4 large eggs

8 ounces (1 cup) sugar

6 ounces (about 1¼ cups) unbleached pastry flour or all-purpose flour

grated zest of 2 lemons or 1 orange

1. Position a rack in the center of the oven and preheat the oven to 375 degrees. Generously butter three large baking sheets.

2. In a large mixing bowl, beat the eggs until fluffy and light. Gradually beat in the sugar, then the flour and zest. Beat until very light, about 1 minute more. Drop scant teaspoons of batter onto the prepared baking sheets, spacing them at least 1 inch apart.

3. Bake until golden brown around the edges, about 6 to 8 minutes. Cool on the pans and loosen with a thin metal spatula. Store in airtight tins.

Apple Fritters

Serves 6 to 8

HISTORICAL NOTES: *As Karen Hess notes, this recipe is classically French and may have come from Lemaire. In her recipe, Mrs. Meikleham specifies lard as the frying fat, and that is what I use here, although the reader who isn't after authenticity may use peanut oil. Mrs. Meikleham suggests either brandy or wine, but Mary Randolph's rendition of the recipe in* The Virginia House-wife *used both, as I have done here. While this is most definitely a European recipe in concept, as historian Jessica Harris notes, fritters are found in the New World wherever there are African cooks in the kitchen. The equipment has not changed over time: a cast iron skillet or Dutch oven remains ideal for deep-frying. Use a wire frying skimmer or tongs to scoop out the cooked fritters, since a slotted spoon does not drain them effectively. Draining on absorbent paper will make the fritters soggy.*

¼ cup brandy

¼ cup white wine

½ cup sugar

1 teaspoon ground cinnamon
  grated zest of 1 lemon

2 medium tart apples, such as Winesap or Granny Smith, peeled, cored, and sliced into thick wedges
  lard or peanut oil, for frying

2 large eggs, separated

1 tablespoon unsalted butter, melted and cooled

½ cup water, plus more as needed

4 ounces (about ¾ cup) unbleached all-purpose flour
  superfine sugar, for dusting (see Historical Notes, page 161)

1. Stir together the brandy, wine, sugar, cinnamon, and lemon zest in a medium bowl. Add the apples, tossing well to completely coat each slice. Set them aside to macerate for at least 1 hour, stirring occasionally to coat evenly.

2. Position a rack in the upper portion of the oven and preheat the oven to 150 to 175 degrees (the warm setting). Put enough lard or oil into a heavy-bottomed Dutch oven or deep skillet to cover the bottom by at least 1 inch but to come no more than halfway up the sides. Heat it over medium-high heat and until very hot but not quite smoking (about 365 to 375 degrees). Position a wire rack over a rimmed baking sheet and set it nearby.

3. Whisk together the egg yolks, butter, and water in a large bowl until smooth. Gradually whisk in the flour and ¼ cup of the macerating liquid, adding more water as needed to make a fairly thin batter. Whisk the egg whites in a large bowl by hand or with an electric mixer fitted with a whisk attachment, until they form soft peaks. Fold about one-third of them into the batter and then fold in the remainder until completely blended.

4. Drain the apples, discarding the liquid, and drop them, two or three at a time, into the batter, turning until coated. Lift them out with a fork or tongs, allowing the excess to flow back into the bowl, and slip them into the hot fat. Fry, turning once or twice, until golden brown, about 6 to 8 minutes. Lift the fritters out with tongs or a wire skimmer, allowing the fat to drain back into the pot, and place them on the prepared rack. Keep them warm in the oven while frying the remaining fritters. Dust with superfine sugar and serve hot.

WHY ARE THERE SO MANY DESSERTS?

THE JEFFERSON FAMILY MANUSCRIPTS are filled with puddings, pastries, and sweets, which in large part shows that at Monticello, as elsewhere, desserts and other baking of upper-class households were the provenance of the mistress. The majority of day-to-day cooking fell to others, but the status and expense associated with desserts brought them under the plantation mistress's careful attention, sometimes to the point that she made them herself. This trend shows itself in the few surviving references to Jefferson family members actually cooking, such as when Jefferson approvingly monitored his daughter Maria's progress in learning to make puddings, or when granddaughter Mary Jefferson

Randolph expressed surprise following the Christmas of 1821, when she neither "ordered the death of a single turkey or helped to do execution on a solitary mince pie."[39] The women controlled desserts in part because sugar was an expensive commodity until late in the nineteenth century. Even wealthy housewives took care to regulate its use, as when Martha Jefferson noted in her account book that she returned "to [M]onticello [and] found half a loaf of sugar & barrel flour opened in my absence."[40] Controlling sugar must have been especially important at Monticello, where a large family and a steady stream of visitors put a continual strain on the household budget.

The dining table in Monticello's Tea Room, laden with faux sweets to interpret the second course of a Jeffersonian dinner.

Bell Fritters Lemaire

Makes about 5 dozen

HISTORICAL NOTES: *Bell fritters are the same delicate, airy fried morsels known in France and New Orleans as beignets. The name "bell" presumably comes from the fact that the hollow puffs resemble bells. Modern beignets are served as a sweet and usually dusted with superfine sugar; since the paste is not sweetened, I think a sugar coating was intended but omitted by the scribes. Readers wishing to be strictly authentic should beat the paste by hand with a wooden spoon, but it is quite stiff, and those lacking strength or a penchant for authenticity may use a hand-held mixer fitted with rotary beaters or a stand mixer with a paddle. When baked instead of fried, this is the classic dough for cream puffs. Both Mary Randolph and Mrs. Burke, Jefferson's great-granddaughter, recorded this recipe, the latter attributing it both to Monticello and Etienne Lemaire, Jefferson's maître d'hôtel at the President's House.*

2 ounces (4 tablespoons) unsalted butter
2 cups water
10 ounces (about 2 cups) all-purpose flour
5 large eggs
  lard or peanut oil, for frying
  superfine sugar, for dusting (see Historical Notes, opposite page)

1. Bring the butter and water to a boil in a medium heavy-bottomed saucepan. Reduce the heat, simmer for about 2 minutes, until the butter is melted, and remove the pan from the heat. Gradually beat in the flour with a wooden spoon to form a thick, smooth paste. Return the pan to medium heat and beat until the paste is glossy, smooth, and begins to pull away from the sides of the pan and to leave a film on the bottom of the pan. (This will happen quickly, in less than 1 minute, and the paste will begin to gather in a clump around the spoon.)

2. Remove the pan from the heat and beat in the eggs, one at a time, beating well after each addition. Continue beating until the batter is glossy, smooth, and light. (This step may also be done in a stand mixer fitted with a paddle; scrape the paste into the mixer bowl and beat at medium speed, adding the eggs one at a time.)

3. Position a rack in the upper third of the oven and preheat the oven to 150 to 175 degrees (the warm setting). Put enough lard or oil into a heavy-bottomed Dutch oven or deep skillet to cover the bottom by at least 1 inch but to come no more than halfway up the sides. Heat it over medium-high heat until very hot but not quite smoking (about 365 to 375 degrees). Place a wire rack over a rimmed baking sheet and set it nearby.

4. Drop heaping teaspoons of paste into the fat, using another spoon or a spatula to push it off the spoon, until the pan is full but not crowded. Fry, turning once, until they are a golden amber, about 2 to 3 minutes per side. Lift out the fritters with tongs or a wire skimmer, allowing the fat to drain back into the pot, and place them on the prepared rack. Keep them warm in the oven while frying the remaining fritters. Dust with superfine sugar and serve hot.

Bread Fritters Monticello

Serves 4 to 6

HISTORICAL NOTES: *The most important aspect of this elegant rendition of French toast is the right bread: it must be firm and substantial, such as the bread baked in Monticello's brick ovens (page 94). Also important is superfine sugar, the closest modern equivalent to the "powdered sugar" Mrs. Meikleham calls for. American confectioners' sugar will not answer because it contains cornstarch as an anti-caking agent. If readers can't obtain superfine sugar, regular granulated sugar can be powdered, as Monticello's cook would have done, with a mortar and pestle. It can also be pulverized in a modern food processor: put a tea-towel over the machine to keep the sugar dust from pluming and process for 3 to 4 minutes or until the sugar is fine. Mrs. Meikleham's recipe did not specify the kind of wine, but Mary Randolph's rendition calls for white wine. Medium dry sherry or Madeira would also work well.*

4   slices (at least ¾ inch thick) firm, home-style bread (page 94)
1   cup white wine
    lard or peanut oil, for frying
2   large eggs
½ - 1   teaspoon freshly grated nutmeg, or 1 teaspoon ground cinnamon
1   cup superfine sugar, for dusting

1. Remove the crust from the bread and cut into 1 x 2-inch strips. Place the strips in a wide shallow bowl and pour ½ cup of the wine over them. Soak for 3 or 4 minutes, or until saturated but not soggy. Transfer the bread to a wire mesh colander to drain.

2. Position a rack in the upper third of the oven and preheat the oven to 150 to 175 degrees (the warm setting). Put enough lard or oil into a heavy-bottomed Dutch oven or deep skillet to cover. Heat it over medium-high heat until very hot, but not quite smoking (about 365 to 375 degrees). Place a wire rack over a rimmed baking sheet and set it nearby.

3. Whisk together the eggs and remaining ½ cup of wine in a wide shallow bowl. Dip the bread one piece at a time in the egg and wine, turning to coat, lift it out with tongs, allowing the excess to flow back into the bowl, and slip it into the fat. Repeat until the pan is full but not crowded. Fry, turning occasionally, until puffed, golden brown, and delicately crisp on the outside but still moist inside, about 5 minutes. Lift them from the fat with tongs or a wire skimmer, allowing the fat to drain back into the pot. Arrange them on the prepared rack and set in the oven to keep warm while repeating with the remaining bread slices.

4. While the fritters are frying, whisk or sift together the spices and sugar. Generously dust this over the fritters just before serving and serve hot.

Lemon Curd Tarts

Makes six 3-inch tarts or 12 tartlets

1 pound prepared or commercial puff pastry
6 medium lemons
1 pound (2 cups) sugar
8 ounces (1 cup) unsalted butter, softened
3 whole large eggs
5 large egg yolks

HISTORICAL NOTES: *This lovely recipe, attributed in Mrs. Trist's manuscript to her mother, Martha Randolph, was given under the old-fashioned name "lemon pudding." Throughout the nineteenth century "pudding" commonly described any custard baked in a crust; these are really just old-fashioned lemon curd tarts. Originally baked in "patty pans with paste in them," the curd is so rich and full-flavored that readers might want to bake it in smaller tartlets. Puff pastry was the usual crust for fancy pies and it is perfect for these tarts, but no recipe appears in the family manuscripts. Readers who wish to make their own can turn to period recipes such as Mary Randolph's. Readers less concerned with absolute authenticity may use commercial puff pastry, but it should be rolled thinner than it comes from the package. Otherwise, it tends to puff too much.*

1. Position a rack in the center of the oven and preheat the oven to 375 degrees. Line 12 individual tart pans with puff pastry, rolling the pastry a little thinner than usual (to a little less than 1/8 inch thick).

2. Grate the zest from 3 of the lemons and juice all of them through a strainer. Mix together the zest, juice, and sugar, stirring until the sugar is nearly dissolved.

3. Prepare the bottom pot of a double boiler with 1 inch of water and bring it to a boil over medium heat. Reduce the heat to a slow simmer. Put the butter into the top portion of the boiler set over direct medium heat. Barely melt it and stir in the sweetened lemon juice, stirring until the sugar is completely dissolved. Set it over the bottom of the double boiler, making sure it doesn't touch the water.

4. Beat together the whole eggs and yolks until smooth. Slowly stir them into the butter, and cook, stirring constantly, until thick, about 8 minutes (the spoon will leave a distinct path in the curd). It will continue to thicken as it cools, becoming completely thick only when completely cool, so take care not to overcook it.

5. Remove from the heat and continue stirring until slightly cooled and very thick. Divide the curd among the prepared tart shells and arrange them on a baking sheet. Bake until the curd is puffed and just set and the pastry is puffed and golden, about 25 to 30 minutes. Serve at room temperature or slightly chilled.

Bread Pudding

Serves 4 to 6

HISTORICAL NOTES: *This is a very old-fashioned pudding, credited to Martha Randolph by her daughter Virginia Trist. Mary Randolph offers a rendition of the same pudding but baked in a pastry; I have left the recipe as Mrs. Trist gave it, adding only the latter recipe's nutmeg, since it is a usual seasoning. The amount given here will fill a standard 9-inch partially baked pastry shell if the reader wishes to experiment. At Monticello, scullions would have made soft breadcrumbs by rasping a stale loaf of bread against a grater, but the food processor makes short work of it today. Roughly break up a sliced stale loaf into the bowl of a food processor fitted with the steel blade attachment. Cover and process until the crumbs are fine. A 9-inch loaf will produce about 6 cups of crumbs. The manuscript recipe includes the accompanying Brandy Butter Sauce, page 171.*

2 cups milk

2 cups finely grated stale bread crumbs (see Historical Notes)

¾ cup sugar

grated zest of 1 lemon

¼ – ½ teaspoon freshly grated nutmeg (optional)

2 large eggs

1 large egg yolk

Brandy Butter Sauce (page 171)

1. Bring the milk to a simmer in a 2-quart pot over medium heat. Stir in the crumbs and simmer until they are saturated and swollen to the consistency of thick oatmeal, about 2 minutes.

2. Pour it into a large mixing bowl. Stir in the sugar until dissolved and stir in the lemon zest and, if using, nutmeg to taste. Let the batter cool slightly.

3. Position a rack in the center of the oven and preheat the oven to 350 degrees. Beat the whole eggs and yolk together until frothy and light. Add the eggs to the batter and stir until smooth.

4. Butter a 2-quart casserole and pour in the batter. Bake until golden brown on top and set, about 45 minutes. Serve warm with Brandy Butter Sauce.

Boiled Custard

Makes about 5 cups

HISTORICAL NOTES: *This artless custard—also known as* crème anglaise—*was so standard in English and American cooking that recipes for it were not all that common. Mary Randolph, for example, calls for it in other recipes but never says how to make it. Mrs. Meikleham's manuscript recipe dates to well after Jefferson's death and is poorly described, so I've also taken clues from Mary Randolph's trifle recipe, which calls for "rich" boiled custard. "Rich" suggests the use of milk from which no cream has been removed, and plenty of egg yolks rather than whole eggs. Using some egg white, as called for in Mrs. Trist's recipe, makes the custard more stable for amateurs and for composed dishes. Vanilla is used in a few custards in* The Virginia House-wife, *and I've included both it and the cinnamon suggested by Mrs. Meikleham, which makes a lovely custard for Trifle (page 153).*

1 cup heavy cream
3 cups whole milk
1 vanilla bean, or 2 cinnamon sticks
2 eggs
6 large egg yolks
4 ounces (1/2 cup) sugar

1. Fill the bottom portion of a double boiler with at least 1 inch of water and bring to a simmer over medium heat. Combine the cream, milk, and vanilla bean or cinnamon stick in the top portion of the double boiler and bring to a simmer over (direct) medium-low heat, stirring frequently. When it is almost boiling, set it over the bottom portion of the double boiler.

2. Whisk together the eggs, egg yolks, and sugar in a medium bowl until smooth. Gradually whisk in 1 cup of the hot milk and cream. Slowly stir this into the simmering milk and cream and cook, stirring constantly, until the custard is thick and thickly coats the back of the spoon. Remove from the heat and stir until slightly cooled. Remove the vanilla bean or cinnamon sticks (both can be rinsed, air-dried, and re-used) and strain the custard through a wire strainer. Cool completely and chill before serving.

• • •

Custard Sauce: This sauce was customarily served with simple pies, tarts, and desserts such as Charlotte Monticello (page 180). To make it, follow the recipe given above, omitting the whole eggs and using only six yolks. For a thicker sauce, add one or two more yolks, depending how thick the sauce needs to be.

JEFFERSON AND VANILLA

It will no doubt disappoint those who love crediting Jefferson with introducing vanilla to America to know that the bean was already around by his day; however, the spice was still rare and expensive, and the relatively cheap extract that we take for granted was still unknown, so it was used with far more restraint than we would exercise today.

Baked Custard

Serves 8

HISTORICAL NOTES: *This is a delicate and very old-fashioned recipe—even more old-fashioned than what we think of as baked custard today. Mrs. Meikleham and Mrs. Trist call it "Plain Custard" and attribute it, respectively, to Monticello and their mother, Martha Randolph. The sisters' recipes differ only in detail, but vary slightly from Mary Randolph's version, which is flavored only with a dusting of freshly grated nutmeg after it comes out of the oven. Before pasteurization, milk was scalded to stabilize it for baking; I call for it here mainly to infuse the milk with the spice. I've cut the quantities to give a more manageable yield for smaller modern families, but the good thing about custards is that they are terrific left over. Monticello's collection includes Jefferson's cups for custards like this, but any small china cups would suffice.*

2   cups whole milk
1   cup heavy cream
1   4-inch stick or 2 small sticks cinnamon
½ - ¾   cup sugar
6   large egg yolks
2   tablespoons white wine or dry sherry

1. Put the milk, cream, and cinnamon in a 2-quart heavy-bottomed saucepan. Bring it to a simmer over medium-low heat, stirring frequently to prevent scorching, and simmer until fragrant, about 5 minutes. Remove it from the heat, let cool until lukewarm, and then remove the cinnamon (it may be rinsed, dried, and re-used).

2. Meanwhile, position a rack in the center of the oven and preheat the oven to 300 degrees. Sweeten the milk with sugar to taste, beginning with ½ cup, and stir until it is completely dissolved. Lightly whisk the egg yolks in a medium bowl, whisk in the milk, and then stir in the wine or sherry.

3. Set 8 *pots-de-crème* or small custard cups in a large rectangular baking pan (such as a 9 x 13-inch sheet-cake pan). Ladle the custard equally into the cups, place the pan on the rack in the center of the oven, and carefully pour boiling water around the cups until it comes halfway up their sides. Bake until just set, about 45 to 50 minutes. Remove the cups from the water bath and let them cool completely. Serve at room temperature or slightly chilled.

Among the porcelain in Monticello's collection is a partial service made in France, decorated with cornflower sprigs and including two custard cups.

Burnt Cream

Serves 4

HISTORICAL NOTES: *Today this elegant but easy dessert is known by its suave French name,* crème brûlée, *but in Jefferson's day, the English translation "burnt cream" was more usual. Although Mrs. Trist credited Honoré Julien, Jefferson's French cook at the President's House, the recipe as she and her sister Mrs. Meikleham transcribed it does not do him justice. I've kept only the manuscripts' subtle flavoring of orange zest, a delicate and nice touch, and note that Mrs. Trist adds, "It is usual to season it with lemon … or any thing else you prefer." Rubbing lemon zest into the sugar is one suggestion; scalding the cream with a cinnamon stick or a vanilla bean (see Boiled and Baked Custards, pages 164 and 165) are two more gleaned from the other custard recipes.*

2   **cups heavy cream**
2 - 3   **large pieces orange zest (about ½ orange) (see** Historical Notes)
¾   **cup sugar (approximately)**
6   **large egg yolks**

1. Position a rack in the center of the oven and preheat the oven to 300 degrees. Meanwhile, scald the cream and orange zest over medium-low heat in a heavy-bottomed 2-quart saucepan, stirring frequently to prevent scorching, until it is fragrant and well flavored. Add ½ cup of the sugar, stirring until it is dissolved. Remove and discard the orange zest.

2. Lightly beat the egg yolks in a medium bowl and beat 1 cup of the hot cream into them. Off the heat, stir the yolks into the remaining hot cream. Divide the custard among 4 shallow ramekins or custard cups set in a close-fitting rimmed pan or casserole dish. Carefully pour boiling water around the cups until it comes halfway up their sides. Cover with foil and bake until the custards are set but still jiggling at the center, about 45 minutes. Remove them from the water bath, cool completely, and then cover and chill.

3. Evenly dust the top of each ramekin of custard with 1 tablespoon of sugar. Heat a salamander until it is red hot or prepare a kitchen blowtorch. Hold the salamander just above the top of the custards or torch them until the sugar is melted and caramelized. Take care not to overheat the custard or it could break. Let the sugar cool and harden before serving.

• • •

Note: Monticello, like well-equipped kitchens of those days, had a salamander, an iron disk set on a long handle that could be super-heated and used to brown or glaze delicate foods. Cookware stores still sell salamanders, along with another good modern alternative, the kitchen blowtorch. I find that the broiler overheats the custard, even when it is well chilled.

Chocolate Cream

Serves 6 to 8

HISTORICAL NOTES: *One of two recipes attributed to the enslaved cook James Hemings, this is old-fashioned rennet-clotted custard. It actually survives in modern American cookery, especially in areas where Scandinavians have settled. The Trist and Meikleham recipes call for either homemade rennet or chicken gizzards, for which we now substitute rennet tablets (also called "Junket" tablets, available at specialty grocers and natural foods stores). In the manuscript recipe, the grated chocolate is boiled with the milk as it reduces, which enhances the thickening. But it also makes the chocolate bitter and uneven in the custard and requires constant attention so that the chocolate doesn't settle to the bottom of the pan and scorch. This recipe, adapted for that drawback and for modern pasteurized milk, does not therefore follow the manuscript to the letter. Variants of this cream, also attributed to Hemings, were flavored with coffee and tea (see Variations).*

1   **quart whole milk**

2   **ounces unsweetened chocolate**

¾   **cup sugar**

2   **rennet tablets (also called "Junket" tablets, about .03 ounces each)**

1. Bring the milk to a simmer over medium heat. Let it return to a simmer and cook, stirring frequently, until the milk is reduced by one-quarter to 3 cups.

2. Meanwhile, finely grate the chocolate onto a sheet of wax paper. Gather up the wax paper and slowly pour the chocolate into the hot milk, stirring constantly, and simmer until it is dissolved and smooth, about 5 minutes. Stir in the sugar until dissolved and turn off the heat. Strain it through a fine mesh sieve and let it cool.

3. Dissolve the rennet in 1 tablespoon of water and stir it into the flavored milk. Divide it among 8 *pots-de-crème* or demitasse cups, or 6 small custard cups. Put enough cold water in a large, heavy bottomed pan that will hold all the cups with a little room on all sides of each to come halfway up the sides of the cups, and put in the cups.

4. Bring the water slowly to a simmer over medium-low heat, but don't let it ever actually boil. As soon as the creams are set but still a little jiggly, remove them from the pan (you should be able to lift them out with your bare fingers). Let cool until fully set and serve at room temperature or cover and chill before serving.

• • •

Variations: For tea cream, allow 1 ounce (a generous half cup) whole tea leaves; for coffee cream, 2 ounces (1 full cup) whole dark-roasted coffee beans. Pour the hot milk over them, let the liquid steep 30 minutes, and strain before adding the sugar and rennet. The coffee beans can be rinsed, dried, and re-used. (Tea makes a stronger infusion than whole beans, so less of it is needed.)

Blancmange

Serves 8

HISTORICAL NOTES: *When Jefferson recorded this recipe for "blanc manger," almond paste had to be made from scratch, but good quality paste is readily available today, and I've used it here. Since bitter almonds are unavailable in America, commercial paste probably tastes more authentic than one made only with sweet almonds. I've also added an optional touch of almond extract to imitate the assertive flavor of bitter almonds. Jefferson carefully directed that the cream be strained to make it absolutely smooth, but that yields a less interesting dish and, since Mary Randolph's rendition doesn't mention it, I omit it here. Determined readers may strain it through a fine wire mesh strainer. The original recipes call for isinglass, for which I substitute unflavored gelatin. Lightly oiling the mold to ease the unmolding is my suggestion; it wasn't mentioned in the original.*

5 ounces (rounded ½ cup) almond paste
2 cups heavy cream
¼ teaspoon almond extract (optional)
½ cup cold water
2 envelopes unflavored gelatin
1½ cups boiling water
4 ounces (½ cup) sugar
Raspberry Cream (opposite page)

1. Break up the almond paste in a medium bowl with a fork or in the bowl of an electric mixer fitted with the paddle. Work in ¼ cup of the cream and, when it is fairly smooth, gradually beat in the remaining cream, mixing until smooth and creamy. Taste, and if the almond flavor is not distinctive, add a few drops of almond extract as needed.

2. In a medium bowl, stir the cold water into the gelatin and let it soften for 10 minutes. Stir in the boiling water and stir until the gelatin is completely dissolved. Add the sugar, again stirring until dissolved.

3. Slowly stir the gelatin into the almond cream. Lightly oil a 1½-quart mold with vegetable oil and pour the blancmange into it. Cover and chill in the refrigerator until it is set and firm, about 4 hours.

4. Dip the mold briefly in warm water and run a sharp knife around the edges to loosen the blancmange. Invert onto a deep-rimmed platter or shallow serving bowl and carefully lift off the mold, tapping it once or twice if necessary. Spoon Raspberry Cream around it and serve cold.

• • •

Note: To speed up the setting (and cut the chilling time by half), after the cream is mixed with the gelatin, set the bowl in an ice bath and stir with a rubber spatula until it begins to thicken, about five minutes, then pour it into the prepared mold.

Raspberry Cream

Makes 2½ cups

½ cup raspberry preserves

2 cups heavy cream

HISTORICAL NOTES: *This recipe is exquisitely simple and really quite lovely. Though Jefferson doesn't mention any accompaniments in his recipe for Blancmange, Mary Randolph indicates that Raspberry Cream is de rigueur. The contrast of pink against creamy white is really handsome, but this cream is also a delicious dessert all on its own. To serve it as such, I'd recommend doubling the recipe: this produces a scant 4 servings when it does not accompany anything else. Like most of the creams, it also freezes beautifully and makes sumptuous ice cream. Chill and freeze it as for Peach Ice Cream (page 176).*

1. Stir the preserves to loosen in a medium bowl. Gradually stir in the cream, a little at a time at first, until the cream is smooth and evenly colored a rich pink.

2. Strain the cream to remove the seeds. Cover and place in the refrigerator to chill. To serve as a dessert cream on its own, spoon it into small sherbet glasses and chill thoroughly.

JEFFERSON'S 'REFRIGERATOR'

On June 21, 1802, a civil engineer and practical farmer wrote, "Thomas Moore respectfully invites the President of the United States to examine the condition of Butter in a newly invented Refrigeratory."[41] Jefferson, who had already planned icehouses at the President's House and Monticello (see 175), apparently viewed Moore's invention, jotting a diagram of the refrigerator along with a description of the cooler made from cedar and tin

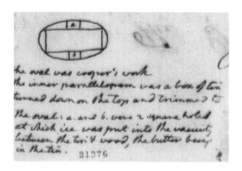

On Thomas Moore's letter inviting Jefferson to view the "refrigeratory," Jefferson jotted his notes and sketch of the device.

and insulated with cloth and rabbit skin. On July 18, 1804, Jefferson recorded in his Memorandum Book that he paid Isaac Briggs, Moore's brother-in-law, thirteen dollars for a refrigerator. Family letters and Jefferson's notes remain silent on the device for fifteen years, until Jefferson visited his retreat home, Poplar Forest, with his granddaughters Ellen and Cornelia. Ellen grumbled to her mother back home that "Grand papa insisted on our using that filthy cooler, (refrigerator, I believe he calls it,) which wasted our small stock of ice, and gave us butter that run about the plate so that we could scarcely catch it, and wine above blood-heat."[42]

—MONTICELLO RESEARCH DEPARTMENT

Savoy Biscuits

Makes 2 dozen

HISTORICAL NOTES: *Jefferson's uneven culinary knowledge is given away by his recipe for sponge cake, or "biscuit de Savoye." While clear as to method, the ingredient amounts are hopelessly wrong; fortunately, Mary Randolph corrected them in* The Virginia House-wife. *I've cut the quantity to bring the yield in line with modern needs. Period methods for sponge cake vary wildly, and I've followed Jefferson's technique, referring to Mary Randolph mainly for proportions. Proper Savoy Biscuits are cooked in oblong molds about the size of a cornstick mold; readers may also use standard muffin or Madeleine tins, though the cooking time for the latter will be less. The tins are usually buttered and coated with superfine sugar, but Mary Randolph suggested lining them with papers much like those for modern cupcakes, and I include them as an alternative. Her recipe also recommends pairing the cake with Wine Sauce (opposite page).*

superfine or granulated sugar, for dusting

6 large eggs

12 ounces (1½ cups) sugar

grated zest of 1 lemon or 1 small orange

5 ounces (1 cup) pastry or cake flour

Wine Sauce, optional (opposite page)

1. Position a rack in the center of the oven and preheat the oven to 350 degrees. Butter 24 Savoy biscuit or standard muffin pans and dust lightly with superfine or granulated sugar, or omit this and line the tins with standard cupcake paper baking cups. Separate the eggs into two bowls. Using a spoon, whisk, or electric mixer fitted with the whisk attachment, beat the egg yolks until smooth. Gradually beat in the sugar until it falls in thick ribbons from the spoon or whisk. Beat in the zest and gradually incorporate the flour. The batter will be fairly stiff.

2. Using a clean bowl, or the bowl of an electric mixer fitted with the whisk, whip the egg whites until they form firm glossy peaks. Fold one-quarter of them into the yolk mixture to soften it, then gently fold in the remaining egg whites, one-third at a time. Spoon the batter into the prepared muffin pans, filling them about two-thirds full. Bake until puffed, golden brown, and set, about 14 to 16 minutes.

3. Place the pans on a wire rack and cool for about 10 minutes. If biscuits were not baked in paper cups, run a sharp knife around their edges to loosen them. Invert the pans, carefully remove the biscuits, and cool completely on wire racks. The biscuits may be served plain, dusted with superfine sugar, or with Wine Sauce.

Wine Sauce

Makes about 1 cup

HISTORICAL NOTES: *This sauce
was frequently used with puddings
and simple cakes. Here, I've used
the same* buerre blanc *whisking
technique recommended for Butter
Sauce over the original methods in
which wine and sugar were either
stirred into Butter Sauce (page 141) or
heated together and gradually beaten
into softened butter. The whisking
technique is easier to control on a
modern range and gives much the
same result. Though Wine Sauce can
be served at room temperature, it must
be made when needed, especially on
a cold day, or the butter may solidify
and become uneven. It should be the
consistency of good thick cream. Mary
Randolph recommended this sauce for
Savoy Biscuits (opposite page) and
it is indeed delicious with them. It
was also commonly served with the
various boiled and baked puddings of
the period.*

½   cup medium dry sherry or Madeira
3 - 4 tablespoons sugar
4   ounces (1 stick) unsalted butter, cut into small bits
¼ - ½ teaspoon freshly grated nutmeg, or the grated zest of ½ lemon

1. Stir together the wine and sugar in a small saucepan until the sugar is dissolved. Bring it to a simmer over medium heat and remove from the heat. Reduce the heat as low as possible.

2. Off the heat, whisk in 3 or 4 bits of butter until almost melted. Whisk in 3 or 4 more and return the pan to the low heat. Continue whisking in butter a few bits at a time until all are incorporated and the sauce is the consistency of thick cream. If it overheats and begins to separate, take it off the heat and whisk in 4 or 5 bits of butter all at once to cool it.

3. Whisk in nutmeg or lemon zest and serve warm or at room temperature.

• • •

Brandy Butter Sauce: Make it exactly as directed for Wine Sauce, substituting ¼ cup of brandy for the wine and omitting the nutmeg and lemon zest.

*This labeled Madeira decanter, excavated from
the Monticello kitchen yard, dates from the 1760s.
English-made, it is decorated with a cartouche and
grapevine motifs. After Jefferson's death, twelve
decanters were recorded in an inventory; some of these
might have been those that he had shipped back from
France in 1790.*

JEFFERSON AND ICE CREAM

"ICE CREAM," AS RECORDED by Jefferson, is certainly the best known—and often, the most misunderstood—of his recipes. Occasionally the recipe serves as a basis

for crediting Jefferson with introducing ice cream to Americans following his return from France. As Karen Hess has observed, however, beginning in 1755 an ice cream recipe appeared in Hannah Glasse's *The Art of Cookery*, a cookbook popular throughout the colonies. Around 1770, the colonial governor of Virginia, Lord Botetourt, served it to guests in Williamsburg.[43] And George Washington acquired a "cream machine for ice" in May 1784, around the same time Jefferson was just leaving for France.[44]

If Jefferson didn't introduce the confection in America, he certainly promoted it. Visitors to the President's House during his administration frequently note ice cream in their observations, and on at least two occasions they enjoyed it enclosed in a warm pastry, perhaps akin to a cream puff. Early in his presidency Jefferson arranged for the installation of an icehouse at the President's House, so the dessert could be enjoyed for much of the year. In anticipa-

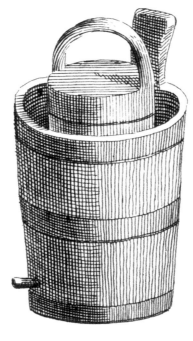

tion of Jefferson's presidential open house on Independence Day 1806, a servant was hired exclusively to turn the ice cream maker.

In his inventory of Monticello's kitchen utensils, cook James Hemings recorded "2 freising molds" that would form ice cream for table presentation, and following Jefferson's death, his daughter Martha Randolph listed an "ice cream freezer" and an "ice cream ladle" among the house's cookware.[45] The family cookery manuscripts contain a wide array of ice cream and ice (sherbet) recipes, all of which would suggest that the Jefferson family enjoyed ice cream regularly.

— B.L.C.

Details from L'Art de Faire Bien de Glace. *Notice the absence of a crank on the early ice cream machines. Courtesy Winterthur Library.*

Vanilla Ice Cream

Makes about 2½ quarts

HISTORICAL NOTES: *This recipe, simply titled "Ice Cream," is possibly the most famous recorded by Jefferson. I present it as he gave it, making an educated guess about the amount of cream since we cannot be sure of the volume of a "bottle." The proportion of egg to liquid is lower than usual, but cream needs fewer eggs, and if we take a bottle to be a quart, the proportion is just right. My guess here, however, is guided more by the amount of sugar, which in ice cream has a function beyond sweetening. If the ratio of sugar to liquid were any less, the cream would freeze harder than could be managed. Use cream that is at least 36 percent milkfat and preferably not ultra-pasteurized. For authenticity and subtlety, use a whole vanilla bean as Jefferson directed; vanilla extract was unknown in those days, and besides, lends a harsh aftertaste.*

- 2 quarts heavy cream
- 1 vanilla bean
- 6 large egg yolks
- 8 ounces (1 cup) sugar

1. Bring the cream and vanilla bean to a simmer in a heavy-bottomed saucepan over medium-low heat, stirring frequently, until fragrant, about 5 minutes. Whisk the egg yolks in a bowl until smooth and whisk in the sugar. It will be quite thick.

2. Slowly beat about 1 cup of the hot cream into the egg yolks and gradually stir this into the hot cream. Cook, stirring constantly, until lightly thickened, enough to coat the back of the spoon, about 5 minutes. Strain the custard through a double layer of cheesecloth or a fine strainer and remove the vanilla bean (it can be rinsed, dried, and re-used). Stir until slightly cooled. Cover and refrigerate until chilled, at least 1 hour or overnight.

3. Freeze the custard in an ice-cream machine according to the manufacturer's directions until set but still a little soft. Scoop the ice cream into a 3-quart mold, or several smaller molds, running the spatula through the ice cream and tapping the mold firmly to remove any air bubbles. Fill the molds completely. Cover and freeze until set, about 2 to 4 hours. The ice cream may also be set without molding it: scoop it into a freezer-safe container and freeze until set.

4. To serve the molded ice cream, dip the mold briefly in hot water, or wrap briefly in a towel heated in the clothes dryer. Run a knife around the top edge to separate the ice cream slightly from the mold. Invert the mold over a serving dish and gently lift the mold from ice cream. If it is not molded, serve in small scoops.

• • •

Note: The ice cream maker of the time, a *sorbetière*, does not produce the smooth, heavily aerated ice cream we know today, nor will a modern churn produce cream that is *glacer au neige*, or "frozen like snow." To imitate that texture, chill the cream in a container (like a rectangular cake pan) in a refrigerator freezer, scraping down the sides and stirring every 10 minutes after the first half hour. Though it can be scooped, ice cream of the day was often set in molds. The molds were usually lidded to seal out the briny ice bath in which it set. An open mold will suffice if care is taken not to completely submerge it when dipping it into hot water before un-molding.

Chocolate Ice Cream

Makes about 1 quart

HISTORICAL NOTES: *Mrs. Meikleham and Mrs. Trist both copied this recipe directly from* The Virginia House-wife, *which may be the oldest American recipe for chocolate ice cream in print. Mrs. Randolph is the first known American cookery writer to give extensive treatment to ice cream—her book provides more than a dozen recipes including a savory one for oyster cream. While it cannot be said that Monticello was the cradle of ice cream in America, Mrs. Randolph's knowledge of the subject was probably fed by the ice creams that were made and served there. Like Jefferson's Vanilla Ice Cream, this is custard based, but there are several important differences: this one uses milk, so there is a higher proportion of eggs (basically double the amount) and more sugar. The texture and flavor of the finished cream is quite different, but equally delicious.*

4   ounces unsweetened chocolate
3   cups whole milk
1   cup heavy cream
1   vanilla bean
8   ounces (1 cup) sugar
    salt
6   large egg yolks

1. Finely grate the chocolate onto a sheet of wax paper. Stir together the milk, cream, and vanilla bean in a heavy-bottomed saucepan. Bring it to a simmer over medium heat, stirring frequently.

2. Add the sugar and a small pinch of salt, stirring until dissolved. Gradually pour in the grated chocolate, stirring constantly, and continue stirring until completely melted.

3. Whisk the egg yolks in a medium bowl until smooth. Gradually beat in about 1 cup of hot chocolate milk and slowly stir the egg yolks back into the simmering liquid. Cook, stirring constantly, until the custard is thickened enough to coat the back of the spoon. Remove from the heat and stir until it is slightly cooled, about 5 minutes. Remove the vanilla bean (it can be rinsed, dried, and re-used).

4. Freeze in an ice-cream machine according to the manufacturer's directions until set but still a little soft. Scoop it into a 3-quart mold, or several smaller molds, running the spatula through the ice cream and tapping the mold firmly to remove any air bubbles. Fill the molds completely. Cover and freeze until set, about 2 to 4 hours. The ice cream may also be set without molding it: scoop it into a freezer-safe container and freeze until set.

5. To serve molded ice cream, dip the mold briefly in hot water, or wrap briefly in a towel heated in the clothes dryer. Run a knife around the top edge to loosen the ice cream from the mold. Invert the mold over a serving dish and gently lift the mold from ice cream. If not molded, serve in small scoops.

THE MONTICELLO ICEHOUSE

IN THE WINTER OF 1802-1803 the summer's harvest of wheat was safely stored in barrels and barns. Monticello overseer Gabriel Lilly had to wait for freezing temperatures before he could harvest his next crop—ice from the Rivanna River. Every available neighborhood wagon was assembled to bring ice from the river to the newly constructed icehouse on the mountaintop. President Jefferson, monitoring the operation from Washington, recorded that it took "62. waggon loads of ice to fill it," and cost $70 for the hire of wagons and food and drink for the drivers.[46]

Jefferson had taken notes on icehouses in Italy and Virginia before he undertook construction of his own. He placed it on the coldest side of the house, under the North Terrace. His drawing shows a cylinder sixteen feet below ground level and six feet above it, with openings at the top "left only 9. I[nches] square that a person may not get in at them."[47]

That specification indicates that more than ice

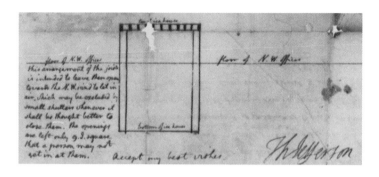

was in the icehouse. "Dishes of butter, cold dressed provisions, salads, etc." were kept in a Philadelphia icehouse of the day, and Monticello's may have been used in a similar way. The preservation of butter and fresh meat was Jefferson's main concern. It would be "a real calamity" if the ice house were not filled, he wrote his overseer in 1809, "as it would require double the quantity of fresh meat in summer had we not ice to keep it."[48] Then there were less critical uses for the ice crop, such as the making of ice cream or the chilling of wine; in 1815, these luxuries were possible until the ice gave out on October 15.

The day before Christmas in 1813, Jefferson wrote: "Filled the ice house with snow."[49] An icehouse at the river took over the primary role while the mountaintop cellar became the "snow house"—and Monticello may be here today because of it. In the spring of 1819 Monticello's North Pavilion caught fire. As Jefferson reported to a friend, "Our snow house enabled us so far to cover with snow the adjacent terras which connected it with the main building as to prevent it's affecting that."[50]

—MONTICELLO RESEARCH DEPARTMENT

Jefferson's March 19, 1802, letter to James Dinsmore, a free workman at Monticello, included a drawing and description of the icehouse at Monticello (above). A modern rendering appears at left.

Peach Ice Cream

Makes about 2 quarts

HISTORICAL NOTES: *This is an important recipe because it is a "real" and not custard-based ice cream. Good cooks generally understood that custard was a substitute for good cream: indeed, one of Mary Randolph's fruit ice cream recipes ends with the note "if good cream can be procured, it is infinitely better—the custard is intended as a substitute when cream cannot be had."[51] It also demonstrates the bounty of flavors of ice cream enjoyed by the Jefferson family—aside from vanilla, chocolate, and peach, the manuscript books also include variations for raspberry, strawberry, citron melons (a variety of musk melon), pineapple, and lemon, as well as recipes for ices (or sherbets) of lemon, cherry, and currant. Mrs. Trist's manuscript attributes the recipe to Mary Randolph, and took it almost verbatim from* The Virginia House-wife, *but it is also credited to Monticello, where it was surely served.*

4 - 6　ripe juicy peaches
　8　ounces (1 cup) sugar
　　　juice of 1 lemon
　　　salt
　1　quart heavy cream

1. Peel the peaches over a large bowl to catch the juice. Pit and roughly chop them, and purée half of them in a food mill or press through a colander into the bowl (a mixture of purée and roughly chopped fruit adds texture). Sprinkle the peaches with about ¼ cup of the sugar and the lemon juice and macerate for at least 30 minutes.

2. Dissolve the remaining sugar and a pinch of salt in the cream. Stir this into the macerated fruit, cover, and chill completely, about 1 hour.

3. Freeze it in an ice-cream machine according to the manufacturer's directions until set but still a little soft. Scoop the ice cream into a 3-quart mold, or several smaller molds, running the spatula through the ice cream and tapping the mold firmly to remove any air bubbles. Fill the molds completely. Cover and freeze until set, about 2 to 4 hours. The ice cream may also be set without molding it: scoop it into a freezer-safe container and freeze until set.

4. To serve molded ice cream, dip the mold briefly in hot water, or wrap briefly in a towel heated in a clothes dryer. Run a knife around the top edge to loosen the ice cream from the mold. Invert the mold over a serving dish and gently lift the mold from ice cream. If not molded, serve in small scoops.

Brandied Peaches

Makes about 4 quarts

HISTORICAL NOTES: *Jefferson copied this recipe out himself, under the title "Pour faire des peches à l'eau-de-vie"—roughly, brandied peaches. As Karen Hess notes, "eau de vie" is really distilled fruit spirits, but we use the term "brandy" loosely in America. Indeed, brandied peaches in many parts of the South are made with bourbon or even moonshine. The recipe is classic, though later renditions do not go through the repeated soaking and boiling given here. Usually, the process is truncated to a single boiling, after which the syrup is boiled down to half its volume and then cut with an equal amount of spirits. The leftover liquid (after the peaches are eaten) makes a potent but delicious cordial. The process is involved but not complicated. Archaeological excavations at Monticello have also unearthed preserved cherries in a bottle, which would've been preserved in much the same way if adventuresome readers wish to experiment.*

4 pounds (about 20 to 24) small slightly under-ripe yellow peaches
1 pound (2 cups) sugar
4 cups eau de vie, brandy, or bourbon

1. Rinse the peaches well under cold running water, rubbing to remove all of the fuzz. Drain well and pierce each one through to the pit in several places with a fork. Fill a large pot with enough water to completely cover the peaches and bring to a boil over medium-high heat. Add the peaches and let it come back to the boiling point. Immediately drain and drop them in cold water. Set aside in a colander to drain.

2. In the same pot, dissolve the sugar in enough water to cover the peaches and bring it to a boil over medium-high heat. Carefully slip the peaches into the pot, let it come back to a boil, and cook until the peaches are tender but still firm, about 20 minutes. Lift them out with a slotted spoon and boil the syrup until it reaches 230 degrees on a candy thermometer. (To test without a thermometer, put a small amount onto a saucer. It should be slightly sticky when rubbed between the fingers.) Let it cool, put the peaches back into it, then cover and let stand for 24 hours.

3. Lift out the peaches, add 2 cups of the brandy or bourbon to the syrup, and bring back to a boil. Remove it from the heat, let cool, and return the peaches to it. Let stand for 24 hours longer.

4. The next day, remove the peaches and boil the syrup one-third at a time, until it registers 230 degrees on a candy thermometer. Stir in the remaining 2 cups of brandy or bourbon and return the fruit to the syrup. Let it come back to a boil and simmer about 5 minutes. Remove from the heat and let cool. Transfer the peaches from the syrup with a clean slotted spoon into sterilized 1-quart jars. Cover with the syrup and seal with sterilized canning lids. Cool and refrigerate, or for prolonged storage, process in a hot water bath for 20 minutes (see Note.)

• • •

Note: For prolonged storage, brandy peaches should be packed in jars especially made for canning, sealed with new lids, and canned using a water-bath processing method following the jar manufacturer's recommended directions.

Snow Eggs

Serves 6

HISTORICAL NOTES: *This is classic French* oeufs à la neige, *which the enslaved cook James Hemings almost certainly learned in France. The recipe appears three times in the Jefferson family manuscripts, twice attributed to Hemings. The manuscripts are quite clear, and I've only cut the scale for a more manageable yield. Orange flower and rose water are old-fashioned flavoring essences that should not be confused with cologne water. Their flavor is subtler and more suave than the ubiquitous vanilla extract that has mostly replaced them. Both are available at specialty grocers and kitchenware stores. The dish survives in modern American cookery as "floating island" (not to be confused with quite a different dish that went by that name in the nineteenth century). The prepared dish is pictured on page 43.*

5 large eggs

5 - 6 ounces (⅔ to ¾ cup) sugar

2 tablespoons orange flower or rose water

2 cups whole milk

2 tablespoons sherry or sweet white wine

1. Separate the eggs, setting aside the yolks, and place the whites in a large metal or glass bowl. Beat the whites with a whisk, or an electric mixer fitted with the whisk, until thick with froth. Gradually beat in 3 to 4 tablespoons of the sugar and continue beating the meringue until it forms firm and glossy peaks. Beat in 1 tablespoon of the flower water.

2. Stir together the milk, remaining sugar, and remaining flower water in a heavy-bottomed 2-quart saucepan. Bring to a simmer over medium heat, stirring frequently to prevent scorching. Reduce the heat to medium low. Drop in heaping tablespoons of meringue (no more than four at a time) and poach, turning once with a skimmer or slotted spoon, until set, about 4 minutes. The meringues will puff considerably as they poach but deflate to half the volume as they cool. Lift them out with a slotted spoon or frying skimmer and drain briefly in a wire mesh colander or towel. Transfer to a serving bowl or individual serving bowls (about three per bowl) and poach the remaining meringue.

3. Whisk the egg yolks in a medium bowl until smooth and gradually beat in 1 cup of the hot milk. Slowly stir this into the simmering milk and cook, stirring constantly, until the custard thickly coats the back of the spoon. Remove from the heat and stir until it has cooled slightly. Stir in the sherry or wine, strain, and keep stirring until cool. Pour the custard over the meringues and serve at room temperature, or cover and chill before serving.

Pancakes Lemaire

Serves 4 to 6

HISTORICAL NOTES: *This recipe entered the family collection when President Jefferson mailed a few recipes gleaned from his butler, Etienne Lemaire, back to his family at Monticello. A little later, he followed up with his daughters, writing: "I presume you were amused with the receipts for making panne-quaiques and other good things."*[32] *What we know today as "pancakes" were then called griddlecakes; "pancakes" were crêpes. The various permutations in the family manuscripts are, unfortunately, rather hopeless, so I've used Mary Randolph's "Quire of Paper Pancakes" in* The Virginia House-wife, *which follows standard French practice and clearly had the same source. Mrs. Randolph says nothing of glazing the top pancake, as the manuscript recipes all indicate, but it was standard practice. I've cut quantities down to suit most modern family tables, but the batter doubles easily. As noted elsewhere, superfine sugar is the closest equivalent to the "powdered" sugar of their day (see Historical Notes, page 161).*

- 2 cups whole milk
- 6 large eggs
- 8 ounces (2 sticks) unsalted butter, melted
- 4 ounces (about ¾ to 1 cup) unbleached all-purpose flour
- ½ teaspoon freshly grated nutmeg
- 1 cup sugar
- ¼ teaspoon salt
- ⅔ cup dry white wine or sherry
  grated zest of 1 lemon
  superfine sugar, as needed
  Wine Sauce (page 171)

1. Scald the milk in a heavy-bottomed saucepan and set aside to cool to about 110 degrees. Whisk the eggs in a large bowl and gradually whisk in the milk and butter until smooth. In another large bowl, sift or whisk together the flour, nutmeg, sugar, and salt. Gradually incorporate the egg and milk mixture into the dry ingredients, whisking until smooth. Whisk in the wine and lemon zest (the batter will be quite thin). Set aside, covered, for at least 1 hour.

2. Lightly dust a warm plate with superfine sugar. Heat a large crêpe pan or non-stick sauté pan (approximately 11 inches in diameter) over medium-high heat and brush lightly with melted butter or vegetable oil. Pour in just enough batter to thinly coat the bottom of the pan and cook until the edges are browned, the bottom is golden brown, and the top is set and completely opaque, about 35 to 45 seconds (they are not turned). Loosen the edges with a spatula, invert it onto the sugar-dusted plate, and lightly sprinkle with superfine sugar. Repeat the process, stacking the pancakes and sprinkling each with sugar to form a cake.

3. Serve warm, slicing them into wedges at the table, with Wine Sauce passed separately.

• • •

Note: The manuscript recipes helpfully suggest stacking the pancakes on an inverted plate (one without a rimmed foot) to make cutting and serving easier. A standard cake plate would also suffice.

Charlotte Monticello

Serves 6

HISTORICAL NOTES: *This charming, old-fashioned recipe had intimate connections to Monticello, as suggested by the fact that Ellen Coolidge requested the recipe from her family. I've followed Mary Randolph's version in* The Virginia House-wife, *which differs little from Mrs. Trist's manuscript but is more coherent. The bread for charlotte must be substantial, preferably made from the recipe included in this book (page 94). Classic French charlottes are baked in molds especially made for them, but we don't know if there was such a mold among those in Monticello's collection of cookware. I use a deep pie plate, but offer an option using a true charlotte mold. A salamander was the original (and still best) utensil used for glazing charlottes, but the oven broiler will do an acceptable job of it. For details on the salamander, refer to the notes for* Burnt Cream (page 166).

3 pounds tart apples, such as Winesap or Granny Smith

4 - 6 ounces (½ to ¾ cup) sugar, plus more for dusting

½ - 1 teaspoon ground cinnamon

½ - 1 teaspoon freshly grated nutmeg

¼ cup water

firm white bread cut in ⅜-inch-thick slices (see step 2)

6 tablespoons unsalted butter

1. Peel, core, and slice the apples. Put them in a large saucepan and add the sugar and spices to taste. Add the water and bring to a simmer over medium heat and cook until the apples are tender but still firm and the juices are almost evaporated and quite thick. Remove from the heat.

2. Trim the crust from enough bread to line the bottom and sides of a 9-inch deep pie plate or 6-cup charlotte mold, slightly overlapping, plus enough to cover the top.

3. Over medium heat, lightly film a large frying pan with some of the butter and add enough bread to fill the pan. Toast until golden on the bottom, remove, add more butter, and toast the second side. Continue in batches until all the bread is toasted.

4. Position a rack in the center of the oven and preheat the oven to 400 degrees. Line the plate or charlotte mold with the bread, overlapping it slightly to completely cover the bottom and sides.

Pour in the apples and cover with the remaining bread, overlapping slightly to completely cover the filling. Put the dish or mold on a rimmed baking sheet.

5. Bake until browned and slightly set, about 15 to 20 minutes for the pie plate, 30 to 40 minutes for the mold. Remove it from the oven and preheat the broiler. Run a knife around the edges to loosen the charlotte, place a heatproof serving plate upside down over it, invert, and carefully lift off the pie plate, leaving the charlotte bottom side up on the plate. If using a mold, wait at least 30 minutes before lifting it away so that charlotte holds its shape. Dust with 2 tablespoons of sugar and broil about 4 inches from the heat until the sugar melts. Watch carefully so that it does not get too brown. Serve warm.

Apple Custard Pie

Makes one 9-inch pie

HISTORICAL NOTES: *Apple custard pies like this survived into modern Southern cooking almost exactly as recorded by both Mrs. Trist and Mrs. Meikleham, except over time they became lighter on butter and are often topped with meringue. At first glance, it may not look like it, but this pie (originally entitled Apple Pudding) is first cousin to Southern pecan pie, since both are buttery transparent custards. There's some disagreement between the sisters' versions and Mary Randolph's rendition. In both manuscripts, the lemon zest is blanched in large pieces and beaten to a pulp. The flavor is of course subtler but also less interesting. I suspect that Monticello's cooks grated the zest into the custard as Mrs. Randolph directed, since it's less fussy, and therefore I've followed her lead in that regard. I've also followed her in baking the apples for the purée rather than boiling them as the sisters directed.*

- 1 pound tart apples, such as Winesap
- ½ recipe puff pastry (see Historical Notes, page 162)
- 4 ounces (1 stick) unsalted butter, softened and creamed
- ½ - ¾ cup sugar, plus more for dusting
- 1 lemon, zest grated and reserved
- ½ - 1 teaspoon freshly grated nutmeg
- 3 large eggs

1. Position a rack in the center of the oven and preheat the oven to 375 degrees. Put the apples in a baking dish and bake until they are tender and soft, about 30 to 40 minutes. Meanwhile, line a 9-inch pie plate with puff pastry, rolling the pastry out a little thinner than 1/8 inch, and prick it well with a fork.

2. Purée the apples through a food mill or wire mesh sieve. (It is not necessary to peel or core them; the utensil will trap the peelings and seeds.) Mix in the butter and sugar to taste while they are warm. Stir in the lemon zest, then halve the lemon and add a little of its juice, as needed, and a generous grating of nutmeg. Lightly beat the eggs in a separate bowl and then stir them into the apple purée. Pour the apple custard into the prepared pastry and bake until the filling is set, about 35 to 40 minutes. Lightly dust the pie with sugar and cool it on a wire rack.

Wine Jelly

Serves 6

HISTORICAL NOTES: *So prized that Jefferson himself copied out a recipe, wine jellies were once delicate and rare confections that have been rendered ordinary by cheap flavored gelatin desserts. The most delicious wine jellies were—and still are—made from gelatin extracted from calves' feet. Unhappily, butchers can rarely supply them, and while veal rib, knuckle (joint), and shank cuts all make very nice jelly, even they have become expensive. I've included notes on the original method, but offer a more accessible, if less delicate, version made with modern powdered gelatin. Because of the structure of powdered gelatin, the flavored liquid should be clarified before it is mixed with the gelatin or it will clog the straining cloth. For cooks who don't care about strict authenticity or pristine presentation, the clarifying step may be omitted, but the jellies will not be as sparkling clear as those served at Monticello (shown on page 64).*

4 large or 6 small lemons

1 teaspoon ground cinnamon

½ teaspoon freshly grated nutmeg

4 cups water

2 cups Madeira or dry sherry

3 cups water

3 large egg whites, shells reserved

8 ounces (1 cup) sugar

¾ ounce (3 envelopes or about 3 tablespoons) granulated gelatin

1 cup cold water

1. Pare the rind from 2 of the lemons in long pieces with a vegetable peeler or sharp paring knife. Juice the lemons and strain into a 2-quart saucepan. Add the rind, spices, and water. Bring it to a boil over medium heat, reduce the heat to medium low, and simmer 5 minutes. Stir in the Madeira or sherry and let it cool.

2. Beat the egg whites until frothy. Crush the shells and beat them into the whites. Stir this into the wine mixture, return it to medium-low heat, and bring it slowly to a simmer. Meanwhile, wet a large piece of muslin (un-dyed plain cotton fabric), wring it out thoroughly, and line a wire strainer with it. Set this over a bowl that will just hold the strainer near its rim.

3. When the egg has solidified and floated to the top, push it to one side and check the clarity of the liquid. If it is clear, skim most of the egg away and ladle the liquid into the strainer. Leave it to slowly drip into the bowl. (This takes some time, so be patient and do not stir or agitate it.) The liquid that drips through the strainer should be perfectly clear.

4. Clean the saucepan and return the clarified liquid to it. Bring it back to a simmer over medium heat, stir in the sugar until dissolved, and simmer until the liquid is clear again. Meanwhile, put the gelatin in a large bowl and stir in the cool water. Let soften for 10 minutes and stir in the hot liquid. Continue stirring until the gelatin is completely dissolved and the liquid is somewhat cooled. To speed up the cooling process, set the bowl in an ice bath and stir constantly until it is cold but not yet beginning to jell.

5. Pour it into small, stemmed glasses or shallow champagne goblets, cover, and chill until set, about 4 hours. Alternatively, the jelly may set in a shallow pan, then be broken up with a spoon or knife, and spooned into stemmed glasses.

**Wine Jelly
(continued)**

To make Wine Jellies the old way, with bones:
Making the jelly as was originally done with veal
bones is involved but not complicated. You will
need to begin at least a day, and preferably two days,
ahead. Rinse 4 pounds of veal shank, rib, or knuckle
(joint) and cover them with 8 cups water in a heavy-
bottomed Dutch oven. Bring slowly to a simmer over
medium-low heat, skimming away any scum that rises,
and simmer gently until the meat scraps are literally
falling off the bones and the liquid is reduced by half,
about 4 hours. Turn off the heat and let it cool. Strain,
cool, cover, and refrigerate the broth until the fat is
hardened on top (4 to 6 hours or overnight). Lift
off the fat and discard it. Put the jelly in a heavy-
bottomed pan, leaving behind the solids at the bottom
of the bowl. Add the wine, sugar, lemon rind, and

spices and heat until the jelly is just melted and the
sugar dissolved. Let it cool slightly and then clarify
and finish the jelly as directed in the recipe above.

• • •

A note on other bones: Wine jelly can be made, as
Mary Randolph noted in *The Virginia House-wife*,
with other bones: the color of beef, lamb, and mutton
jelly is deeper, pork is lighter and similar in color to
veal jelly, and chicken is more golden. Cooks who wish
to experiment with other bones might try beef, lamb
or pork ribs, shank or neck bones, or chicken wing
tips, backs and feet (the latter are often available in
ethnic markets).

*Three different styles of Monticello jelly glasses are known (above). Following Jefferson's death,
Martha Randolph's inventory noted "21 cut & 3 plain jelly glasses."*

Beverages at Monticello

ALTHOUGH THE BEVERAGE most commonly associated with Monticello is wine, a variety of drinks appear in family records, visitors' accounts, and correspondence.

Jefferson wrote that "malt liquors & cyder are my table drinks."[53] The North Orchard at Monticello was dedicated to cider apples, and Jefferson's records include dozens of references to cider production. Bottling cider was no easy task. One Monticello overseer recalled that the process took two weeks, noting, "Mr. Jefferson was very particular about his cider."[54] After a bottling in 1793 Martha Randolph informed her father: "Of the 140 bottles [of cider] that were put away you will hardly find 12. It flew in such a manner as to render it dangerous…. Those that were carelessly corked forced their corks, the rest burst the bottles amongst which the havoc is incredible."[55] When Monticello's cider production was unequal to its demand, Jefferson purchased the drink from neighbors. Like all provisions in the cellars, cider was carefully guarded. In 1801 Thomas Mann Randolph wrote to President Jefferson when 80 gallons of cider disappeared from a storage room despite two locks.[56]

Beer was also produced at Monticello, beginning with Jefferson's marriage in 1772 to Martha Wayles Skelton, whose account book shows almost biweekly brewings of about 15 gallons of "small beer" (with relatively low alcohol).[57] Following her death, brewing activity halted, and Jefferson's accounts include regular purchases of the beverage. Beginning in 1793, Jefferson's letters occasionally suggest an interest in resuming beer production at home, an idea that came to fruition during the War of 1812, when Joseph Miller, an English brewer, was interned in Albemarle County. Jefferson befriended Miller, who then oversaw Jefferson's establishment of a brewhouse and trained cook Peter Hemings in the art of brewing. Hemings learned so well that Jefferson suggested James Madison send someone from nearby Montpelier for him to train in turn, writing: "our malter and brewer is uncommonly intelligent and capable of giving instruction if your pupil is as ready at comprehending it."[58]

Jefferson deemed coffee "the favorite drink of the civilised world,"[59] and it appeared regularly on his grocery orders. He preferred the "well ripened coffee of the W. Indies." Karen Hess notes that not only was his coffee imported, but so also were the proportions of his recipe, far stronger than typically prepared in America. In retirement, Jefferson estimated that his household consumed one pound of coffee daily and one pound of tea in three weeks, often specifying "Hyson" tea.

A host of other drinks appear in documents, such as family letters suggesting that a silver service vessel was called "the duck" and used for serving chocolate.[60] A granddaughter's recipe mentions lemonade, and Jefferson recorded the production of peach mobby, a form of brandy. Grocery orders sometimes included "syrop of punch" to be mixed, presumably, with rum, which also appears among purchases, along with whiskey and French brandy. Perhaps this rum punch is the one the Chevalier de Chastellux enjoyed with Jefferson in the Monticello Parlor: "And before we realized it, book and bowl had carried us far into the night."[61]

—Monticello Research Department

Chocolate

Serves about 12

HISTORICAL NOTES: *Housewives rarely recorded beverages that they enjoyed daily. For example, the recipe that survives in Jefferson's hand for brewing coffee is the exception because it differed from standard practice. Likewise, Mary Randolph details a recipe for cakes that are eaten with chocolate in* The Virginia House-wife, *but gives no recipe for the beverage, nor do we find one in the manuscripts. For chocolate that would have been served in the "duck" (see page 78) at Monticello, Karen Hess directed me to Maria Eliza Rundell,* A New System of Domestic Cookery *(third edition, Exeter, 1808), a copy of which was at Monticello. There we find: "Cut a cake of chocolate in very small bits; put a pint of water into the pot, and, when it boils, put in the above…. When wanted, put a spoonful or two into milk, boil it with sugar, and mill it well."*

2 cups water

4 ounces unsweetened chocolate, finely grated

10 cups whole milk, for serving

sugar, for serving

1. Bring the water to a boil in a heavy-bottomed saucepan. Remove from the heat and whisk in the chocolate until completely melted. Return the pan to medium-low heat and cook, whisking constantly, until it begins to simmer and is smooth and thick. Remove from the heat. If making ahead, pour into a bowl to cool, transfer it to a jar, seal, and store in a cool place. It will keep about 2 weeks.

2. To serve, allow 2 to 3 tablespoons for every 6 ounces of whole milk (for the entire amount, allow 10 cups). Whisk them together in a heavy-bottomed saucepan until smooth and sweeten to taste with sugar. Bring to a simmer over medium heat, whisking constantly until hot and frothy.

Serve in a warm chocolate pot, pitcher, or in mugs.

• • •

Note: The size of "a cake" of chocolate is challenging. Typically it was 1 ounce, but in this instance, 1 ounce makes a thin, watery elixir, a spoonful of which barely tinted 6 ounces of milk, let alone added flavor. I added grated chocolate an ounce at a time until I had an elixir that made something that would reasonably flavor the milk with chocolate and 4 ounces was just about right—jiving roughly with the proportions of other period recipes, though still not quite so rich.

Raspberry Vinegar

Makes about 2½ cups for use as vinegar, or 3½ cups for use as syrup

HISTORICAL NOTES: *Although used mostly as a salad condiment today, originally this beautiful ruby-red vinegar was used as a beverage. Before the advent of soft drinks, vinegar syrups mixed with ice water were popular as a cooling summer drink. This recipe first entered the family collection when Jefferson requested a recipe for vinegar syrup from Lemaire, likely to be used in making rum punch. In his reply, Lemaire added a variation for raspberry vinegar. The recipe was later adapted and copied out into an account book at Monticello, and Mary Randolph gives an extravagant and aromatic rendition of it in* The Virginia House-wife. *Both Lemaire and Mrs. Randolph called for sweetening the vinegar to make a syrup, but I have here followed the account book version, so that readers may use the vinegar as they choose, either as an excellent salad vinegar or sweetened as a beverage.*

1 pound (4 cups) fresh or frozen raspberries

2 cups red wine vinegar

1 cup Simple Syrupm, optional (recipe follows)

1. If using fresh berries, rinse them under cold running water and drain well. Put them into a stainless steel or glass bowl and lightly crush them. If using frozen berries, put them in the bowl while still frozen. Crushing them is not necessary. Stir in the vinegar, cover with cheesecloth or wire mesh screen (a large mesh colander or frying splatter screen would be ideal), and let stand 48 hours.

2. Strain the vinegar through a wire strainer (lined with cheesecloth if the mesh is not fine enough to catch all the solids). The vinegar can be bottled, sealed, and used as is, both as a base for beverages and as a condiment. To use it as a beverage, allow 2 to 3 tablespoons per 8 ounces of ice water and sweeten to taste.

3. To make raspberry vinegar syrup for use as a beverage, mix the vinegar with Simple Syrup. Allow 3 to 4 tablespoons (or to taste) for every 8 ounces of ice water.

⋯

Simple Syrup: Stir 1 cup sugar and 1 cup water together in a heavy-bottomed saucepan. Bring to a simmer over medium heat and simmer until it is reduced to the consistency of honey (230 degrees on a candy thermometer), about 1 cup. Take it from the heat and cool it before using.

Short Titles and Abbreviations

Bear	James A. Bear, Jr., ed., *Jefferson at Monticello.* Charlottesville: University Press of Virginia, 1967.
DLC	Library of Congress.
EWRC	Correspondence of Ellen Wayles Randolph Coolidge, Albert and Shirley Small Special Collections Library, ViU. Transcriptions posted online as part the Family Letters Project, Thomas Jefferson Foundation, Inc., 2004. http://familyletters.dataformat.com/.
Family Letters	Edwin M. Betts and James A. Bear, Jr., eds., *The Family Letters of Thomas Jefferson.* Charlottesville, 1986.
FB	Thomas Jefferson's original Farm Book, reproduced in facsimile in FBB.
FBB	Edwin M. Betts, ed., *Thomas Jefferson's Farm Book.* Princeton, 1953. Reprint, Charlottesville: Thomas Jefferson Memorial Foundation, Inc., 1999.
GB	Edwin M. Betts, ed., *Thomas Jefferson's Garden Book.* Philadelphia: The American Philosophical Society, 1944. Reprint, Charlottesville: Thomas Jefferson Memorial Foundation, Inc., 1999.
Jefferson Library	Jefferson Library, Monticello, Charlottesville, VA.
MB	James A. Bear, Jr., and Lucia C. Stanton, eds., *Jefferson's Memorandum Books: Accounts, with Legal Records and Miscellany, 1767-1826.* Princeton, 1997.
MHi	Massachusettes Historical Society, Boston.
MJR	Martha Jefferson Randolph.
Papers	Julian P. Boyd, et al., eds., *The Papers of Thomas Jefferson.* 31 vols. to date. Princeton, 1950– .
Papers, Retirement Series	J. Jefferson Looney, et al., eds., *The Papers of Thomas Jefferson, Retirement Series.* 1 vol. to date. Princeton, 2005–.
Smith	Smith, Margaret Bayard, *The First Forty Years of Washington Society.* Edited by Gaillard Hunt. New York: Charles Scribner's Sons, 1906. Reprint, New York: Frederick Ungar Publishing Co., 1965.
TJ	Thomas Jefferson.
TJR	Thomas Jefferson Randolph.
ViU	Special Collections, Alderman Library, University of Virginia, Charlottesville.

NOTES

Jefferson's Place in American Food History

1. In Dumas Malone's six-volume, Pulitzer Prize-winning biography, *Jefferson and His Time,* for instance, the index for volume six contains entries for architecture and books, but the few (and terse) references to hospitality are buried under the "Monticello" entry. There are no entries or sub-entries referring to food, wine, cooking, or the like.

2. The entire quote as often cited is "Thomas Jefferson came home so Frenchified, he abjured his native victuals in favor of French cuisine." Dumas Malone, however, refers to this quote as a "'purported' saying" in *Jefferson and His Time* (Boston: Little, Brown & Company, 1948-1977), 6:384. The earliest known citation of the quote appears in Henry S. Randall, *The Life of Thomas Jefferson* (New York, 1858), III:508.

3. Katherine E. Harbury, *Colonial Virginia's Cooking Dynasty* (Columbia: University of South Carolina Press, 2004), 58.

4. Jefferson to William Short, 7 May 1784, *Papers,* 7:229.

5. Grevin packing list, Short Papers, DLC, *Papers,* 18:34-38.

6. TJ to Maria Jefferson Eppes, 18 Jan. 1803, *Family Letters,* 241.

7. TJ to James Madison, 28 Oct. 1785, *Papers,* 8:683; TJ to James Madison, 17 Sept. 1787, *Papers,* 12:137.

8. TJ to Nicholas Lewis, Paris, 17 Sept. 1787, *Papers,* 12:134.

9. Charles Willson Peale to TJ, 2 Mar. 1812, DLC, *GB,* 483.

10. TJ to Bernard McMahon, 16 Feb. 1812, DLC, *GB,* 479. Jefferson notes that it was never grown before in the U.S.

11. TJ to John Wayles Eppes, 24 Mar. 1811, CSmH, excerpted in Karen Hess, *Mr. Jefferson's Table: The Culinary Legacy of Monticello* (Chapel Hill: University of North Carolina Press, forthcoming).

12. According to E. M. Sowerby's *Catalogue of the Library of Thomas Jefferson* (Charlottesville: University Press of Virginia, 1983), #1182, Jefferson owned Sir Benjamin Thompson, Count von Rumford's multi-volume *Essays, Political, Economical, and Philosophical (1798-99),* which features the essay on fireplaces and kitchen arrangements.

13. First quote and second quotes from *William Plumer's Memorandum of the Proceedings in the United States Senate* (New York, 1923), 212-3 and 547. Third from Thomas Jefferson Randolph Memoirs, 1805-06 winter, ViU.

14. TJ to David R. Williams, 31 Jan. 1806, DLC.

15. Marquis de Chastellux, *Travels in North America,* ed. by Howard C. Rice, Jr. (Chapel Hill, 1963), II:392. He is specifically referring to after-dinner conversation in the Monticello Parlor.

16. Diary of Hetty Ann Barton, May 1803, at the Historical Society of Pennsylvania, Philadelphia.

17. William Plumer, 3 Dec. 1804, in *Memorandum of Proceedings,* 212-13.

18. Mahlon Dickerson to Silas Dickerson, 21 Apr. 1802, at New Jersey Historical Society, in Donald Jackson, *Letters of the Lewis and Clark Expedition with Related Documents, 1783–1854* (Urbana and Chicago: University of Illinois Press, 1978), 2:677.

19. Smith, Aug. 1809, 65; August 1809; Daniel Webster, Dec. 1824 in Charles M. Wiltse and Harold D. Moser, eds., *The Papers of Daniel Webster* (Hanover: University Press of New England, 1974), 1:371. (Hereafter *Webster Papers.*)

20. George Ticknor, Feb. 1815, in *Life, Letters, and Journals* (Boston, 1876), I:36.

21. TJ to Dr. Vine Utley, 21 Mar. 1819, in Merrill D. Peterson, ed., *Thomas Jefferson: Writings* (New York: Library of America, 1984), 1416. (Hereafter Peterson, *Writings.*) Ellen Randolph Coolidge to Henry S. Randall, 13 Feb. 1856, Ellen Wayles Coolidge Letterbook, ViU. TJR to Henry S. Randall, Randall, III:675. Webster's notes of a visit to Monticello in 1824, in *Webster Papers,* IV:371. Bacon recollections in Bear, 73.

Nourishing the Congress

1. Smith, 12, 391.

2. TJ to Philippe Létombe, 22 Feb. 1801, MHi.

3. Ellen Randolph Coolidge to Henry S. Randall, 13 Feb. 1856, Ellen Coolidge Letterbook, 48, ViU.

4. Philippe Létombe to TJ, 26 Mar. 1801, DLC. Jefferson had at first hoped to persuade his former slave James Hemings to come to the President's House as chef. Hemings, after several years of training with Parisian chefs, presided over Jefferson's kitchens in Paris and Philadelphia until his emancipation in 1796. For reasons that are not entirely clear, negotiations broke down and Hemings continued in his post at a Baltimore tavern, except for several months spent preparing meals at Monticello in the summer of 1801. James Hemings died a suicide in October; see Lucia Stanton, *Free Some Day: The African-American Families of Monticello* (Charlottesville: Thomas Jefferson Foundation, Inc., 2000), 125-129.

5. TJ to Joseph Rapin, 17 Apr. 1801, MHi.

6. Augustus John Foster, *Jeffersonian America,* ed. Richard Beale Davis (San Marino, CA, 1954), 9.

7. As TJ wrote to Thomas Lomax, "If we can once more get social intercourse restored to it's pristine harmony, I shall believe we have not lived in vain" (25 Feb. 1801, DLC).

8. A number of printed invitation cards in this format, with names filled in by TJ's secretaries, as well as blank invitation cards in other formats, survive.

9. Smith, 391.

10. William Plumer, *Memorandum of Proceedings,* 213 (3 Dec. 1804); Benjamin H. Latrobe to Mary Elizabeth Latrobe, 24 Nov. 1802, *The Correspondence and Miscellaneous Papers of Benjamin Henry Latrobe,* ed. John C. Van Horne et al. (New Haven, 1984) 1:232. (Hereafter *Latrobe Papers.*)

11. Hetty Ann Barton diary, May 1803.

12. Thomas J. Randolph recollections, ViU: 1837.

13. Details of the presidential servants' livery are in the invoices of tailor Thomas Carpenter in ViU and MHi.

14. William Parker Cutler and Julia Perkins Cutler, *Life Journals and Correspondence of Rev. Manasseh Cutler* (Cincinnati, 1888) 2:71-72.

15. Cutler, *Life,* 2:155 (23 Feb. 1804); Latrobe, *Latrobe Papers,* 1:232 (24 Nov. 1802); Plumer, *Memorandum of Proceedings,* 212-213 (3 Dec. 1804).

16. Cutler, *Life*, 2:155 (23 Feb. 1804); Samuel Latham Mitchill to Catharine Mitchill, 10 Jan. 1802, *Harper's New Monthly Magazine* 58 (Apr. 1879): 744; William Plumer, Jr., *Life of William Plumer*, ed. A. P. Peabody (Boston, 1857), 246 (24 Dec. 1802); Latrobe, *Latrobe Papers*, 1:232 (24 Nov. 1802); Charles Willson Peale diary, June 1804, *The Selected Papers of Charles Willson Peale and His Family*, ed. Lillian B. Miller et al. (New Haven, 1988) 2:693; Plumer, *Memorandum of Proceedings*, 212 (3 Dec. 1804).

17. Smith, 391.

18. Isaac A. Coles diary, 31 Mar.-3 Apr. 1807, copy in Jefferson Library.

19. TJ to Philippe Létombe, 22 Feb. 1801, MHi. Lemaire's recipes outnumber those of Julien in the collection preserved in Jefferson's family.

20. Latrobe, *Latrobe Papers*, 1:232 (24 Nov. 1802); Plumer, *Memorandum of Proceedings*, 547 (27 Dec. 1806); Mitchill to Mitchill, 10 Feb. 1802, *Harper's New Monthly Magazine* 58: 744 (Apr. 1879).

21. Lemaire accounts, 1806-1809, Henry E. Huntington Library, San Marino, CA.

22. Ibid.

23. Lemaire list of provisions from Bordeaux, Feb. 1806, MHi.

24. Isaac A. Coles diary, 31 Mar.-3 Apr. 1807.

25. Thomas J. Randolph recollections, ViU: 1837.

26. TJ to Etienne Lemaire, 25 Apr. 1809, MHi.

27. TJ to William Short, 24 Nov. 1821, College of William and Mary.

28. Smith, 391-2.

French Influence in Monticello's Kitchen

1. Bear, 12-13. Much of our understanding of the Monticello kitchen derives from the work of Ann Lucas and Kathy Revell.

2. *Webster Papers*, 1:371.

3. Jefferson owned several editions of Andrea Palladio's *Four Books of Architecture* over the course of his lifetime. The architectural treatise illustrates antique Roman buildings and Palladio's own designs, and served as one of the primary sources for Jefferson's interpretation of classicism in American architecture.

4. Bear, 3; TJ to Archibald Thweatt, 29 May 1810, DLC.

5. TJ, contract regarding the emancipation of James Hemings, 15 Sept. 1793, MHi, in *FB*, 15.

6. "Monticello Historic Structure Report, Vol. 4: Description and Analysis of Cellars and Dependencies," Mesick Cohen Waite Architects, February, 1992, and "Analysis of the Cellars and South Offices at Monticello," Mark R. Wenger, et al, Colonial Williamsburg Foundation, December, 2000. For architectural plans and commentary, see William L. Beiswanger, *Monticello in Measured Drawings* (Charlottesville: Thomas Jefferson Memorial Foundation, 1998).

7. R.L. Mégroz, *The Cook's Paradise being William Verral's 'Complete System of Cookery'* (London: Sylvan Press, 1948), 26.

8. TJ to William Short, 7 May 1784, *Papers*, 7:229.

9. For a detailed discussion of James Hemings, Peter Hemings, Edith Fossett, and other enslaved workers at Monticello, see Lucia Stanton, *Free Some Day: The African-American Families of Monticello*.

10. Few original stew stoves survive in historic American kitchens (an example can be found at the Rundlett-May House in Portsmouth, NH), but several have been re-created at sites such as the Governor's Palace in Williamsburg, the Octagon in Washington, D.C., and the Hermann-Grima House in New Orleans, to name a sampling. As several of his cooks learned French cookery on it, Jefferson obviously knew of the stew stove at the President's House. In addition to the eight-opening stew stove in Monticello's kitchen, Jefferson had a smaller one installed at Poplar Forest, his retreat in Bedford County, VA.

11. Jefferson owned Sir Benjamin Thompson, Count von Rumford's multi-volume *Essays, Political, Economical, and Philosophical* (1798-1799), which contains relevant essays such as "On the Construction of Kitchen Fireplaces and Kitchen Utensils" and "Of the Construction of Saucepans and Stewpans for Fixed Fireplaces"). Listed in Sowerby, #1182.

12. See Thomas Webster, *An Encyclopedia of Domestic Economy* (NY: Harper & Brothers, 1845), 808.

13. Grevin Packing List, July 17, 1790, Short Papers, DLC, *Papers*, 18:34-38.

14. Thomas Jefferson to Henry Foxhall, March 24, 1809, MHi. Jefferson ordered eight two-piece sets of 'cheeks' and grates, in three different sizes: three small, three medium, and two large.

15. July 17, 1790, Short Papers, DLC.

16. February 20, 1796, DLC.

17. MJR inventory, circa 1826, MHi.

Women and Housekeeping at Monticello

1. "Song Dreamed at Daybreak this, April 1. 1818," Thomas Mann Randolph, Jr., in the commonplace book of Virginia Jefferson Trist, ViU. I would like to thank Diane Ehrenpreis, Ann Lucas, and Cinder Stanton for conversation that inspired and contributed to my thinking for this essay.

2. Martha Wayles Skelton Jefferson died after bearing six children in ten years. Two children survived to adulthood and only Martha Jefferson Randolph outlived Thomas Jefferson. Maria Jefferson Eppes died in 1804 from complications of childbirth.

3. See the family tree, page 30. Martha Jefferson Randolph had her first child in 1791 at age nineteen and her twelfth in 1818 at age forty-five. Eleven lived to adulthood.

4. Diary entry from 11 Jan. 1839, Ellen Randolph Coolidge diary, 1838-1839, MHi.

5. Mary Randolph to Virginia Randolph, 27 Dec. 1821, Nicholas P. Trist Papers, Southern Historical Collection, University of North Carolina Library, Chapel Hill (NcU).

6. Virginia Randolph to Nicholas Trist, 2 Jan. 1823, Nicholas P. Trist Papers, DLC; Mary Randolph to Ellen Randolph Coolidge, 11 Sept. 1825, Jefferson-Coolidge Family Collection, ViU. For further reading see Catherine Clinton, *The Plantation Mistress: Woman's World in the Old South* (New York: Pantheon Books, 1982).

7. Virginia Randolph to Nicholas Trist, 2 Jan. 1823, Nicholas P. Trist Papers, DLC; Mary Randolph to Ellen Randolph Coolidge, 11 Sept. 1825, Jefferson-Coolidge Family Collection, ViU.

8. For slavery and the Monticello plantation, see Lucia Stanton, *Slavery at Monticello* (Charlottesville: Thomas Jefferson Foundation, 1996) and *Free Some Day: The African-American Families of Monticello*.

9. Bear, 3.
10. Virginia Randolph to Nicholas P. Trist, 21 July 1823, Nicholas P. Trist Papers, DLC.
11. Martha Jefferson Randolph and Mary Randolph Account Book, ca. 1822-1827, Private collection. Copy at Jefferson Library. I am grateful to Leigh Sellers and Heidi Hackford for assistance with the account book.
12. Anne Cary Randolph Account Book, 1805-1808, DLC.
13. Bear, 114.
14. Mary Randolph to Virginia Randolph, 31 Jan. 1822, Nicholas P. Trist Papers, NcU.
15. Virginia Trist to Nicholas Trist, 4 Sept. 1822, Nicholas P. Trist Papers, DLC.
16. Ellen Randolph to Nicholas Trist, 30 Mar. 1824, Nicholas P. Trist Papers, DLC.
17. Ellen Randolph to MJR, 27 Sept. 1816, ViU: 9090.
18. TJR's assertion in a draft letter ca. 1873, ViU: 8937.
19. Ellen Randolph to Virginia Randolph, 31 Aug. 1819, Jefferson-Coolidge Family Collection, ViU.
20. Bear, 121.

African Americans and Monticello's Food Culture

1. Bear, 51.
2. Peter J. Hatch, *The Gardens at Thomas Jefferson's Monticello* (Charlottesville: Thomas Jefferson Foundation, Inc., 2005 edition), 45. Hatch compiled information from family account books; microfilm at Jefferson Library.
3. TJ to Thomas Mann Randolph, 4 Feb. 1800, *Papers*, 31:360.
4. TJ to MJR, 2 Nov. 1802, in *Family Letters*, 238-239.
5. Ellen Wayles Randolph Coolidge to MJR, 20 Nov. 1825, EWRC.
6. Recorded by Septimia Randolph Meikleham, in the collection of the Thomas Jefferson Foundation. Printed as SRM 74 in Hess, *Mr. Jefferson's Table*.
7. Ellen Wayles Randolph to MJR, 28 July 1819, ViU. "Miss Edgeworth" is Maria Edgeworth (1767-1849), author of moral tales for young people.
8. Salt: TJ to Jeremiah Goodman, 8 Sept. 1813, *FBB*, 185. Peas and potatoes: *FB*, 46 (July 1795); TJ to Thomas Mann Randolph, 1 June 1797, DLC. Milk: TJ memorandum, 29 Sept. 1806, Bear, 63; TJ to Jeremiah Goodman, Dec. 1811, *GB*, 167.
9. TJ to Jeremiah Goodman, 8 Sept. 1813, *FBB*, 185.
10. Eliza Trist to Nicholas P. Trist, 25 Aug. 1819, DLC.
11. *FB*, 77, undated.
12. Russell Smith account, traveling across Virginia to Richmond and Charlottesville, summer 1844, transcription at Jefferson Library.
13. TJ to Jeremiah Goodman, 8 Sept. 1813, *FBB*, 185.
14. TJR recollections, ViU: 1397.
15. 28 May 1811, *FB*, 137.
16. TJR recollections, ViU: 1397.
17. Wendell P. Dabney, *Cincinnati's Colored Citizens* (Cincinnati, 1926), 180, 349.
18. *Cincinnati Enquirer*, 13 Aug. 1901. For more information about slavery and African American families at Monticello, see Lucia Stanton, *Slavery at Monticello* and *Free Some Day: The African-American Families of Monticello*, both invaluable in the preparation of this essay.

19. TJ to William Short, 7 May 1784, *Papers*, 7:229.
20. TJ, contract regarding the emancipation of James Hemings, 15 Sept. 1793, MHi, in *FB*, 15.
21. Etienne Lemaire to TJ, 6 May 1809, MHi, *Papers, Retirement Series*, 1:189.

Provisioning the Table

1. Bear, 73.
2. TJ to James Brown, 8 Aug. 1790, *Papers*, 17:321-22.
3. TJ to George Jefferson, 12 June 1809, *Papers, Retirement Series*, 1:267-8.
4. Ibid., 1:268.
5. TJ to Edmund Rogers, 14 Feb. 1824, Colonial Williamsburg Foundation, Inc., Williamsburg, VA. Transcription from microfilm.
6. TJ to Gordon, Trokes & Company, 25 July 1809, *Papers, Retirement Series*, 1:368-9.
7. TJ to Mr. Ashlin, 20 Apr. 1812, and TJ to Mathew Wills, 26 Apr. 1812, *GB*, 485, 487.
8. TJ, 29 July 1814, *GB*, 525.
9. Ibid., 583.
10. See Anne Cary Randolph's Records at Monticello, DLC, and, with a greater number of fish entries, the Randolph Memorandum Book, copy at Jefferson Library.
11. TJ to Stephen Cathalan, Jr., 3 July 1815, DLC. During Jefferson's public service, he kept business and personal letters entirely separate.
12. TJ to William Few, 3 Jan. 1808, *GB*, 361-62.
13. TJ to his overseer, Jeremiah Goodman, 6 Jan. 1815, *GB*, 539.
14. Etienne Lemaire to TJ, 6 May 1809, *Papers, Retirement Series*, 1:188.
15. TJ to TJR, 16 Apr. 1810, *Family Letters*, 396-97.
16. TJ to Bernard Peyton, 19 July 1819. MHi.
17. TJ to George Jefferson, 19 June 1808, *FB*, 205-06.
18. TJ to George Jefferson, 11 Feb. 1805, *FB*, 186. For information on TJ's problems with the dilution of wine, see Sir Augustus John Forster, *Jeffersonian America*, Richard Beale Davis, ed. (San Marino, CA: The Huntington Library, 1954), 153.
19. TJ to George Jefferson, 19 June 1808, *FB*, 205-06. See also TJ to MJR, 12 May 1793, in which he stated that some items must "remain at Richmond till they can be carried up by water, as to put them into a wagon would be a certain sacrifice of them." *Papers*, 26:18.
20. TJ, inventory of cellar holdings, 1 Feb. 1826, *MB*, 1415.

Jefferson's Favorite Vegetables

1. TJ to Dr. Vine Utley, 21 Mar. 1819, in Peterson, *Writings*, 1416.
2. TJ to William Thornton, 11 Oct. 1809, *GB*, 416; TJ to Thomas Mann Randolph, 30 Mar. 1792, *GB*, 175.
3. "The 1806 Market Accounts of Etienne Lemaire," translated by Amy Rider (19 Aug. 1996) for the Colonial Williamsburg Foundation, served as the source for information about produce purchased for Jefferson's presidential dinners.
4. Mary Randolph, *The Virginia House-wife*, ed. by Karen Hess (Columbia: University of South Carolina Press, 1984), 116.
5. TJ, "Notes of a Tour into the Southern Parts of France, &c," 19-23 Mar. 1787, *Papers*, 11:424; TJ to John Rutledge, Jr., 19 Jan. 1788, *GB*, 134.
6. TJ to Anne Cary Randolph, 22 Mar. 1808, *GB*, 368.

7. "Thomas Mann Randolph's Speech before Albemarle Agricultural Society," 18 June 1824, in *American Farmer*, vol. VI, no. 13, 97.
8. General John Mason to TJ, 22 Jan. 1809, *GB*, 403.
9. *Virginia House-wife*, 126.
10. *GB*, 474.
11. TJ to Benjamin Hawkins, 1 Apr. 1792, *GB*, 176.
12. *Virginia House-wife*, 121.
13. *Virginia House-wife*, 122.
14. *MB*, 16 Sept. 1821.
15. From "Receipts Recorded by Virginia Randolph Trist," catalogued as "Martha Jefferson Randolph Recipes," #5385-F, ViU. Printed as "VRT S 83" in Hess, *Mr. Jefferson's Table*.
16. Nicholas P. Trist to Virginia R. Trist, Oct. 1829, Trist Papers, NcU.

Jefferson's Table: Evidence and Influences

1. Earliest citation appears in Randall, III:508.
2. TJ to Dr. Vine Utley, 23 Mar. 1819 in Peterson, *Writings*, 1416.
3. MJR to Ellen Wayles Randolph Coolidge, 26 Nov. 1825, EWRC. Also at ViU is a manuscript traditionally known as the "Cookbook of Martha Jefferson Randolph," but this title is erroneous. For a discussion, see page 89; for further analysis of family recipes and manuscripts, see Hess, *Mr. Jefferson's Table*.

Dining at Monticello: The Feast of Reason

1. Smith, Aug. 1809, 65.
2. Ellen Wayles Randolph to MJR, 28 Jan. 1818, ViU.
3. Francis Calley Gray, Feb. 1815, *Thomas Jefferson in 1814* [sic], (Boston, 1814), 69-70.
4. Martha Trist Burke, List of "Monticello Relics," 1907-1908, Trist-Burke Collection (#6696), ViU.
5. "The Autobiography of Judith Walker Rives," Rives Family Papers (#2532, Box 1) ViU. Farmington was the Albemarle County plantation of George and Martha Divers.
6. Smith, 69.
7. *Webster Papers*, 1:371.
8. Smith, 387-388.
9. Ellen Wayles Coolidge to Henry S. Randall, 5 July 1858, Ellen Coolidge Letterbook, ViU. Transcription at Jefferson Library.
10. George Ticknor, *Life, Letters and Journals* (Boston, 1876), I:36.
11. Septimia Anne Randolph Meikleham, "Everyday Life at Monticello," [after 1838], TJF, on deposit at ViU.
12. Both Ticknor and Smith observed that the second bell announced that food was "on the table."
13. *Webster Papers*, 1:371.
14. Bear, 13.
15. Gray, 70.
16. Ticknor, 1:36.
17. Meikleham, "Everyday Life."
18. Ticknor, 1:36.
19. Gray, 70.
20. *Webster Papers*, 1:371.
21. Smith, 69.
22. *Hope with Cupid*, c. 1785, was signed by Jossé-François-Joseph Le Riche.
23. TJ to John Trumbull, 5 Aug. 1789, DLC.
24. Joseph Coolidge to Nicholas P. Trist, 5 Jan. 1827, DLC.
25. Ibid.
26. Martha Jefferson Randolph to TJ, 23 June 1808, MHi.
27. *Webster Papers*, 1:371.
28. Peter Fossett recollections, in unidentified Cincinnati newspaper, 1900, Clippings Scrapbook, p. 978, Cincinnati Public Library.
29. TJ to Elbridge Gerry, June 11, 1812, *FBB*, 488.
30. For selections from visitors' written recollections, see Merrill D. Peterson, ed., *Visitors to Monticello* (Charlottesville: University Press of Virginia, 1983).
31. Randall, III:330.
32. TJ to James Monroe, 18 Dec. 1786, *Papers*, 10:612.
33. Anna Maria Thornton Diary, Sept. 1806, DLC.

Jefferson and Wine

1. Entry dated 1 Sept. 1769, MB, 1:148.
2. Philip Mazzei, *Memoirs of the Life and Peregrinations of the Florentine Philip Mazzei, 1730-1816*, trans. Howard R. Marraro (New York: Columbia University Press, 1942), 206-07.
3. TJ to John Bannister, Jr., 19 June 1787, *Papers*, 11:476-77.
4. TJ, "Notes of a Tour through Holland and the Rhine Valley," *Papers*, 13:15-16, and TJ, "Hints on European Travel," ibid., 13:265.
5. Ibid., 13:19.
6. TJ, 1784-89, "Notes on French Wines by Region," DLC.
7. Lynn W. Turner, *William Plumer of New Hampshire* (Chapel Hill: published for the Institute of Early American History and Culture by UNC Press, 1962), 95.
8. Theodore Roosevelt, *Gouverneur Morris, American Statesmen Series* (Boston: Houghton Mifflin, 1899), 287.
9. TJ to John F. Oliveira Fernandes, 16 Dec. 1815, DLC.
10. TJ to Dr. Vine Utley, 23 Mar. 1819 in Peterson, *Writings*, 1416.
11. TJ to Thomas Appleton, 14 Jan. 1816, Albert Ellery Bergh, *The Writings of Thomas Jefferson*. 20 vols. (Washington, D.C.: Thomas Jefferson Memorial Association, 1907), 19:231. Hereafter L&B.
12. TJ to Baron Hyde de Neuville, 13 Dec. 1818, ibid., 15:178.
13. TJ to C.P. de Lasteyrie, 15 July 1808, ibid., 12:91.
14. Thomas Pinney, *A History of Wine in America* (Berkeley: University of California Press, 1989), 129.
15. TJ, "1807 Vineyard Plan," in Weather Memorandum Book, Historical Society of Pennsylvania, Philadelphia.
16. Edward Antill, "An Essay on the Cultivation of the Vine, and the Making of Wine, Suited to the Different Climates in North-America," American Philosophical Society, *Transactions 1* (Philadelphia, 1771, 2d ed.), 201-10.

Recipes

1. Many of the hand-written recipes are at DLC; some were reprinted in *The Congressional Cookbook* (1933). The Garden Book and Farm Book are in the collection of the MHi. For provenance and a transcription of any given recipe, see Hess, *Mr. Jefferson's Table*.

2. Jefferson's menu notes from the President's House are at the MHi.

3. The account books of Martha Wayles Skelton Jefferson and Anne Cary Randolph are at DLC; that of Martha Jefferson Randolph is in a private collection, with microfilm at Jefferson Library.

4. The Meikleham manuscript is in the collection of the Thomas Jefferson Foundation; the other three collections are at ViU.

5. Smith, 81.

6. TJ to Nicholas Lewis 17 Sept. 1787, *GB*, 130; MJR to Ellen Wayles Randolph Coolidge, [1829], EWRC.

7. Ellen Wayles Randolph Harrison and Martha Jefferson Trist Burke, *Monticello Child Life* (trans. Mrs. Burke, 1888), at Jefferson Library.

8. Ellen Wayles Randolph Coolidge to MJR, 20 Nov. 1825, EWRC.

9. Bear, 20-21.

10. Randolph account book, microfilm at Jefferson Library, May 28, p. 41.

11. Samuel Brown to TJ, 13 June 1813, *GB*, 514.

12. Ellen Wayles Randolph Coolidge to MJR, 24 Aug. 1819, EWRC.

13. Ellen Wayles Coolidge: Letters Used and Omitted by Randall, 5 July 1858, ViU.

14. Thomas Jefferson, *Notes on the State of Virginia* (London, 1787; reprint, with notes, William Peden, ed., Chapel Hill: University of North Carolina Press, 1955), 43.

15. This story is recorded in *Saga of a City, Lynchburg, Va. 1786-1936* (Lynchburg: 1936), 58.

16. Jacob Crowinshield to TJ, 13 July 1804, DLC; TJ to Ellen Randolph Coolidge, 14 Nov. 1825, *Family Letters*, 462; Ellen Randolph Coolidge to TJ, 8 Mar. 1826, *Family Letters*, 473.

17. Thomas Jefferson to Mr. Ashlin, 20 Apr. 1812, *FB*, 485; *MB*, 980 and 1015.

18. Sir Augustus John Foster, *Jeffersonian America*, Richard Beale Davis, ed. (San Marino, CA: The Huntington Library, 1954), 20.

19. TJ to TJR, 16 April 1810, *Family Letters*, 396.

20. TJ's menus notes for President's House are in the Coolidge Collection, MHi.

21. TJ to John Wayles Eppes, 24 Mar. 1811, *Thomas Jefferson's Table*.

22. Ibid.

23. TJ to N. Herbemont, 3 Nov. 1822, *GB*, 604; references to olive trees at Monticello from *GB*, 50, 61, 77; TJ to Stephen Cathalan, 22 Mar. 1804, DLC.

24. TJ to TJR, 16 Apr. 1810, *Family Letters*, 396; TJ to John Rutledge, Jr., 19 Jun. 1788, *Papers*, 13:263.

25. TJ to William Few, 3 Jan. 1808, DLC, *GB*, 361-2; TJ to Anne Cary Randolph, 22 Mar. 1808, MHi, *GB* 368; TJ to Dr. Gustavus Honer, 15 May 1808, *GB*, 370-1.

26. TJ to Horatio G. Spafford, 14 May 1809, *L&B*, 12:278-282; TJ to John Milledge, 5 June 1811, DLC (excerpt in *GB*, 457-8).

27. 11 Aug. 1807, Weather Memorandum Book, 1776-1829, given in *GB*, 336.

28. Jefferson's "Notes on Macaroni," *Papers*, 14:544.

29. William Short to TJ, 11 Feb. 1789, *Papers*, 14:540-1; William Short to TJ, 3 Apr. 1789, *Papers*, 15:29; Stephen Cathalan, Jr., to TJ, 2 Aug. 1789, *Papers*, 15:324; TJ to Stephen Cathalan, Jr., 30 Aug. 1789, *Papers*, 15:372; Stephen Cathalan, Jr., to TJ, 10 Sept. 1789, *Papers*, 15:409.

30. TJ to MJR, 8 Apr. 1793, *Papers*, 25:521 and Adrien Petit's List of Packages Sent to Richmond, c. 12 May 1793, *Papers*, 26:19.

31. TJ to Gordon, Trokes, and Company, 30 Dec. 1809, MHi (transcribed from microfilm).

32. TJ to Edward Rutledge, 14 July 1787, DLC.

33. Ralph Izard to TJ, 10 Nov. 1787, *GB*, 131.

34. TJ to William Drayton, 1 May 1791, *GB*, 163-64.

35. Ellen Wayles Randolph Coolidge to MJR, 24 Aug. 1819, EWRC.

36. MJR to Ellen Wayles Randolph Coolidge, 26 Nov. 1825, EWRC.

37. Ibid.

38. Ibid.

39. Mary Randolph to Virginia Randolph, 27 Dec. 1821, Trist Papers, NcU. For exchanges between TJ and Maria (Mary) Jefferson, see TJ to Mary Jefferson, 11 Apr. 1790, and subsequent correspondence in *Family Letters*.

40. Martha Wayles Skelton Jefferson's Account Book, 22 Feb. 1773, DLC.

41. Thomas Moore to TJ, 21 June 1802, DLC.

42. Ellen Wayles Randolph Coolidge to MJR, 24 Aug. 1819, EWRC.

43. See also Louise Conway Belden, *Table Decorations and Desserts in America, 1650-1900* (New York: W.W. Norton & Company and Winterthur, 1883), 145-146.

44. George Washington, Ledger B Manuscript, 198a, George Washington Papers, DLC.

45. Hemings inventory, 20 Feb. 1796, DLC; MJR inventory, 1826, MHi.

46. *GB*, 281.

47. TJ to James Dinsmore, 19 Mar. 1802, DLC, *GB*, 278.

48. TJ to Edmund Bacon, 3 Jan. 1809, Huntington Library, *GB*, 400.

49. *GB*, 497.

50. TJ to John Barnes, 5 May 1819, MHi.

51. *Virginia House-wife*, 175.

52. TJ to MJR, 27 Jan. 1803, *Family Letters*, 242.

53. TJ to Vine Utley, 21 Mar. 1819, DLC, Peterson, *Writings*. For more on cider and Jefferson's preferred cider apples, and for information on peach mobby, see Peter J. Hatch, *The Fruits and Fruit Trees of Monticello* (Charlottesville: University Press of Virginia, 1998), 64-66.

54. Bear, 100.

55. MJR to TJ, 26 June 1793, *Family Letters*, 121.

56. Thomas Mann Randolph to Thomas Jefferson, 14 Mar. 1801, Jefferson-Coolidge Family Collection, ViU.

57. Martha Wayles Skelton Jefferson Account Book, DLC.

58. TJ to James Madison, 11 Apr. 1820. For further information on Jefferson and beer, see Ann Lucas, "The Philosophy of Making Beer" (April 1995), http://www.monticello.org/reports/life/beer.html.

59. TJ to Edmund Rogers, 14 Feb. 1824, Colonial Williamsburg Foundation.

60. Joseph Coolidge to TJR, 16 Dec. 1826, Edgehill-Randolph papers, ViU.

61. Marquis de Chastellux, *Travels in North America*, ed. Howard C. Rice, Jr. (Chapel Hill: Univerity of North Carolina Press, 1963), 11:392.

Suggested Further Reading

What follows is a highly selective list. A more extensive listing, "Selected Books and Videos," is available on our web site at http://www.monticello.org. Web visitors may also "browse by interest," selecting "Food and Cooking" to find related reports published online (or go directly to http://www.monticello.org/browse/food.html).

Bear, James A., Jr., ed., *Jefferson at Monticello* (1967).

Bear, James A., Jr., and Lucia C. Stanton, eds., *Jefferson's Memorandum Books* (1997).

Beiswanger, William L., *Monticello in Measured Drawings* (1998).

Beiswanger, William L., et al., *Thomas Jefferson's Monticello* (2002).

Belden, Louise Conway, *The Festive Tradition: Table Decoration and Desserts in America, 1650-1900* (1983).

Betts, Edwin M., ed., *Thomas Jefferson's Farm Book* (1953; rept. 1999).

Betts, Edwin M., ed., *Thomas Jefferson's Garden Book* (1944; rept. 1999).

Betts, Edwin M. and James A. Bear, Jr., eds., *The Family Letters of Thomas Jefferson* (1966; rept. 1985).

Boyd, Julian P., et al., eds., *The Papers of Thomas Jefferson* (1950-).

Carson, Barbara G., *Ambitious Appetites: Dining, Behavior, and Patterns of Consumption in Federal Washington* (1990).

Fowler, Damon Lee, *Classical Southern Cooking: A Celebration of the Cuisine of the Old South* (1995).

Gabler, James M., *Passions: The Wines and Travels of Thomas Jefferson* (1995).

Hatch, Peter J., *The Fruits and Fruit Trees of Monticello* (1998).

Hatch, Peter J., *The Gardens of Monticello* (1992).

Hess, Karen, *Mr. Jefferson's Table: The Culinary Legacy of Monticello* (forthcoming).

Looney, J. Jefferson, et al., eds., *The Papers of Thomas Jefferson: Retirement Series* (2005-).

Malone, Dumas, *Jefferson and His Time*, 6 volumes (1948-81).

Malone, Dumas, *Thomas Jefferson: A Brief Biography* (1993).

Peterson, Merrill D., *Visitors to Monticello* (1989).

Randolph, Mary, *The Virginia House-wife* (1824; facsimile ed., introduction by Karen Hess, 1984).

Randolph, Sarah N., *The Domestic Life of Thomas Jefferson* (1871; rept. 1985).

Stein, Susan R., *The Worlds of Thomas Jefferson at Monticello* (1993).

Stanton, Lucia, *Free Some Day: The African-American Families of Monticello* (2000).

Stanton, Lucia, *Slavery at Monticello* (1996).

Wheaton, Barbara Ketchum, *Savoring the Past: The French Kitchen and Table from 1300-1789* (1983).

Wilson, Douglas L. and Lucia C. Stanton, eds., *Jefferson Abroad* (1999).

About the Contributors

The Thomas Jefferson Foundation, Inc., is the private, nonprofit organization that owns and operates Monticello in Charlottesville, Virginia. Established in 1923, the Foundation has a dual mission of preservation and education.

Beth L. Cheuk coordinates the publications program for the Thomas Jefferson Foundation, which publishes books for both scholarly and general audiences. Responsible for all aspects of these publications, she also served as Monticello's first webmaster.

Elizabeth V. Chew, Ph.D., is an art historian with expertise in relationships between architecture, material culture, and gender and family politics. Associate Curator of Collections at Monticello, she is involved in research on the house's interiors and collections and their interpretation to the public. She has a particular interest in Jefferson's granddaughters and their lives at Monticello.

Damon Lee Fowler is a culinary historian and food writer living in Savannah, Georgia. He has edited two historical cookbooks and has written five cookbooks of his own, including *Classical Southern Cooking: A Celebration of the Cuisine of the Old South*, nominated for two Julia Child awards and one from the James Beard Foundation.

James M. Gabler lectures frequently on the subject of Jefferson's wines and travels and has written several wine books. *Passions: The Wines and Travels of Thomas Jefferson* won the 1995 "Veuve Clicquot Wine Book of the Year" award. Mr. Gabler has written wine articles for a variety of publications, taught courses on wine, and serves as the wine columnist for "The Daily Record," Baltimore, MD.

Peter J. Hatch has served as Director of Gardens and Grounds since 1977, responsible for the care, restoration, and interpretation of the Monticello landscape. He is an authority on Jefferson's gardening interests and on the history of plants in American gardens. His most recent book is *The Fruits and Fruit Trees of Monticello.*

Karen Hess is a culinary historian living in New York City and author of *Mr. Jefferson's Table: The Culinary Legacy of Monticello* (forthcoming) and *The Carolina Rice Kitchen: The African Connection*. She has also edited numerous historical cookbooks, including *The Virginia House-wife.*

Jennifer Lindner McGlinn is a pastry chef, food writer, and historian. She is a graduate of the University of Pennsylvania, the Culinary Institute of America, and the Winterthur Program in Early American Culture. Coauthor of *The City Tavern Baking and Dessert Cookbook*, she also hosts historic baking demonstrations.

Justin A. Sarafin serves as Project Coordinator for the ongoing restoration of Monticello's dependencies, which involves the physical restoration, furnishing, and re-interpretation of the service-oriented spaces where members of Jefferson's enslaved population worked and lived. A graduate of Wheaton College (Mass.) and the University of Virginia, Mr. Sarafin also teaches architectural history.

Lucia Stanton is Shannon Senior Historian at Monticello and is the former Director of Research. The author or co-editor of various books on Jefferson, including *Jefferson's Memorandum Books, Free Some Day: The African-American Families of Monticello*, and *Slavery at Monticello*, she is currently involved in an oral history of the descendants of Jefferson's slaves and working on a book about the Monticello plantation.

Susan R. Stein is Curator of Monticello, with responsibility for Thomas Jefferson's world-famous house and the wide variety of artifacts that relate to Jefferson's life on the mountain. She organized the landmark 1993 exhibition that commemorated the 250th anniversary of Jefferson's birth and produced the exhibition catalog, *The Worlds of Thomas Jefferson at Monticello.*

Dianne Swann-Wright, Ph.D., served as Director of African-American and Special Programs at Monticello before becoming Curator at the Frederick Douglass - Isaac Myers Maritime Park in Baltimore, Maryland. Author of *A Way Out of No Way: Claiming Family and Freedom in the New South*, she co-developed the Thomas Jefferson Foundation's *Getting Word* oral history project.

Gaye Wilson has been a staff member of Monticello's Research Department since 1996. She has authored several papers and articles, made presentations at scholarly conferences, and served as a guest speaker for a variety of groups. Previously she taught History of Dress at the University of Texas at Austin, where she managed the historic clothing collection for the Theatre Department.

ACKNOWLEDGMENTS AND PHOTO CREDITS

Research conducted by the Thomas Jefferson Foundation, Inc., over more than two decades has yielded important information and a greater understanding of Monticello's food culture. For investigation that has reframed the context of this research, we thank our own Lucia Stanton for bringing to light the rich activity and life outside of Monticello's main house, and on the plantation at large. Many other individuals have made significant contributions to this book as well as to the restoration of the dependencies, including Anna G. Koester, Ann Lucas, Sally Meyer, and Katherine G. Revell. For early conversations that intrigued us and sparked further research, we also wish to credit the late Rosemary Brandau, who managed the historic food programs at Colonial Williamsburg.

All books published by the Thomas Jefferson Foundation, Inc., receive generous support from the Martin S. and Luella Davis Publications Endowment. However, this book also owes its existence to the work and support of many organizations and individuals who have furthered our understanding of Monticello's food culture and have made possible the restoration of many of Monticello's food-related spaces. The Thomas Jefferson Foundation and its Curator, Susan Stein, wish to thank the Florence Gould Foundation and the National Endowment for the Humanities for grants that supported the planning and implementation of our restoration and interpretation of the cook's room, storage room, kitchen, and beer storage room. The beer storage room received additional support from the Anheuser-Busch Foundation and Mr. and Mrs. John L. Nau III.

v	Charles Shoffner; Renée Comet, styled by Lisa Cherkasky
vi	Leonard Phillips
1	Thomas Jefferson, Recipe for *Biscuit de Savoy*, no date, Jefferson Papers, Library of Congress
2-3	Robert C. Lautman
4	Peter J. Hatch
5-8	Charles Shoffner. Basket of Monticello vegetables styled by Lou Hatch
9-10	Edward Owen
11	Detail from "The presidents house in the City of Washington, Sepr. 1811" by Benjamin H. Latrobe. Courtesy, Mrs. John M. Scott, Jr.
12	Pen and Ink Drawing of the State Floor Plan of the Jefferson White House by Benjamin H. Latrobe, 1803. Library of Congress
13	Robert C. Lautman
14	Design for a dessert of forty-three sweetmeats and fruits for from twenty to twenty-five people. Detail from François Massialot, *Nouvelle Instruction*, new ed., facing p. 516. Courtesy, The Winterthur Library: Printed Books and Periodical Collection
15	Detail from Jefferson's account book for 5 May 1806. Courtesy Massachusetts Historical Society
16	Thomas Jefferson, "A Statement of the vegetable market of Washington...." Original unlocated. First printed in Henry S. Randall, *The Life of Thomas Jefferson* (New York, 1858), in volume 1, facing p. 44.
17-18	Charles Shoffner
19	Grevin Packing List, July 17, 1790. Short Papers, Library of Congress
20	Ottavio Bertotti Scamozzi, *Le fabbriche e i disegni di Andrea Palladio....* (Trento: La Roccia, 1975), 2 vol. Reprint of the 1776-1783 edition published by F. Modena, Vicenza; Robert C. Lautman
21	Thomas Jefferson Foundation, Inc.
22	Charles Shoffner
23	Thomas Jefferson Foundation, Inc.
24	Charles Shoffner
25	Edward Owen
26	Bailey, N. (Nathan). *Dictionarium Domesticum, being a new and compleat houshold dictionary....* By N. Bailey, London, 1736. Based on information from English Short Title Catalogue. Eighteenth Century Collections Online. Gale Group. http://galenet.galegroup.com/servlet/ECCO
27	Charles Shoffner
28-31	Edward Owen; bust on page 30 photographed by H. Andrew Johnson and shown courtesy of the family of Margaret and Olivia Taylor and Page Taylor Kirk
32	Henry Sargent, American, 1770-1845. *The Dinner Party* (detail), about 1821. Oil on canvas. 156.53 x 126.36 cm. Museum of Fine Arts, Boston. Gift of Mrs. Horatio Appleton Lamb in memory of Mr. and Mrs. Winthrop Sargent. 19.13
33	Charles Shoffner
34	Robert L. Self
35-36	Charles Shoffner
37	Page 128 of Thomas Jefferson's Farm Book. Courtesy Massachusetts Historical Society
38	Skip Johns
39	Account Book of Anne Cary Randolph, 1805-1808. Jefferson Papers, Library of Congress
40	Charles Shoffner
41	Detail from *Life in Philadelphia. Sketches of Character: At home. Abroad.* Ca. 1833. Lithograph by H. Harrison after E.W. Clay. Plate 10. Courtesy Library Company of Philadelphia
42	Kitchen Furniture Inventory by James Hemings, page two. February 20, 1796. Jefferson Papers, Library of Congress

43 Renée Comet, styled by Lisa Cherkasky; Snow Eggs recipe recorded by Virginia Jefferson Randolph Trist, Alderman Library, University of Virginia. 5385-F

44 Peter Fossett, Wendell P. Dabney, *Cincinnati's Colored Citizen's*, Cincinnati, 1926

45 Charles Shoffner

46 Renée Comet, styled by Lisa Cherkasky

47 Dodge & Oxnard to Thomas Jefferson, September 27, 1821, Wine Shipping Bill. Jefferson Papers, Library of Congress

48 *William Coats, Takes this method of acquainting the Public in general … that he has for sale …* Philadelphia, 1772. Broadside printed by John Dunlap. Courtesy Library Company of Philadelphia; Edward Owen (bottom)

49 From *Food and Drink: A Pictorial Archive from Nineteenth-Century Sources*, selected by Jim Harter. (New York: Dover Publications, Inc., sec. revised edition, 1980)

50 Renée Comet, styled by Lisa Cherkasky; Charles Shoffner

51 Thomas Jefferson to Stephen Cathalan, Jr., June 6, 1817. Jefferson Papers, Library of Congress

52 "Vignette of a batteau," from *An Essay on Landscape*, Vol. 2. 1798-99. Benjamin H. Latrobe. Courtesy The Library of Virginia

53-54 Charles Shoffner. Basket of Monticello vegetables styled by Lou Hatch

55 Page 46 of Thomas Jefferson's Garden Book. Courtesy Massachusetts Historical Society

56 Charles Shoffner

57 Leonard Phillips

58-59 Charles Shoffner

60 Leonard Phillips

61 Peter J. Hatch

62 Charles Shoffner

63 Leonard Phillips

64 Renée Comet, styled by Lisa Cherkasky

65 Edward Owen

66 St. Mémin, engraving of Mary Randolph. Courtesy Corcoran Gallery of Art, Washington, D.C.; Thomas Jefferson Foundation, Inc.

67 Charles Shoffner

68 Thomas Jefferson, no date, Ice Cream Recipe; Household accounts of Martha Wayles Skelton Jefferson, 1772-1782. Jefferson Papers, Library of Congress

69 Renée Comet, styled by Lisa Cherkasky

70 Robert C. Lautman

71 Edward Owen

72 Robert C. Lautman

73 Portrait of James Madison by Gilbert Stuart, 1804, accession #1945-23, A&B, image #TC92-23. Courtesy The Colonial Williamsburg Foundation. Portrait of Dolley Payne Todd Madison by Gilbert Stuart, 1804. Courtesy The White House

74-76 Charles Shoffner

77 Charles Shoffner (left); Thomas Jefferson, urn, circa 1794-1796. N507/ K2311. Courtesy Massachusetts Historical Society; Edward Owen (bottom right)

78-79 Edward Owen

80 Charles Shoffner

81 Thomas Jefferson to Alexander J. Dallas, February 26, 1816. Jefferson Papers, Library of Congress

82 Archaeology Department, Thomas Jefferson Foundation, Inc.

83 Robert C. Lautman

84-85 Charles Shoffner

86 Leonard Phillips

87-88 Charles Shoffner

90 Renée Comet, styled by Lisa Cherkasky

93 Edward Owen

95 Charles Shoffner

96 *Harper's New Monthly Magazine*, July 1853

98 Renée Comet, styled by Lisa Cherkasky

107 Peter J. Hatch

108 Renée Comet, styled by Lisa Cherkasky

113 Edward Owen

119 Richard Peters, "On Tunis Sheep" (detail) from *Memoirs*, vol. 2. PSPA S 108 P54 v.2. Courtesy Philadelphia Society for Promoting Agriculture

121-125 Charles Shoffner. Monticello vegetables on p. 122 styled by Lou Hatch

127 Jefferson's plan for the dependencies at Monticello (detail), dated circa 1796 (N150/K152). Courtesy Massachusetts Historical Society

128 The Atlantic Tom Cod. *Microgadus tomcod* (Walb.), Gill. Plate 59. (figb0315); The Shad. (Female) *Clupea sapidissima*, Wilson. Plate 213. (figb0480); The Shad. (Male) *Clupea sapidissima*, Wilson. Plate 212. (figb0479). Historic NMFS Collection. Courtesy National Oceanic and Atmospheric Administration/Department of Commerce

132 Renée Comet, styled by Lisa Cherkasky

137 Leonard Phillips

145 Thomas Jefferson, no date, Maccaroni Recipe and Press Design. Jefferson Papers, Library of Congress

147 Renée Comet, styled by Lisa Cherkasky

150 "Harvesting the Rice," from *Harper's Monthly Magazine*, November 1859. Courtesy The Library at The Mariners' Museum

151 Charles Shoffner, styled by Lou Hatch

152 Renée Comet, styled by Lisa Cherkasky

159 Robert C. Lautman

165 Edward Owen

169 Detail from Thomas Moore to Thomas Jefferson, June 21, 1802. Jefferson Papers, Library of Congress

171 Edward Owen

173 Details from Emy, *L'Art de bien faire les glaces d'office…*, pl. 1, p. 72. Courtesy, The Winterthur Library: Printed Books and Periodical Collection

175 Thomas Jefferson to James Dinsmore, March 19, 1802. Jefferson Papers, Library of Congress; *Monticello Historic Structure Report, Volume IV, Description and Analysis of Cellars and Dependencies*, prepared by Mesick Cohen Waite Architects (February 1992)

176-181 Charles Shoffner

183-184 Edward Owen

187 Charles Shoffner

Recipe Index

GENERAL INDEX

Pour faire des pêches à l'eau-de-vie.

Il faut essuyer les pêches pour ôter le duv[et]
ensuite les piquer avec une fourchette dans 5
à 6 endroits. vous faites ~~blanchir~~ bouillir d[e]
l'eau. quand elle bout, vous jetter vos pêch[es]
pour les blanchir, seulement. laisser faire u[n]
billon, ensuite vous les retirer, et mettez
[de] suite à l'eau froid. vous les retirer
[de] l'eau pour les egoutter. vous faites clarif[ier]
[du] sucre et les laisser bouillir, pour retirer l'e[au]
[vo]us verrer quand il sera asser bouilli entre[z]
[met]tant le doigt dedans, et frotter les deux doig[ts]
[s]i vous sentez que vos doigts tiennent ensem[ble]
[el]le, c'est qu'il est asser. vous le laisser refro[idir]
[qua]nd il est froid, vous y metter les pêch[es]
[po]ur les y laisser 24 heures. ensuite vous fait[es]